D1557289

Mexico and the Foreign Policy of Napoleon III

Mexico and the Foreign Policy of Napoleon III

Michele Cunningham
Visiting Research Fellow
Department of History
Adelaide University
Australia

DC
59.8
M6
C86
2001

First published 2001 by
PALGRAVE
Houndmills, Basingstoke, Hampshire RG21 6XS and
175 Fifth Avenue, New York, N. Y. 10010
Companies and representatives throughout the world

PALGRAVE is the new global academic imprint of
St. Martin's Press LLC Scholarly and Reference Division and
Palgrave Publishers Ltd (formerly Macmillan Press Ltd).

ISBN 0–333–79302–1

This book is printed on paper suitable for recycling and
made from fully managed and sustained forest sources.

A catalogue record for this book is available
from the British Library.

Library of Congress Cataloging-in-Publication Data
Cunningham, Michele, 1948–
    Mexico and the foreign policy of Napoleon III /
    Michele Cunningham.
        p. cm.
    Includes bibliographical references and index.
    ISBN 0–333–79302–1
    1. France—Foreign relations—Mexico. 2. Mexico—
    —Foreign relations—France. 3. France—Foreign relations–
    –1852–1870. 4. Napoleon III, Emperor of the French,
    1808–1873. 5. Mexico—History—European intervention,
    1861–1867. I. Title.
    DC59.8.M6 C86 2000
    327.72044—dc21
                                                00–066882

10   9   8   7   6   5   4   3   2   1
10   09 08 07 06 05 04 03 02 01

Printed and bound in Great Britain by
Antony Rowe Ltd, Chippenham, Wiltshire

For Dad and Mum

Contents

List of Maps

(*Source*: Pierre de la Gorce, *Histoire du Second Empire*, Vol. 4 (Librairie Plon, Paris, 1899).)

Preface

My interest in Napoleon III and the Second Empire was first encouraged by the late Professor Austin Gough with his enthusiasm and talent for making history come alive. My fascination with this period was further inspired by the writings of a contemporary journalist and former British diplomat, Grenville Murray, who wrote numerous satirical articles on the Second Empire, many of which appeared in *Cornhill Magazine* and were collected in a book, *French Pictures in English Chalk*. His early papers were so critical that they encouraged me to determine whether there was any substance to Napoleon III and his Empire. One of the interesting aspects of Murray's writings is that his later articles move from undisguised ridicule of the Emperor to a very warm acceptance of the man and his work for France. I cannot help but feel this change occurred after he went to live in France in 1868 and perhaps met the Emperor himself. A chance discovery in the Archives Nationales of a letter from Murray to the Empress Eugenie confirmed that view. Murray wrote a week before the defeat at Sedan expressing his admiration for the Emperor and all he had tried to achieve, and offered his assistance in enlightening the English public in the face of anti-French propaganda being disseminated by the Prussians. His opinion of the Emperor was one of many that urged me to try and understand that enigmatic man who inspired so much criticism and even vitriol from republican opponents and historians. Although there are now many historical studies more favourable to Napoleon III, there is still much controversy over his achievements in France and his place in history. This volume, it is hoped, will contribute to an understanding of Napoelon III's foreign policy, although, as James McMillan remarked, the definitive history of Napoleon III's foreign policy is still to be written.

I am extremely grateful for the assistance I received from staff in both the French and British archives. In the Archives Nationales I was directed to sources of which I had been unaware, and the guidance afforded to me both in the archives and by correspondence is appreciated. Similarly, the staff in the Service Historique de l'Armée de Terre at Vincennes, and in the Archives du Ministère des Affaires Étrangères made my limited time there very productive. My thanks go to the Research Branch at the University of Adelaide and the Department of History for travel grants to facilitate my research, and to staff in the Department of History for their support and assistance. Special thanks go to Kerrie Round, Noelle Cochran and Vesna Drapac for their valuable comments and suggestions at various stages in the development of this work. I also acknowledge the helpful comments of William Echard and William H. C. Smith on my doctoral thesis, which formed the basis for this book. Their guidance has contributed to the many revisions undertaken. My grateful appreciation is extended to Professor Peter Mühlhäusler and Marie-Noelle Mirza for their assistance with the translation of French quotations throughout the text. Most importantly, without the support of my husband, John, and my family I would never have been able to do this.

Readers will observe throughout the text that the terms 'England' and 'Britain' are both used to describe what we now call Britain. Today we refer to England only if we wish to differentiate it from Scotland, Wales and Northern Ireland. In the period of this narrative, however, Britain was referred to as England, both by the British and foreigners, perhaps more often than as Britain, although the government was generally called the British government. When correspondence has been directly quoted, or referred to, I have maintained the use of 'England' or 'English' if that was used. At times in my own narrative I have also used 'England' because it seemed more appropriate for the event being described. In the diplomatic correspondence Britain was generally referred to as 'Angleterre' or 'Grande-Bretagne', and French feelings were generally directed against the English!

M.K.C.

List of Abbreviations

AD	*Archives Diplomatiques: Receuil de Diplomatie et d'Histoire*
AMAE	Archives du Ministère des Affaires Étrangères, Paris
AMG	Archives du Ministre de la Guerre, held by the Service Historique de l'Armée de Terre, Chateau Vincennes
AN	Archives Nationales, Paris
AP	Archives privées. Private records in the Archives Nationales
CP	Correspondance politique in the Archives du Ministère des Affaires Étrangères, Paris
FO	Foreign Office records in the Public Record Office, London
PA–AP	Papiers d'agents – archives privées. Private papers in the Archives du Ministère des Affaires Étrangères, Paris
PRO	Public Record Office, London
RDM	*La Revue des Deux Mondes*
SHAT	Service Historique de l'Armée de Terre at Chateau Vincennes
State Papers	*British and Foreign State Papers* (Blue Books)

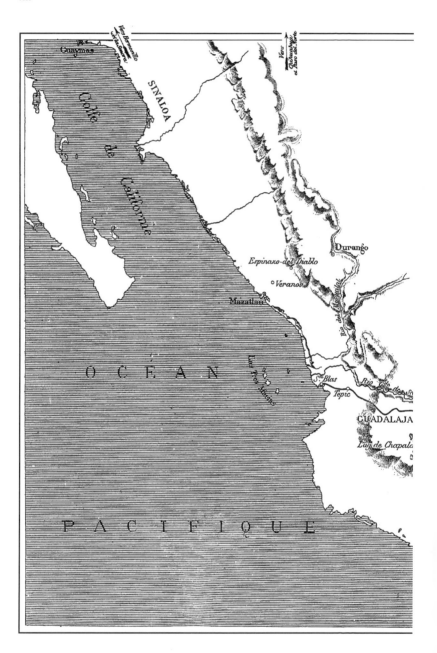

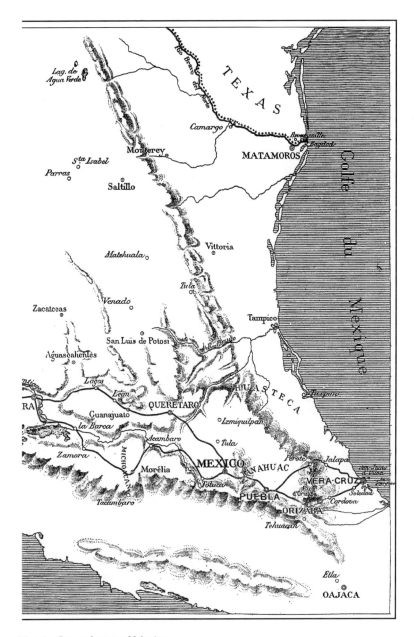

Map 1 General map of Mexico

Introduction

The French intervention in Mexico between 1862 and 1867, undertaken initially in conjunction with Britain and Spain, has challenged historians, who have sought to understand and explain why Napoleon III became involved in what many saw as a hopeless cause. A number of conclusions have been reached, the most widely accepted being France's need to find resources such as silver and cotton, and Napoleon III's determination to establish a Latin, Catholic, monarchical bloc to prevent further encroachment by the United States into Central and South America. While each of these theories contains an element of truth, they should be challenged as the analyses have not gone far enough. Eugene Rouher, Napoleon's Minister of State, declared the Mexican intervention was *la plus grande pensée du règne* [the loftiest idea of the reign], but the term has since been used as a criticism, some claiming the venture failed because of the ineptitude of its author, while others said it was because Napoleon was a Utopian dreamer out of touch with reality. However, if this campaign is considered within the context of Napoleon's foreign policy, it can be shown that it might indeed have been *la plus grande pensée du règne*, and that Napoleon III had a broader vision than maintaining Latin and Catholic influences in the Americas.

Napoleon III's policy, developed from the political writings of his youth, embraced a world view that few of his contemporaries could comprehend or appreciate. In the case of his foreign contemporaries, their views were always tinged with fear and suspicion that he intended to subjugate Europe as his uncle had done. Neither have historians accepted his world view in the spirit in which it was intended, which was to establish a basis for peace. Many have dismissed it as the ruminations of a dreamer, others have seen it as a plan to gain territory for France and hegemony in Europe. Few have understood that Mexico provided an opportunity for Napoleon III to extend his vision for maintaining peace beyond Europe to embrace the world. Instead the intervention has been seen as a naïve opportunistic attempt to extend France's influence into the New World. While Napoleon's aims were not achieved due to a number of factors, many of which were beyond his control, he should still be given credit for his greater world view. Had his contemporaries been less conservative and shared his vision it is possible that some of the problems in international relations arising in the twentieth century might have been avoided.

An analysis of the historiography of the Mexican intervention reveals that a diverse range of motives has been attributed to Napoleon III. The earliest works on Mexico, largely memoirs or observations of contemporaries, were almost entirely critical of France's involvement in general, and of Napoleon III in particular. One of the few historical works on the Mexican intervention that has been sympathetic is that of Paul Gaulot. His work was based on the correspondence of General Bazaine, the French commander in Mexico from late 1863, with the Emperor, the Minister of War, Marshal Randon, and others, and it revealed how the Emperor was misinformed and badly served by his minister and commanders in Mexico.[1] Little more appeared, however, until 1928 when Egon Corti gained access to the archives of Maximilian. His monumental work, *Maximilian and Charlotte of Mexico*, addressed the negotiations between Maximilian and Napoleon III, and Maximilian and the Mexican emigrants in Europe, then followed the progress of the Mexican Empire until its collapse in 1867.[2] Drawing on the correspondence between Napoleon and Maximilian held in the Viennese archives, published sources and secondary works, Corti concluded that Napoleon was determined to impose a monarchy on Mexico, and that he only ever made a token gesture to universal suffrage to decide Mexico's destiny. His support for this claim is far from conclusive, however, and, while others have agreed with his assertion, none has given anything other than anecdotal evidence or conjecture to support his arguments.

Napoleon's economic adviser, Michel Chevalier, wrote a large work on Mexico in which he justified intervention on the basis that France needed to ensure its greatness by preventing the spread of Protestantism into the Americas and preserving the Latin Catholic culture.[3] While there is no evidence that Napoleon shared Chevalier's views – in fact there is much to deny it – Daniel Dawson, in 1935, claimed that this was Napoleon's prime motivation for intervention, simply because of his close relationship with Chevalier. Dawson added a study of the

British Foreign Office papers from the embassies of Paris, Madrid, Vienna and Washington, and of the legation in Mexico City, to the sources used by Corti, and concluded that Napoleon III's reason for being involved in Mexico was to pose a threat to the expansion of the United States by developing a Latin Catholic bloc in Central America.[4] In 1939 Christian Schefer, the first to use the archives of the French Ministry of Foreign Affairs, examined the origins of the expedition. He saw that the primary aim of Napoleon III's foreign policy was to cement alliances with Britain and at least one European neighbour, and that the Mexican venture, in conjunction with Britain and Spain, provided an ideal opportunity to do this. Such an expedition might also help to ensure that the Americas remained open to the commerce of Europe and the rest of the world – a more humanitarian motive than others had ascribed to the Emperor. Schefer, however, concluded that the Mexican venture failed to become *la plus grande pensée du règne* because of Napoleon III's ineptitude.[5] But, again, his archival support was limited because he consulted neither the many private papers in the Archives Nationales, nor the records of the Minister of War, and ignored the British archives.

In the 1960s Carl Bock did an exhaustive study in the French and British Foreign Ministry archives for his analysis of the negotiation and breakdown of the Tripartite Convention, which was signed by Britain, France and Spain on 31 October 1861.[6] Although he provided a valuable understanding of the forces acting on all sides, he commented that only a few letters written by Napoleon III were on file in the Archives du Ministère des Affaires Étrangères. He did not consult the Archives napoléon in the Archives Nationales and his conclusions were strongly influenced by the opinions of his predecessors. Like Corti, he was convinced that the Emperor searched for an excuse to impose a monarchy in Mexico, and that he and the Empress were obsessed with the idea, but he has little to support this argument other than the comments of contemporaries such as Lord Cowley, the British minister in Paris.

Alfred and Kathryn Hanna reached similar conclusions to Dawson, even though they consulted a wider range of documents. However, they consulted mainly the Mexican and United States sources to show that Napoleon was forced to conclude the intervention because of pressure from the United States. Ralph Roeder provided some interesting information on the intervention in his work on Juarez, the Mexican President opposing the intervention, using Juarez's private archives, the Bazaine archives kept in Texas, and an exhaustive list of secondary sources. He was able to provide views from numerous Mexican sources to support and supplement the European sources, particularly in relation to the activities of the Comte de Gabriac and Dubois de Saligny, the French Ministers in Mexico in the 1850s and 1860s. His portrayal of the Mexican political and social situation in this period provides valuable background for the study of the intervention.[7]

Works in the 1970s focused on different aspects of this interlude: on Maximilian and Charlotte; on the British involvement in the intervention; or on analysis of possible economic motives for Napoleon's intervention.[8] Many concluded that the expeditions carried out in the 1850s by French adventurers such as Count Gaston de Raousset-Boulbon, to exploit silver mining in the Sonora, were to gain exclusive economic benefits for France. There is no evidence that Raousset-Boulbon's efforts were officially supported by the French government, yet Shirley Black remarked that 'there is often the implied hint that he was fulfilling an important, and assigned, mission'.[9] Statements such as this have been used as evidence to support conclusions that the mining of silver was a primary motive for Napoleon's intervention. While Black shows that there was an increasing demand for silver in France, the exploitation of the mines in Mexico was by no means a prominent theme in the correspondence of the Emperor during the campaign. As will be seen in Chapter 6, the mines were to be developed by private companies which would give a portion of the produce to the French government. This in turn could be taxed by the Mexican government to provide a source of income. While Napoleon did seek benefits for France, his determination was that all countries would have access to the markets and produce of Mexico, as Schefer has shown. Publications other than those mentioned have simply been revisions of previous work, except for the most recent work of Jean-François Lecaillon, who has presented an analysis of the conduct of the campaign from the point of view of the soldiers who served in Mexico. To do this he has used journals, memoirs and collections of private letters of the soldiers to add to the existing studies.[10]

While most historians have recognised that others, such as the minister in Mexico, Dubois de Saligny, and the commanders, Admiral Jurien de la Gravière, General de Lorencez and General Forey, misled Napoleon, they have treated this fact lightly and concluded that when these representatives appeared to be contravening their written instructions, they were in fact carrying out Napoleon's secret orders. The only support for such a claim appears to be a comment made by the Austrian ambassador, Prince Richard de Metternich, that Jurien had been given secret instructions to ensure that a monarchy was chosen as the form of government in Mexico. Napoleon's written avowals that he was happy for Mexicans to choose the government they wanted, whether monarchical or republican, were said to be masking his real intentions. It can be shown, however, that when reports from his commanders revealed that they had misinterpreted their instructions he took great pains to clarify his intentions. Perhaps it was assumed that, because his agents acted in opposition to their written instructions, there must have been secret ones. The correspondence of Jurien and Forey, however, shows that they consciously acted on their own initiative and either justified not following their instructions, or took responsibility for their decisions. These dispatches have until now been overlooked or ignored.

In summary, the analyses of the Mexican intervention that have been based on archival research have each been limited because of the unavailability of documents, at least in the 1930s, or selective because of a bias towards either the American, the British or the French viewpoint. It is a long time since anyone has returned to the archives, where correspondence not used by previous analysts has been found, particularly in the Archives napoléon in the Archives Nationales. In reconsidering this intriguing aspect of the history of the Second Empire, as wide a range of sources as possible in the French and British archives has been consulted, primarily because the relationship between France and Britain had considerable bearing on the development and outcome of the intervention. Apart from the British and French Foreign Ministry archives and those of the French Minister of War, valuable documents were found in the files of the Ministry of Marine and Colonies as well as among private papers, particularly those of the Bonaparte family. In the Archives Nationales there were also two cartons of papers relating to the Mexican campaign amongst those found in the Tuileries in September 1870, and many other valuable documents in the same series. Among these additional sources many more original letters and instructions written or received by Napoleon were found, and these have been invaluable in analysing his intentions throughout the campaign.

The intervention in Mexico attracted more criticism in France than earlier foreign ventures, but this is perhaps not surprising when one considers at what stage in the development of the Second Empire the campaign took place. In November 1860 Napoleon introduced some liberal reforms which allowed for discussion of the annual address, the right to propose amendments to bills, and the publication of parliamentary debates. The following year, parliament was given 'the right to discuss the budget clause by clause',[11] which gave it unprecedented influence on government expenditure. Thus, for the first time, opposition to the Emperor's policy could influence the carrying out of that policy, and

Mexico was the first foreign involvement, apart from the Italian question, to be subjected to extensive debate and questioning in the *Corps législatif*. Mexico was also to be the first lengthy military campaign of the Empire, and for this reason it attracted opposition from not only political opponents, but also from the public, who were used to the short decisive campaigns of recent years. While some were concerned that France should not withdraw from Mexico in defeat, the majority did not understand the reasons France was involved, and Mexico's distance from France meant it was not as important to them as resolving the problems that were developing on their doorstep.[12] Although the influence of the pressure from the parliament, and of public opinion, is difficult to determine, it is highly probable that the verbal and written opposition to this campaign has had an impact on how it has been regarded by historians.

The Mexican problems also arose shortly after Napoleon had concluded one of the major achievements of his reign, the Commercial Treaty with England, which not only boosted France's exports but was a profound indication of his intention to preserve peace with England. The idea, then, of a campaign in conjunction with England and Spain was, to him, an ideal opportunity to further develop his relations with his neighbours and pursue his goal of a united Europe. That this campaign was to be in the Americas was an added bonus, because achieving a world free of trade barriers would be the final step towards a universal agreement to maintain peace. While many have concluded that Napoleon III had a simplistic world view, which entailed maintaining a Latin Catholic culture in the Americas to contain the spread of republicanism and Protestantism, I would suggest his policy was much more far-sighted. An analysis of this policy – from its very early development in the writings of his youth, from his addresses and notes regarding foreign policy during his reign, and from his numerous proposals for the convening of a European Congress – suggests that he had a consistent ideal, in the context of which Mexico can be placed. From the evidence it is then possible to dismiss the claims of many analysts and contemporaries that his main aim was a determination to restore Latin, Catholic influence in Central and South America. While he did wish to contain the expansion of the United States, his reasons were less self-seeking than his contemporaries believed.

It is feasible that Napoleon III's Mexican policy was misunderstood simply because his overall foreign policy has been misunderstood, the most common interpretations being that he was inconsistent, impulsive, determined to extend France's borders and regain mastery of Europe, and that he did not know with whom to form a strong alliance. At various times he courted each of the major powers, although with limited success, and this has been interpreted as a lack of any real direction in his policy. However, in recent years William Echard has shown quite convincingly that there was indeed a consistent aim in Napoleon's foreign policy. By focusing on his repeated attempts to convene a European Congress, Echard showed that Napoleon was faithful to the ideas, revealed in the writings of his youth, that envisaged a united Europe free from internal struggles. His attempts at cementing alliances with different powers are seen to be purposeful steps along the way to achieving his goal.[13] My own ideas on Napoleon III's foreign policy have developed along similar lines to those of Echard, as a result of studying *Des Idées napoléoniennes, Rêveries politiques*, and other writings, which show that Napoleon envisaged that his ideas relating to Europe would one day be extended to encompass the world. The Mexican intervention can thus be seen as an illustration of how his world policy might have been achieved. This idea, however, goes against the general survey of Napoleon III's foreign policy, which maintains that he was constantly seeking opportunities to 'prepare the way for the general reorganisation of the map of Europe that was his consuming ambition'.[14]

It is, though, in the context of the writings of his youth that the apparently contradictory nature of his policy can be understood. As Stuart Campbell remarked:

Historians have attributed the seemingly mysterious and contradictory policies of the Second Empire to the unpredictable character of its Emperor. The fact is that few pretenders have so thoroughly advertised their plans before taking power, and Napoleon III remained amazingly true to the proposals of Louis Napoleon.[15]

Accepting this is essential to realising what Napoleon was trying to achieve. In writing *Des Idées napoléoniennes*, Louis Napoleon was interpreting what he believed was the policy of his uncle, the Emperor Napoleon, and he wished to see it brought to fruition. Louis Napoleon saw this policy as, fundamentally, the founding of 'a solid European association by basing his system upon complete nationalities and upon general interests fairly satisfied'. This would have resulted in a European code and court of appeals, uniform coins, weights and measures, and eventually national interests would have given way to European interests and, Louis Napoleon added,

l'humanité eût été satisfaite; car la Providence n'a pu vouloir qu'une nation ne fût heureuse qu'aux dépens des autres, et qu'il n'y eût en

Europe que des vainqueurs et des vaincus, et non des membres réconciliés d'une même et grande famille.[16]

[mankind would have been satisfied; for Providence could not have wanted a nation to be happy at the expense of others, and that there might be in Europe only conquerors and the conquered, but rather, reconciled members of one large family.]

Émile Ollivier defined Napoleon III's own policy as 'that of nationalities', and he also showed that it embraced the principles of the 1848 Revolution. He referred to a pre-1848 speech by Thiers, calling for the union of Italy; another by Cavaignac, in May 1849, calling on the Minister to safeguard the independence and liberty of the people; and the order of the day of 24 May 1848 proclaiming 'the future politics of France: close ties with Germany, reconstitution of an independent Poland, enfranchisement of Italy'.[17] Napoleon III's efforts to convene European congresses are testimony to his intention to implement both his uncle's policy and those principles of 1848 described above. In the 1840s he wrote an article about the benefits of constructing a canal in Nicaragua to connect the Atlantic and Pacific oceans, and it illustrated how he saw that policy extended to encompass the world, believing that prosperity could be achieved only by removing all the barriers that separate people. Improved communications and commerce were now the ways to bring nations closer together, and an essential element in bringing about unity was the lowering of trade barriers.

In the aftermath of the Mexican intervention, it was easy to accuse Napoleon III of having intervened in Mexico because he had been obsessed with the strategic position of Central America and the prospect of constructing a canal there. American historians, particularly, have used that reasoning. Alfred and Kathryn Hanna, for example, suggest that 'Louis Napoleon's serious reflections on an American canal to connect the Atlantic with the Pacific would appear to provide irrefutable evidence in tracing the origin of Napoleon III's Grand Design'.[18] To a certain extent they were correct, for the genesis of *la grande pensée* of Napoleon III is revealed in his pamphlet on a canal in Nicaragua, as it is in other political writings of his youth. At the conclusion of his pamphlet Louis Napoleon wrote:

La prospérité de l'Amerique centrale se rattache aux intérêts de la civilisation en général, et le meilleur moyen de travailler au bien-être de l'humanité, c'est d'abattre les barrières qui séparent les hommes, les races et les nations ... La religion chrétienne nous enseigne que nous sommes tous frères, et qu'aux yeux de Dieu, l'esclave est égal au maître, – de même que l'Asiatique, l'Africain et l'Indien sont égaux à l'Européen. D'un autre côté, les grands hommes de la terre ont, par leurs guerres, mêlé ensemble les differents races, et laissé derrière eux quelques-uns de ces impérissables monuments, tels que l'aplanissement des montagnes, le percement des forêts, la canalisation des rivières, monuments qui, en facilitant les communications, tendent à rapprocher et à réunir les individus et les peuples. La guerre et le commerce ont civilisé le monde. La guerre a fait son temps; le commerce seul poursuit aujourd'hui ses conquêtes. Ouvrons-lui une nouvelle route. Rapprochons de l'Europe les peuplades de l'Océanie et de l'Australie, et faisons-les participer aux bienfaits du christianisme et de la civilisation.[19]

[The prosperity of Central America is linked to the interests of civilisation in general, and the best way to work towards the well-being of humanity is to knock down the barriers which divide men, races and nations ... The Christian religion teaches us that we are all brothers, and, in the eyes of God, the slave is equal to the master – as well as that the Asian, the African and the Indian is equal to the European. From another point of view, the great men of the earth have, through their wars, mixed different races, and left behind them some undying works, such as levelling of mountains, piercing of forests, channelling rivers, monuments which, by facilitating communication, attempt to bring human beings and populations closer together. War and commerce have brought civilisation to the world. War has had its day; commerce alone carries on today with its conquests. Let it open a new road. Let us bring closer to Europe the people of Oceania and Australia, and allow them to share in the benefits of Christianity and civilisation.]

What these writings do show is not an obsession with Central America for narrowly strategic reasons, but, rather, an awareness of the advantages for world harmony of another avenue to facilitate communication between nations and the mixing of peoples of varied origins. The most important point in this passage is his comment that the only way to 'civilise' the world was no longer through war but through commerce. *This* was the 'grand idea' of Louis Napoleon, not the maintenance of conservative monarchical institutions in the Americas to oppose the growing number of republican governments.

Instead, what is evident here, is the core of the policy of Louis Napoleon as Emperor.

These ideas were also reflected in many of Napoleon III's speeches, writings and discussions during his reign, and they remained remarkably consistent. In his address to the *Corps législatif* in 1854 he declared that 'the era of conquests is over, and cannot return; for it is not by extending her territorial boundaries that a nation in our days can be honoured and powerful; it is by placing itself in the lead of generous ideas, by causing everywhere the rule of law and justice to prevail'.[20] Yet if extending territorial boundaries was not necessary to achieve greatness, one might be tempted to ask why Napoleon wanted to obtain Nice and Savoy and the Rhineland for France. Perhaps the answer lies in an observation made in 1860 to the French Ambassador to Austria on his departure from Paris. Napoleon remarked that if France were able to obtain her 'natural' borders, for example the Alps, this would mean she could spend less on defence and devote more money to commercial developments as England did. He had observed that England's commercial superiority was a result of her isolation and that, therefore, there was not as much need to spend money on defence. Every year France lost a large portion of her male population to conscription, when they could be used productively at home to improve France's commercial situation.[21] To our eyes, perhaps, a legitimate argument, but to the statesmen of the mid-nineteenth century Napoleon III's motives would always be suspect. Although Nice and Savoy were annexed to France in 1860 by peaceful means, Britain and the rest of Europe were convinced that Napoleon would ultimately claim the Rhineland for France, too, despite his protestations that he would never act against the will of the people in those lands.

Napoleon's comments were supported by his minister, Persigny, in the same year, and many years later by Ollivier, in an article on Napoleon's foreign policy. Persigny said to the Conseil général de la Loire:

Dans l'état actuel des sciences militaires, un fleuve comme le Rhin n'est pas une frontière stratégique. Ce n'est donc pas pour un avantage illusoire que la France irait s'exposer à une nouvelle guerre européenne.[22]

[Given the present state of military science, a river like the Rhine is not a strategic border. France will thus not expose herself to a new European war for some illusory advantage.]

Ollivier also dismissed the idea of Napoleon wanting to extend France's frontiers as being totally incompatible with his policy:

> L'Empereur, sous la pression de l'opinion publique et quoique cela lui fût personnellement indifférent, eût peut-être souhaité, sans toucher aux provinces rhénanes, une rectification de frontières vers le Palatinat. Mais comme toute combinaison de ce genre dépendait du libre assentiment des populations et qu'il savait cet assentiment impossible, il n'a jamais rien sacrifié à cette convoitise mesquine.[23]

> [The Emperor, under pressure from public opinion, and though he was not personally concerned, may have wished the borders to be moved towards the Palatinate, without touching the Rhine provinces. But, as any change of this kind depended on the free consent of the population, and as he knew that this consent was impossible, he had never sacrificed anything to this mean desire.]

Although there is little evidence to support the claims of his opponents, Britain remained constantly alert for any signs of French aggrandisement and attempts to overturn the Treaties of 1815.

Napoleon did want to overturn the Treaties of 1815, but not in an effort to make France once again Master of Europe. He saw, instead, a Europe united to improve social, industrial and commercial conditions for everyone, rather than divided over territorial squabbles and rivalries. According to the young Louis Napoleon, the Treaties of 1815 had not only left France weaker, but had based European equilibrium on the rivalries of the great powers rather than on the interests of all nations. He believed that if his uncle's idea of a European association founded on complete nationalities and on satisfied general interests had been achieved, the problems caused by the Vienna 'settlement' would never have happened, because communal interests would have taken priority over individual interests. He described the situation that would have existed with such an association:

> Chaque pays, circonscrit dans ses limites naturelles, uni à son voisin par des rapports d'intérêt et d'amitié, aurait joui à l'intérieur des bienfaits de l'indépendance, de la paix et de la liberté. Les souverains, exempts de crainte et de soupçon, ne se seraient appliqués qu'à améliorer le sort de leurs peuples, et à faire pénétrer chez eux tous les avantages de la civilisation![24]

[Each country, defined within its natural borders, united with its neighbour by links of common interest and friendship, would have enjoyed internally the benefits of independence, peace and liberty. The monarchs, free from fear and suspicion, would have applied themselves only to the betterment of the people, and to the introduction of the advantages of civilisation.]

It was this notion of sharing ideas and civilisation that was fundamental to the foreign policy of Napoleon III, and William Echard concluded that 'only within the context of a certain idea of Europe does the foreign policy of Louis Napoleon begin to make sense.'[25] He believed the reason that others have been unable to find an explanation for Napoleon's apparent difficulty in deciding with whom he wanted an alliance was because they have tried to interpret his policy 'in terms of the *ends* sought' when it was

in fact developed in terms of the *means* by which those ends were to be achieved. The consistent purpose of the alliances and ententes entered into or sought by Napoleon between 1849 and 1863, then, would have been to make the concert of Europe function as he wished it to function, that is, to bring the powers together in general congresses that would reorganize Europe, solve its most urgent problems and thereafter regulate the new arrangements.[26]

His contemporaries, however, preferred to classify his 'ideas' as the dreams of a romantic because they seemed too esoteric or grandiose to be achieved. Prévost-Paradol saw them as the dreams of a 'mediocre visionary', while Napoleon's unrelenting critic, Zola, said he had 'more imagination and reverie than judgement. He tried to live the life dreamt of by the prisoner of Ham.'[27] But their greatest criticism was that he did not ever outline a comprehensive foreign policy with clearly stated objectives, which left his opponents and his fellow sovereigns apprehensive about his intentions. Instead, he preferred not to be bound by a fixed programme but to follow his uncle's philosophy of adjusting his system according to events and circumstances. His proposals for European congresses were rejected on similar grounds. He refused to propose a definite programme of issues to be resolved by the congress to avoid preconceived ideas about an outcome, but this led Britain and Austria, particularly, to be anxious about his intentions for Europe.

In reviewing his foreign policy in 1859 Napoleon said that what he had consistently tried to do was to reassure Europe regarding France's intentions; return France to her rightful place as a power in Europe; secure France's alliance with England and confirm his relationship with other continental powers. Of these, he placed most emphasis on the alliance with England, which he considered so useful to world peace. He believed that his desire for a secure alliance with England was reciprocated by the Queen and men of State there, but though this was outwardly England's desire, he did not appreciate the very real fear that was maintained in England of an invasion by France.[28] The main cause of this suspicion was that the English views on how best to maintain peace in Europe were almost diametrically opposed to those of the Emperor. Lord Palmerston, alternately Prime Minister and Foreign Minister between the 1840s and 1860s, was convinced that the territorial settlements of 1815 were still the best guarantee of peace, because they helped maintain the balance of power. By this he meant that no one state could assume a position of hegemony, in particular France or Russia, so any suggestion of an adjustment in territorial frontiers he saw as a threat to that balance of power. Prior to, and in the early years of, the Second Empire, Palmerston believed that the conservative elements in France would cooperate in the maintenance of that balance so 'he made friendship with France a prominent feature of his policy.'[29] This changed to concern, however, after the Empire was proclaimed in 1852, and in the late 1850s Palmerston became almost paranoid about a possible invasion by France when it appeared that France's navy, employing the new ironclad ships, might rival Britain's own.

Unaware of the depth of Palmerston's anxieties, Napoleon maintained his determination to achieve a strong alliance with Britain. This was the basis of his decision to become involved in the Crimea in 1854, in China in 1860 to protect Catholic missionaries and Britain's opium trade, and in Mexico in 1861. Nevertheless England, particularly in the person of Lord Palmerston, was to remain suspicious of France and convinced that Napoleon III, like his uncle, was intent on invading England, regardless of any evidence to the contrary. This was particularly so after the negotiations by Napoleon for the cession, by Sardinia, of Nice and Savoy to France, which followed his role in organising the ceding of Tuscany to Sardinia in January 1860. Britain was not affected by these changes, and the people of each of the provinces voted in favour of them, but Palmerston feared this move presaged further demands for French expansion, which would threaten the balance of power in Europe. Combined with a perceived challenge to Britain's naval supremacy, these concerns had considerable impact on relations between the two governments for several years.

It was within this atmosphere that the problems of a politically unstable and economically devastated Mexico were discussed by France, Britain and Spain in the late 1850s and early 1860s. The conflicting policies and attitudes of Britain and France, particularly, in relation to both Europe and the Americas, form the bases from which these two nations tried to develop a mutually acceptable approach to the problems affecting their interests in Mexico. This process was further complicated, however, by some fundamental differences between the two countries, one of the most important being in their systems of government. In France, foreign policy was developed almost solely by the Emperor, with the opportunity for the Senate and *Corps législatif* to propose amendments being introduced only in late 1860. France also did not begin publishing diplomatic correspondence until 1861, while in Britain the *Blue Books*, containing diplomatic correspondence, had been published since early in the century, providing the opportunity for widespread criticism of government foreign policy. No other country had its policy so exposed to public scrutiny, and this exposure increased with the availability of transcripts of parliamentary debates and the use of newspapers and journals for politicians to espouse or defend their views.[30] This practice was to create noteworthy problems during negotiations between France and Britain because concern over parliamentary and public opinion dictated the actions of senior British ministers.

This is one of the factors that needs to be given more consideration when studying the Mexican intervention. Most commentators have played down the contribution of others to the failure of the campaign and have placed the blame squarely at the feet of Napoleon III. Yet the prelude to the campaign involved discussions between Britain and France and also Spain, each ultimately having different motivations which were bound to affect the outcome of their accord. For this reason, this analysis will review the attitudes to Central America of the United States, Britain and France, and to a lesser degree, Spain, during the first half of the nineteenth century. A brief history of the troubled years of Mexican independence will then form a background to the decisions of the governments of France, Britain and Spain to intervene in Mexico, and to a discussion of the controversies that have persisted about the motives of Napoleon III relating to Mexico, the management of the campaign, and the offering of the throne to the Archduke Maximilian of Austria. A prominent part of this discussion will relate to the actions of various individuals and will draw significantly on the correspondence of Napoleon with his commanders, his ministers and with

Maximilian to determine to what extent Napoleon should be blamed for the failure of the intervention. Should he be exonerated from blame because of the actions of others, and should he be given credit as a visionary when the reality turned out to be a disaster?

1
Prelude to Intervention

For many – both contemporaries and later analysts alike – the significance of the French intervention in Mexico between 1861 and 1867 lies in the fact that it was an overwhelming failure. Behind that failure, however, is a complex web of historical facts, international rivalries, vested interests, and conflicting ideological bases of the foreign policies of the nations concerned with the attainment of political stability in Mexico. These nations included, most importantly, France, Britain and the United States and, to a lesser degree, Spain. The interests and concerns of these nations thus form the background to one of the most controversial episodes of the mid-nineteenth century. The turmoils that had wracked Europe in the early years of the century, culminating in the overthrow of Napoleon I and the 'settlement' of Europe by the Treaties of 1815, also had an impact on the Spanish American colonies, which began to revolt against their weakened Spanish masters and demand independence. Mexico, Spain's largest colony, gained independence in 1821, but this was only the beginning of a period of revolution and anarchy that was to devastate the country for more than forty years. In addition, an independent Mexico then began to assume a position of strategic and commercial importance to Britain, the United States and Europe, becoming a pawn in their challenges for supremacy in the region.

The British had shown interest in Mexico ever since Napoleon's Continental System had excluded them from European markets, and Mexico's independence from Spain had encouraged an aggressive commercial interest in the area. Since Britain was still diplomatically isolated from Europe, she wished to protect the newly-independent Latin American markets from interference by European governments, and proposed that she and the United States sign an agreement 'to prevent any European intervention in the Western Hemisphere.'[1] The United States, however, decided to issue an independent statement, which became known as the Monroe Doctrine, which had more far reaching effects than the British proposal. It stated, in part:

(1) That the United States did not wish to take part in the politics or wars of Europe.

(2) That the United States would regard as manifestations of an unfriendly disposition to itself the effort of any European power to interfere with the political system of the American Continents, or to acquire any new territory on these continents.[2]

By this statement the United States was announcing its determination to protect the republican American nations from conservative European influence, its refusal to allow Latin America to become a protectorate of Great Britain, and that the United States was becoming 'a power among nations that had to be reckoned with'.[3] So Britain, instead of improving her position in the Americas, found that even her own navigational rights and colonies in the American sphere were under threat.

The United States was still in a period of great expansion, and was determined to possess a large part of the American continent, particularly as far as the west coast, which to this point was controlled by Britain with her Canadian provinces and the territory of Oregon, and by Mexico, which owned California. The United States was also anxious to annex Texas, which had been populated by settlers from the United States when Mexico became independent. Texas had become independent in 1836, but in 1845 was annexed by the United States under the expansionist policy of President James Polk. This policy also saw Polk threaten war with Britain over the territory of Oregon, but Britain acquiesced to his demands in order to protect her trading interests with the United States and reduce the burden of her colonies. While the United States had gained access to the Pacific seaboard, it did not yet own the only reasonable port, San Francisco, which could only be achieved by taking California from Mexico. Mexico conveniently declared war on the United States in 1846 over the annexing of Texas, the war lasting two years and resulting in the defeat of Mexico and the ceding of California to the United States. In three years the area of the United States had nearly doubled. Continental security also was almost achieved, with possession of the west coast, including a valuable port, and removal of a threat to its southern flank through Texas.

Despite Britain's acquiescence over the Oregon territories, the United States harboured an intense concern over her possible strategic control of a Central American communication route. Polk, however, failed to realise that Britain was no longer interested in extending her Empire, wanting only to develop her trading and commercial interests and protect them from competition with Europe. Polk feared that, as Britain possessed several islands in the Caribbean as well as having a protectorate along the Mosquito coast of Honduras and Nicaragua, she might also acquire Cuba from Spain and thus control the Caribbean and the approaches to Central America. Britain could, by 'asserting its existing control of the high seas ... render California as useless as it had been under Mexico – forcing California and parts of the West to break off from the Union in their own best interests'.[4] In a bid to prevent such an occurrence Polk offered Spain $100 million in 1848 to purchase Cuba, but was unsuccessful.

In 1850 the United States and Britain signed the Clayton–Bulwer Treaty, which prevented either government gaining control over a canal that might be constructed in the isthmus, or colonising or assuming 'any dominion over Central America'.[5] From Britain's viewpoint it also provided some control over the expansion of the United States. But the prospect of a canal in the region encouraged private American adventurers, or filibusters as they became known, to try and gain control of Nicaragua and the passageway between the Atlantic and Pacific Oceans. Although not officially sanctioned, their actions raised awareness in Britain that the United States considered the Americas theirs, and the British public could see no reason why Britain should contest that fact. Public opinion on the situation was expressed in such newspapers as *The Times* and *The Economist* in June 1856. *The Times* believed that they should not resist the expansion of the United States unless a British community was threatened or some real interest was at stake, and added: 'It must be for our interest to see North America under strong, civilized, uniform and prosperous government ... It does not become us to play the dog in the manger with our fast-growing progeny across the Atlantic.'[6] *The Economist* went even further:

We could not hinder the ultimate absorption by the Anglo-Saxon republicans of the whole of Central America if we would ... We can have no interest in upholding the present wretched and feeble governments of Spanish America. Our interest lies all the other way. We wish ourselves for no extension of territory on that continent ... Desiring no territory, we desire only prosperous, industrious,

civilized and wealthy customers...Central America peopled and
exploited by Anglo-Saxons will be worth to us tenfold its present
value.[7]

Guided by such opinions, Palmerston, the British Prime Minister, recognised that Britain's commercial interests demanded a policy of maintaining peace with the United States, and that it would be impossible to
contain the activities of the American filibusters without antagonising
the United States. For this reason, both parties agreed to abrogate the
Clayton–Bulwer Treaty in 1858, and British opposition to expansion
by the United States effectively ended. This new position was later to
have an impact on the discussions with France and Spain relating to
intervention in Mexico.

France was not disinterested in the situation in Central America at this
time, and, along with the United States and Britain, had signed treaties in
the 1850s 'with the various Central American countries...and all parties
were insured territorial integrity and free rights of transit across the Isthmus'.[8] The idea of a canal, somewhere between Panama and the south of
Mexico, to improve this transit, had been seriously investigated and
discussed for many years, having been originally suggested in the
sixteenth century. With the independence of the Spanish American
colonies, many nations became interested in ensuring freedom of access
to such a communication route and, also, to trade with the surrounding
countries. Individuals from various nations then began making proposals
for the construction of a canal.

In the 1840s approaches were made to foreign governments, including
that of Louis-Philippe in France, to support the construction of a canal,
and his government had sent an engineer to determine the suitability
of Panama. Another approach, from the States of Guatemala, Honduras
and San Salvador, was rejected by Louis-Philippe, however, so their
representative asked to visit Prince Louis Napoleon, who was at that
time imprisoned in the fortress at Ham,[9] and who had shown an interest in such a project after visiting the Americas. He was offered the
opportunity to organise a company to construct a canal in Nicaragua,
and, while he awaited the results of a request to be released from prison
to travel to America, he wrote a comprehensive brochure on the
importance of a canal, with an analysis of a number of the proposed
sites and details of the construction, the costs involved and the estimated revenue that could be generated by its use. As a prisoner with
time to think, Louis Napoleon was able to ruminate over such projects,
and this one offered a feasible opportunity to obtain his release and to

be assured of a worthwhile occupation while he awaited a favourable time to pursue his 'destiny' in France. As approval for his release was not forthcoming, and he wished to see his dying father, he decided to escape from Ham and go to England, where he waited some months for permission to visit his father in Tuscany. The changing political situation in France, however, kept Louis Napoleon in England until the collapse of the Orleanist regime in 1848 and the idea of going to America was then abandoned – but not forgotten, many later claimed.

In the meantime, an independent Mexico was suffering turmoil within while much of her territory was being absorbed by the United States. For forty years a struggle persisted between two factions, the Conservatives and the Liberals, and those forty years saw as many governments, and even more presidents, each taking the place of the previous one by use of a Mexican system, in the Spanish tradition, called a *pronunciamento*. This changing of the government simply by making a proclamation, meant the country was doomed to continual anarchy and instability. In addition, the most dominant element in the search for power was the Church, which had managed, with the help of Fernand Cortez and numerous bequests from wealthy Mexicans, to accumulate almost a third of the wealth of the country. The Church was supported by the Conservative Party, which struggled against the Liberals, who wished to reduce the power and influence of the Church. It was not until 1833, however, that the Liberals, under the direction of Antonio Lopez de Santa Anna, made any serious attempt to address the issue of the political influence of the Church. As well as curbing the political influence of the clergy, Santa Anna secularised public education, determined that the clergy should be allowed to renounce their vows, and began the secularisation of Church property. But when his government moved to reduce the size of the army, which was firmly under the influence of the Church, both the army and the Church united against the government, and eventually Santa Anna decided to side with the Church and the Conservatives.

In the following twenty years three new constitutions were drawn up, and while each addressed the issue of providing a franchise, the limitations of each franchise differed, as did the attitudes to the Church. In 1836, under the Conservatives, the rights and duties of Mexican citizens were defined, and the franchise was given to adult males with an income of 100 pesos. But in 1843 these same Conservatives raised the income threshold for voters to 200 pesos, which automatically excluded the Indians, who worked mainly as farm-hands or labourers, despite the fact that the Indians constituted approximately one half of the population of about eight million. The rest was comprised of about one million whites and three million Creoles. This latest constitution also declared that the Roman Catholic religion was the only one allowed in Mexico, which dealt another blow to the Liberals.[10] The struggle for freedom continued, resulting in a constant state of anarchy, which led some Mexicans to consider approaching European governments to provide Mexico with a sovereign, in the hope this might bring some stability. In 1855 Santa Anna commissioned José Miguel Gutierriz Estrada, a Mexican exiled in Europe since 1840, to find a European sovereign, but Estrada's approaches were rejected everywhere and Santa Anna himself was soon ousted from power by the Liberals.

The Liberals, led first by Diego Alvarez and then Ignacio Comonfort, immediately began introducing reforms which seriously attacked the position of the Conservatives. Some Church property was confiscated, and on 5 June 1856 an order was issued suppressing the Jesuits and allowing the forswearing of vows by members of religious orders and the clergy. This was followed by the abolition of the right of civil and ecclesiastical corporations to hold real property, except that directly used for worship. The idea was 'to force all large property holders to disgorge and sell their enormous holdings, so as to get the land into the hands of the middle and poorer classes and give them the incentive which comes from private ownership'.[11] A Constituent Congress then drafted a new constitution that was presented in February 1857 and accepted by Congress in September that year. The Liberal Constitution gave the franchise to males aged 18 if they were married, and 21 if not; provided for a constitutional federal government; provided freedom and protection to slaves; freedom of religion; freedom of the press; encouraged immigration from all countries, and enterprise in industry, especially mining and international imports. The military was to be under civil authority, and military and ecclesiastical privileges were abolished; and Church property worth $200,000,000, the income from which was worth $20,000,000, was to be nationalised.[12]

After the constitution was presented, however, President Comonfort declined to support it because of its impact on the Church. He then made a pact with the Conservatives, accepting a counter proposal by them and breaking with the Liberals. The Conservative plan proposed: the inviolability of Church property and revenues and re-establishment of former exactions; re-establishment of privileges for the army and clergy; the Roman Catholic religion as sole and exclusive religion in Mexico; censorship of the press; immigration only from Catholic countries; overthrow of the Constitution of 1857 and use of a central dictatorship subservient solely to the Church; establishment of a monarchy if possible, but, if not, a European protectorate.[13] It was, in effect, the complete antithesis of the Liberal Constitution and became effective because of Comonfort's defection to the Conservatives. Comonfort, however, was then ousted by General Felix Zuloaga, who declared himself President of a now Conservative government, in January 1858. This was the beginning of a civil war that raged for three years, and it was in this time that calls for intervention by European governments became stronger. In reaction to Zuloaga's *coup d'état*, Benito Juarez, a senior minister in Comonfort's cabinet, declared an alternative government in February 1858, which eventually took up residence in Vera Cruz. This government was considered the legal and constitutional government, because it was supported by the majority of State governors and by public opinion in 16 out of 22 States.[14] While turmoil reigned in Mexico, the foreign governments dealing with the country were faced with the dilemma of deciding which of the two Mexican governments they should recognise, and whether they should heed the calls from both Mexicans and their own representatives to become involved in the crisis.

Although over the years Mexican emigrants made several informal approaches to the European governments, the first official one was made by Zuloaga in 1858, in accordance with the alternative proposal to the Constitution of 1857. It met with varied but cautious reactions, however, from France and Britain. Zuloaga asked the French and British representatives in Mexico, de Gabriac and Otway, to request assistance from their governments for the re-establishment of order and security in the country, as well as the complete reorganisation of its administration. The French Minister of Foreign Affairs, Count Walewski, commented to his minister in London that it was evident that no Mexican government would be able to prevent a dissolution 'which was incontestably imminent'. He felt that Zuloaga's request was made in the fear that one day Mexico would be absorbed by the United States, and the situation was therefore worthy of close examination by England and France, in view of the prospect of interoceanic communication being controlled by the United States.[15] The view of the British Foreign Minister, Lord Malmesbury, was that he did not think that Mexico had reached a stage where she would be prepared to submit herself to outside protection and, besides, England was not prepared to undertake such a mission. He also thought it highly likely that Mexico would one day be absorbed by the United States, to him a solution most advantageous for Europe because it would improve trading opportunities with the Southern

States of America and probably lead to a division, and, later, the dissolution of the United States. He thought this was probably why the United States had not already tried to annex Mexico.[16]

Meanwhile, in October 1858, reports reached Paris that the Spanish were preparing the departure from Cadiz of an expedition to Mexico to press their claims against the government, thus pre-empting any joint venture, just as they were to do again in 1861. General Almonte, the Mexican minister in Paris for Zuloaga, asked Britain and France to mediate between Spain and Mexico, but Spain rejected such an offer. In early November Marshal O'Donnell, the Spanish Prime Minister, told the French and British ministers in Madrid, Fournier and Buchanan, that if Mexico did not accept its forthcoming ultimatum, Spain was prepared to go to war – with the United States as well if necessary. Buchanan, the British minister,was convinced that Spain wanted to drag France and Britain into a war with Mexico and the United States, purely to prove her strength.[17] Buchanan advised Lord Russell, now Foreign Minister, of this, adding that Marshal O'Donnell was determined to be firm and that Spain had plenty of ships in the vicinity.[18]

These moves for intervention in Mexico did not come to fruition for various reasons which will be discussed shortly, but it is valuable to consider the proposed aims and actions in this earlier situation. Buchanan wrote to Russell that both Calderon Collantes, the Minister of State for Foreign Affairs, and O'Donnell had more than once suggested that 'it will be the interest and duty of England and France to adopt measures in concert with Spain for encouraging the re-establishment of some legitimate authority in Mexico and for restraining the aggressive policy of the United States towards their southern neighbours'.[19] At this time they suggested that 'moral influence' alone would probably be sufficient to achieve this end if the European powers adopted a firm policy. Buchanan believed, however, that Spain's motives were really more basic than this. He thought Spain was looking to renew her prestige and interests in the West Indies and South America, and that the Spanish government was convinced that if problems arose with the United States, Britain and France would eventually become involved. He informed O'Donnell and Collantes, however, that if Spain did engage in a war to further this end, it was most unlikely that Great Britain and France would wish to become involved.

It seemed that the United States was then occupied with difficulties in Paraguay, and Spain was hoping to take advantage of this opportunity. The United States had also been making suggestions about buying Cuba from Spain, and, according to Fournier, it was Spain's fear of losing Cuba if she went to war with the United States that made her decide to maintain peace with Mexico and gain satisfaction through other means. Fournier also thought the Spanish Government was making 'lots of noise' about foreign affairs in an effort to gain some glory for Spain and take the focus off internal affairs.[20] The 1850s had been an unstable period in Spain, with a revolution in 1854 and constant battles between the various factions in succeeding years. O'Donnell had taken control of the ministry in June 1858 and maintained his position until March 1863. Although his was 'the most stable ministry constitutional Spain had seen', O'Donnell was constantly faced with revolt by political notables and was finally forced to resign on 27 February 1863.[21]

Although Spain's apparent determination to use force against Mexico dissipated over the following weeks, Collantes began discussions with France on the advantages of seeing a stable government re-established in Mexico. He wrote to Alesandro Mon, his minister in Paris, that he thought France, England and Spain should adopt a firm attitude regarding the integrity of the territory of the Mexican Republic and the conserva-tion of her nationality. He thought that if they guaranteed that none of them wished to make Mexico a protectorate, they could encourage the formation of a stable government without actually interfering in the country's politics.[22] He later said that Spain only wished to re-establish good relations with her former colony and to see Mexico happy and prosperous because of the factors, such as religion and language, that bound the two nations together. All that Spain wanted for Mexico was to see her grow by being at peace with other countries and achieving internal order.[23]

In July 1859, Collantes again suggested to Britain that the three nations should help resolve the internal problems of Mexico, which might prevent her being annexed one day by the United States. Russell did not think that interference by the European powers was likely to settle Mexican affairs permanently so was not inclined to be involved; nor was he moved by Collantes's concerns about the United States.[24] British residents had also appealed to their government to protect Brit-ish commerce and prevent Mexico being exploited by the United States, who 'would soon acquire a most undue . . . nay, dangerous preponder-ance, and would have it in their power to wield a formidable weapon against the mercantile interests of other nations', but this did not stir the British government either.[25]

Despite all these discussions no action was taken against Mexico in 1859, one of the reasons being Spain's involvement in a dispute with Morocco which was not resolved until April 1860. This engagement possibly satisfied Spain's need to enhance her prestige in the world, for the time being at least, and this is perhaps why the government decided to settle its differences with Mexico. Negotiations in Paris between the Spanish minister, Alesandro Mon and Almonte, the Mexican minister for the Conservative government, resulted in the Mon–Almonte Treaty signed on 26 December 1859 and ratified on 25 January 1860. It provided for the prosecution of those responsible for the assassination of Spanish nationals in two separate incidents in 1856, and for the payment of compensation to others who suffered damages at the same time. It was agreed that other claims would also be finalised in discussions between the two governments.

The political situation in Mexico had not improved, however, for the divisions in Mexico were fundamental and deep, and unlikely to be resolved easily. In January 1859, Zuloaga, the Conservative president in Mexico City, was ousted by his colleague, Miguel Miramon, who increased the pressure on the Juarez administration in Vera Cruz with strong military offensives against Liberal strongholds throughout the country. In July, Juarez introduced a number of reforms, which included: nationalising Church property; separation of Church and State; exclaustration of monks; establishment of a civil registry for certificates of births, marriages and deaths; secularisation of cemeteries; and secularisation of public holidays. In reply Miramon pledged to champion 'the interests of the Church, vigorously sustaining the prerogatives and independence of that institution'.[26] Early in 1860, in an attempt to resolve this anomalous situation, Britain and France thought mediating between the two leaders might help establish a government that would be accepted by the entire nation. Edouard Thouvenel, successor to Walewski as French Foreign Minister, suggested the formation of a Constituent Assembly to determine what form the new government should take, and to resolve all the difficulties facing the country. Capitalising on these ideas, Collantes instructed his ministers in London and Paris to discuss with the respective Foreign Ministers how the three powers and the United States, if it wished to be involved, could intervene in Mexico to achieve a stable government. He believed that the news that such an intervention was to take place would be enough to give courage 'to the honourable people' in Mexico to work towards establishing a government which would end forever 'the spirit of rebellion that had caused so much damage in this unfortunate country'.[27]

Russell's response to Collantes's proposal was that he would consider any suggestions as long as the employment of material force was not contemplated in their execution.[28] Thouvenel said that no decision could be made about action until the American Senate had voted on whether to ratify a proposed treaty between the United States and the Juarez government in Vera Cruz, as this would naturally have an effect on what the European powers decided to do.[29] Collantes then suggested to Russell that if England, France and Spain all adopted a strong policy it would show the United States that they were not prepared to tolerate its attitude of exclusion of European nations from the New World. He did not elaborate on what he meant by 'strong policy', but a treaty between Juarez and the United States would be to the detriment of Europe, because it would give the United States more strength in its determination to exclude Europe from the Americas. Apart from these reasons, Collantes insisted that Spain was acting from humanitarian motives, which would not let her see Mexico continue to be weakened by the prevailing anarchy in the country.[30]

The three governments finally agreed to act in concert to mediate between the two Mexican leaders, but circumstances prevented this occurring. One was the continued outrages being committed against European nationals, which included murder and physical abuse, thefts and forced loans, and another was the change of each of their representatives in Mexico. Between March 1860, and May 1861, all three governments replaced their ministers for various reasons. In June 1860, the Spanish ambassador, Joaquin Francisco Pacheco, arrived in Mexico to replace the consul who had been managing Spain's affairs. The British minister, Otway, had left Mexico in late 1859, and, pending the arrival of the new minister, Sir Charles Wyke, British representation was maintained by George Mathew, Secretary of the British Legation in Mexico City. The Comte de Gabriac, the French minister, was on leave for some months for personal reasons, so a replacement had to be found for him also. De Gabriac's replacement, Dubois de Saligny, did not arrive until November 1860, and Wyke until May 1861.

By August 1860 the British government had lost patience with the two parties in Mexico, and Russell wrote to Mathew that Her Majesty's government could no longer tolerate the outrages committed against British subjects and the continual forced loans imposed by the Miramon government. He was, therefore, to withdraw the legation from Mexico City and break off relations with Miramon. He was not to go to Vera Cruz, though, as Britain did not wish to show any partiality towards the Juarez government even though they had not been as 'utterly regardless . . . of the representations of Her Majesty's Government'. Although Russell admitted that this might only have been due to the presence of a British squadron off Vera Cruz, he stressed that Britain would stay 'aloof from both parties' until a government with some chance of stability was established.[31] This action was applauded on behalf of British residents in Mexico by a correspondent from Mexico City, who confirmed the deeds of the Miramon government and added that the Constitutional Party of Juarez was the only one with whom British nationals could feel secure.[32] Pacheco, on the other hand, had decided that Miramon was more worthy of support than Juarez and in August he had presented his letter of credence to him.

Saligny left France with orders to work with his British and Spanish colleagues to impose a truce and bring about a meeting of a constituent assembly. On his arrival in November, however, he decided that he had no faith in anybody being able to regenerate Mexico, and believed the country was doomed to perpetual civil war.[33] In any case his instructions were soon out of date because Juarez's army defeated Miramon and took over the capital on 25 December 1860. The day after Juarez's arrival in Mexico City, Pacheco and several other foreign representatives, including the Apostolic Delegate and all the bishops, were expelled from the country for having supported Miramon. Saligny then took over responsibility for Spanish affairs.

In the months ahead Saligny was to play a crucial role in determining the course of events and influencing the policy of his government towards Mexico, and he was perhaps the most significant of those who must be held responsible for the controversy that has persisted regarding Napoleon's intentions in Mexico. For this reason, it is necessary to understand the situation he was inheriting from his predecessor, de Gabriac, and the character and background of Saligny himself. De Gabriac had made an unfavourable impression on all his colleagues in Mexico and, according to the American minister, Forsyth, was an 'open and active partisan of the Zuloaga party', spending 'a large part of his time *daily* in the Palace', and dreaming of a 'European protectorate' and monarchy for Mexico.[34] He was also described as a 'restless and irresponsible intriguer' who 'provided a conspicuous example of the latitude that diplomats of his stripe allowed themselves in out-of-the-way corners of the service like Mexico.'[35] Dubois de Saligny was to prove an even more controversial diplomat than de Gabriac, and his choice as de Gabriac's replacement is, at first glance, both interesting and puzzling. It has been the behaviour of Saligny, and his insistence that he was carrying out the Emperor's instructions, that has led the majority of analysts of the Mexican campaign to believe, despite evidence to the contrary, that Napoleon III intended, come what may, to impose a monarchy on Mexico to achieve *la plus grande pensée du règne.*

Saligny's career in the diplomatic service did not make him an obvious choice for the post. From 1831 to 1839 he had been in Hanover, Athens and Washington and was then Chargé in the independent Republic of Texas until its annexation by the United States in 1845. After this he had no post until sent to the Hague during the Second Republic. In 1851 he was recalled, possibly because of his Orleanist connections, and remained without assignment until called on to go to Mexico for an interim period of six months while de Gabriac was on leave. His choice for this short term was probably a result of his friendship with the Duc de Morny, a half-brother of Napoleon III, who, in previous years, had influenced the choice of representatives in Mexico. This influence was most probably linked to his financial investments in Mexico.[36] Apart from apparently also being supported by de Gabriac, there seems to be no other reason for his selection. The fact that he remained in Mexico far longer than the intended six months, was due solely to the defeat of Miramon by Juarez in December 1860. Nancy Barker observed: 'Since Gabriac was detested by the Juaristas, who were well aware of his interventionist policies, he could not return after their victory. Dubois de Saligny, in residence in the legation, received the post virtually by default.'[37]

Before leaving Paris, however, Saligny had renewed his association with Judah P. Benjamin, a United States senator from Louisiana, whom he had known when he was Chargé in Texas. Benjamin was in Paris trying to raise capital to rescue his company which planned to construct a railway across the Isthmus of Tehuantepec. Saligny was invited to join the enterprise, and his role while in Mexico was to try and convince the French government to become involved. Saligny's reward, if successful, was to be a considerable sum of money. Another associate of Saligny's, the Marquis de Radepont, a former army officer who had been in Mexico since 1847, was also in Paris at this time. In Mexico he had played the role of middle-man in pressing claims of French nationals against the Mexican government. This was a fairly common practice in Mexico and it was inevitable that claims would be greatly inflated to provide an income for the middle-man. Among Radepont's acquaintances was the Duc de Morny and the Swiss banker, Jecker, for whom he had pursued claims during the 1850s. As Radepont had business in the United States with Senator Benjamin, to whom Saligny had introduced him, Saligny agreed to take over pursuit of all the claims that Radepont had been looking after, when he arrived in Mexico.[38] As will be seen in Chapter 4, Saligny was to continue the practice of inflating claims, adding to them the controversial

Jecker bonds, a loan which had been negotiated by the Miramon government.

It was not long before the Mexicans had cause to complain of Saligny's behaviour, although it would appear that little regard was to be paid to those complaints in Paris. In April 1861, Andrés Oseguera, the First Secretary of the Mexican legation in Paris, wrote to the Duc de Persigny, then Minister of the Interior, to gain support for the new government in Mexico. The Mexican people, he said, felt they had nothing to fear from the politics of the Emperor because his system 'was the happy combination of order, justice, progress and a genuine liberty', to all of which the new Mexican government aspired. It wanted to introduce civil and religious liberty and reduce the power of the Church, which had so often interfered with past governments and dominated the country with its fanaticism and 'the bribing of the army with its excessive wealth'.[39] Because of this affinity in ideals between the two countries, Oseguera said it was difficult to understand why Saligny was behaving in such a hostile manner. He referred to an incident when the Juarez government had ordered a search of the Convent of the Sisters of Charity for 'money and valuables concealed there in violation of the law nationalizing Church property'. The Spanish Sisters had appealed to Saligny, as the Spanish representative, for protection, although there was no intimidation involved during the search. Saligny had complained on behalf of Spain, and then on behalf of himself and the French government, threatening not to renew relations with the Mexican government on the basis that the Sisters of Charity were under the Emperor's protection throughout the world – which they were not.[40] Roeder commented that Saligny's 'position was weak' because he had been forbidden to interfere in any internal affairs, and if he had been asked to show 'the imperative orders under which he claimed to be acting, he would have been hard put to attribute them to the French Government'.[41]

There seems to be no response from Persigny or Thouvenel to this letter, but Saligny's ensuing reports did not help the cause of Juarez with the French government. In March he wrote to Thouvenel that foreigners, particularly the French and the Germans, were being attacked continually in the streets of Mexico City, and when the government finally organised a police force to control the 'assassins', attacks began to occur on the roads out of the city.[42] At the end of April Saligny reported that there was disagreement among the various parties about what kind of government was appropriate for Mexico. Many also complained of the ineffectiveness of the constitution of 1857, which was supposed to save the country. He continued with the following observations and suggestion to his government:

> Dans l'état d'anarchie, on pourrait dire de décomposition sociale, où se trouve ce malheureux pays, il est bien difficile de prévoir la tournure que prendront les événements. Une seule chose me paraît démontrée, s'est l'impossibilité de rester dans le *statu quo*. Tout indique que nous touchons à une nouvelle révolution. Dans cette situation, il me paraît absolument nécessaire que nous ayons sur les côtes du Mexique une force matérielle suffisante pour pourvoir, quoi qu'il arrive, à la protection de nos intérêts.[43]

[In the state of anarchy, we could even say social break-down, in which this unfortunate country finds itself, it is difficult to predict the turn events may take. The only thing which seems clear is that the *status quo* is not possible.

Everything indicates that we are close to a new revolution. In this situation, it seems to me that it is absolutely necessary, whatever happens, to have on the Mexican coast enough material strength to provide protection for our interests.]

Saligny then requested extraordinary powers, and that he be authorised to take, on his own responsibility, any action dictated by circumstances. He asked for naval reinforcements, which would be responsible to him, and allow him to make Mexico respect the rights of foreign nations and end the abuses being committed in the country. To support his recommendation, Saligny made a broad observation that all Spanish American republics had similar histories of successive revolutions. To end this cycle, any violation of the Rights of Man needed to be suppressed immediately, otherwise the powers, after useless negotiations, would be compelled to undertake distant and fruitless expeditions, because at the moment of their arrival the culpable government would have disappeared and been replaced by two or three others.[44]

Yet it has been seen in the letter of Oseguera that the Mexican government aspired to all the liberal policies espoused by France, and when the Constitution of 1857 was drafted, the Constitutional Committee said: 'Two principal sources serve to inspire that political code: for the declaration of the rights of man, the doctrine [is] that of the French Revolution of 1789, and for the political organization of the Republic [it is] the Constitution of the United States.'[45] It might be recalled that the first article of the French Constitution of 1852 stated: 'The Constitution recognizes, confirms and guarantees the great principles proclaimed in 1789, which are the basis of the public law of the French people', for example, public liberties, legal equality and property rights.[46] Saligny, however, concluded the above dispatch to Thouvenel by recommending that Thouvenel seriously consider the idea of establishing a monarchy in Mexico as it was the only system capable of bringing an end to the abuses being committed, and of making the country respect the rights and dignity of other nations.

Saligny had little confidence in the Juarez administration, believing its position to be precarious, so he began to press for settlement of the French claims he had discussed with the Mexican Minister, Zarco, in March. He gave the government until 11 June to repay the money, but on 12 June Leon Guzman, the Foreign Minister, said that although the government wished to fulfil its obligations, it was impossible to repay one particular claim as there was not enough money in the treasury. He promised, however, to have the money from another claim, the Penaud convention, by 15 June. Saligny did not believe him, and advised Thouvenel that the French government should make preparations to press their claims by force if necessary, because he felt Mexico was trying to buy time to avoid its responsibilities.[47] He reported in July that the government had refused to repay the Penaud convention, so he reiterated his conviction that force was the only way to make the government fulfil its obligations to France.[48] An observer, however, accused Saligny of being an *agent provocateur*, saying that 'the government had approached the creditors of the French Convention with an offer of pledges and promissory notes secured by Church property, which they were inclined to accept; but on consulting their Minister [Saligny], they were advised to refuse any settlement'.[49]

While Saligny was condemning the Mexican government and accusing it of deliberately avoiding its responsibilities, Mathew wrote more perceptive observations of the situation to Russell, based no doubt on his rather longer time in Mexico. He thought Juarez was 'an upright and well-intentioned man', but not strong enough to handle the present crisis. In addition, the fact that he was an Indian put him at a disadvantage with the Spanish sections of society and with those of mixed blood. The main hope for Mexico, Mathew believed, was for a prolonged period of peace to allow for 'the development of constitutional principles, and for the gradual enlightenment of the people'. The only chance for this to occur was if England or the United States supported the government, or 'principles of government' by a protective alliance or 'by the declaration that no revolutionary movements would be permitted in any of the seaports on either ocean'. Mathew commented further on the deplorable state of the country's finances, saying that without the consent of the various States the government could not raise taxes, and, despite the possession of 'great internal wealth', Mexico's finances had been exhausted by the last period of war. The income that the government did have access to could only meet less than half its required expenditure. Although Church property had been nationalised and much of it sold, most of the proceeds had paid debts incurred by the war, while rumours calculated 'to prevent the restoration of confidence, and the consequent investment of money in the purchase of nationalized property', had reduced the expected income to the government.[50]

These contradictory views would have confused the French and British governments if read together, but Sir Charles Wyke arrived in Mexico in May 1861, and his attitudes and politics were to prove far different from those of Mathew, and somewhat similar to Saligny's. Unlike Saligny, Wyke had had several years experience in Central and South American countries, so the choice of him as minister in Mexico is logical. It may have been, though, that he came with preconceived ideas about the people and the situation, which can be seen by his early insistence that strong action was required on the part of his own government. His role in Mexico was to prove almost as controversial as Saligny's, although not as destructive, and his and Saligny's reports were the catalyst for their governments to intervene in Mexico.

Wyke left England on 2 April 1861, armed with lengthy instructions from Russell regarding both Britain's policy towards Mexico and demands for Mexico to meet its international obligations. He was to advise the Mexican government that the policy of the British government was one of non-intervention, and that they only wished to 'see Mexico free and independent, and in a position to regulate civil administration of the country, to maintain internal peace, and to discharge its international duties without the intervention of any foreign power whatever'.[51] Russell felt sure that 'such assurances' would encourage the Mexican government to accept any advice that Wyke had to offer as being impartial. He went on to caution Wyke about becoming involved in the differences between the various parties in Mexico:

A British Minister can never safely interfere in such matters; but as the representative of a country possessing liberal institutions, and therefore desiring to see other nations enjoying the same blessing, he will always be looked upon with respect and will have more real influence for good in proportion as he keeps aloof from the factions or disputes of rival parties in the State.[52]

Wyke's first duty was to demand reclamation for British bond-holders under an agreement that had been signed by the Juarez government in Vera Cruz two years earlier. The bond-holders had also lost money stolen from the British legation by Miramon's government. If Juarez denied responsibility for this, Wyke was at liberty to refer 'quietly' to the presence of British ships of war on the Mexican coasts, leaving the Mexican government 'to infer that those ships are available for your support if your just demands should be rejected, or if the engagements entered into with you should be disregarded'.[53] He was also to use every opportunity to emphasise the need to develop the country's resources, thereby providing the means of covering the government's own expenses as well as its foreign debts. In addition, he was to offer advice regarding the exercise of religious freedom in Mexico – the only question in international politics on which Britain felt authorised to offer an opinion. Wyke was reminded that the British government did not seek in Mexico, or in any other part of the world, exclusive political influence or commercial advantages that she was not prepared to share with other nations.[54]

Wyke quickly came to very different conclusions than Mathew had about the Mexican government and its ability to meet its foreign obligations. As far as he was concerned the government had either destroyed Church property or dissipated the money from its sale without using it to pay its debts.[55] It therefore had to be coerced to pay them, and one way to do this was by using naval forces against the ports on both coasts of the country 'when the moral effect produced would equal the material pressure, and ensure prompt compliance with any conditions which we might choose to impose'.[56] Wyke had been influenced in his opinion by a Captain Aldham, who had been in Mexico or thereabouts for three years. Aldham's view was that the Mexicans were very adept at 'evading their engagements', and it was time to show that Britain was not going to allow Mexico to continue 'to set every principle of justice at defiance with impunity'.[57] Wyke believed a show of determination by Britain would receive the respect and support of the Mexican people. Ralph Roeder commented that Wyke brought 'to the diagnosis of the organic troubles of Mexico . . . the peremptory judgement of the bailiff, the diplomacy of a commercial traveler, and the impatience of a vigorous invalid'.[58]

It is evident that it took neither Wyke nor Saligny very long to consider themselves completely *au fait* with the politics of the country, the abilities and motivations of individual personalities both in the government and other parties, and with the character of the Mexican people. How justified they were in their opinions is open to debate, but it is obvious that the opinions of both were taken seriously by their respective governments. In July they were to be provided with a reason to call on their governments for an intervention, when the Mexican Congress issued a decree which included the suspension of payment of foreign debts for two years. In a prolonged correspondence with Manuel Zamacona, the Mexican Foreign Minister, about this decree, Wyke scathingly criticised it as 'a gross violation of [Mexico's] most sacred obligations towards other nations'.[59] Zamacona responded that this was not the case, and that it was due 'solely to the force of circumstances, which have rendered it morally and physically impossible for the nation to continue making those payments which have hitherto been made by means of the most strenuous exertions'. The government, he said, had only two choices: 'either to respond to public opinion by adopting the only existing means of preserving order and reorganizing the whole administrative system, or to look quietly on and leave society to become an easy prey to the prevailing anarchy'.[60] Peace, order and administrative reform would be impossible to achieve if the government had to expend nearly all its income on servicing the national debt. In effect, Mexico was asking for the support and understanding of its creditors while the government embarked on the regeneration of its country; suspension of payments to foreign nations was to be a temporary exercise to allow time for a solid base to be established for regeneration.

Wyke, however, could see no justification for Mexico taking this step without prior consultation with her foreign creditors and, rather pompously, proceeded to liken Mexico's reasons for her action to the justification of a starving man who had stolen a loaf of bread, claiming that:

> imperious necessity impelled him thereto ... but such an argument cannot, in a moral point of view, justify his violation of the law, which remains as positive, apart from all sentimentality, as if the crime had not had an excuse. If he was actually starving, he should have first asked the baker to assuage his hunger, but doing so of his own free will, without permission, is acting exactly as the Mexican Government has done towards its creditors on the present occasion.[61]

He then added, 'for reasons so evident that I will not now advance them', he thought that the intended action would in fact aggravate the difficulties facing the government rather than provide relief. The following day he went on to advise that spoliation was not the answer, and what was needed was

> a determination to make every sacrifice, and incur every privation, with a view of maintaining your honour and fulfilling your engagements. This determination once adopted and manfully put in practice would at once inspire confidence and rally round you those whose sympathies you now appeal to in vain, because they doubt from past experience both your prudence and your sincerity.[62]

Wyke concluded with a declaration that unless the decree was withdrawn in 48 hours he would suspend all correspondence with the Mexican government until he received further instructions from his own government.

Zamacona made a final attempt to convince Wyke that the Mexican government was not disavowing its obligations, whether incurred by previous governments or not, but merely seeking a suspension of payments for a given period of time, and that the decree would actually provide a greater security for creditors. The government had almost concluded an agreement with some of their foreign creditors, with guarantees regarding maintenance of their present rate of interest, but it could not be finalised because Wyke refused to sanction it, as Saligny had done earlier with the French creditors. Zamacona then rejected the aptness of Wyke's simile, as well as the accusation that his government was committing further spoliation with this decree. He felt instead that the action of the government was

> rather that of a father overwhelmed with debts, who, with only a small sum at his disposal, scarcely sufficient to maintain his children, employed it in the purchase of bread instead of in the payment of his bills. Were Her Britannic Majesty's Representative a member of the family, would his Excellency be eager to qualify his father's conduct by the name of spoliation?[63]

Wyke was unmoved, and immediately advised Russell that things would continue to get worse while this 'dishonest and incapable Administration' remained in power. It was therefore essential that Great Britain 'put a stop, by force if necessary, to its present state of anarchy'. He then dismissed any possibility of sincerity on the part of the Mexican government:

> From the tone of their notes to me anybody not on the spot would imagine that dire necessity had alone compelled them thus to act, whereas in reality 6,000,000 of hard dollars have actually passed through their hands within the last half year, to say nothing of the immense amount of church property in this district alone which has been dissipated in a manner, according to public rumour, utterly discreditable to the members of the Government.[64]

To support his belief that this administration should be changed, Wyke mentioned the existence of the Moderate party which, though presently 'cowed by the two opposing ultra factions', would emerge, if supported by foreign intervention, and form a stable and reliable government. Two days later he wrote that things were going from bad to worse and the government was now 'generally detested'. There were, he said, various conspiracies in train against the government, including one to replace Juarez with ex-president Comonfort with support from a party in the capital.[65] Finally, on 30 July, Wyke wrote to Zamacona that he was suspending relations with Mexico because his government had 'dared to issue [the decree] without consulting with me as the Representative of that Power which was the other Contracting Party to a Convention which said Decree shamefully violated.' He considered that the government had possessed ample resources to meet its obligations, and that it was only its 'wilful recklessness and want of common prudence' that had forced it to repudiate its obligations, which would only aggravate its poverty.[66]

Wyke offers no proof other than 'public rumour' to justify his claim that the government had frittered away its money, and though he had been in the country for only a few weeks he felt qualified to dismiss Mathew's reasonable explanation for the shortfall in expected revenue from the sale of Church property. Wyke used the anarchy prevailing in the country as further proof that Juarez's government was weak and ineffective, when perhaps it may have been better to support a government that was making an open declaration about its position and its intentions while asking for the understanding and support of other nations.

Saligny, however, shared Wyke's views, although the two were to become bitter rivals once the intervention began. Zamacona had written also to Saligny, acknowledging the difficulty the government would have of rising above the actions of previous regimes, but asking that it be judged on its own merits because of its determination to carry out the administrative reorganisation of the country.[67] Saligny was no more receptive than Wyke, and in a letter to Thouvenel he, too, focused on the appalling state of the country and advised he had broken off relations with Mexico. This rupture, Saligny claimed, had led the vast majority of Mexicans to look forward to a war which they hoped would solve the country's troubles. He added that, with few exceptions, the French population in Mexico was also anxious for the French government to take strong action.

Saligny seemed determined to discredit Juarez's government, for he warned Thouvenel against the special envoy that Juarez was sending to Paris and London to explain, and ask for acceptance of, its plans for reform and financial reorganisation. He said categorically that nobody in Mexico, 'beginning with the administration', took seriously these so-called imaginative plans put forward by a desperate government whose only aim was to find an excuse to get hold of the money already put aside to pay its foreign debts.[68] His words bore fruit, for when, four days after receiving this dispatch, Thouvenel was approached by Juan Antonio de la Fuente, the Mexican minister in Paris, he refused to hear any explanations for the July decree. Instead he told de la Fuente that the French government entirely approved Saligny's conduct, and that, with England, they had already given orders for a squadron of ships from the two nations to demand due satisfaction from the Mexican government. Following this meeting de la Fuente suspended diplomatic relations with France.[69]

The day after the visit of de la Fuente, Thouvenel advised Saligny that the government entirely approved of his actions and his decision to sever relations with Mexico. He spoke of the hope the government had entertained that the new administration would honour its obligations, and how hope had increased when Zarco signed the convention in March. Now that the Mexican government had no intention of honouring its obligations, Saligny was to demand the immediate retraction of the July decree, and insist that commissioners be placed in the ports of Vera Cruz and Tampico to collect the customs duties to pay the foreign conventions. If they refused, he was to remove the entire French legation from Mexico City.[70]

In the meantime, Saligny's actions in Mexico began to alienate him even further from his fellow Frenchmen in Mexico. In August, when a large crowd gathered to welcome General Ortega's return from a successful battle against the Conservative army, Saligny reported to Zamacona that an attempt had been made against his life during the demonstration. He claimed that a bullet had been fired and hit a post near where he was standing at his residence. However, there were no other witnesses and no mark could be found on the post. He also made other claims of threats against French nationals, which could not be corroborated either, but this did not stop him. Roeder commented:

> Far from representing the French colony, which was predominantly Liberal in its sympathies, he was denounced even by its conservative members as a menace to their interests, and the leading bankers and merchants proposed to draw up a representation against his interference and war-mongering.[71]

In 1863, in a memorandum to the French commander, General Bazaine, a long-time French resident, Schlœsing, remarked that this incident was not taken seriously by 'any one of our impartial compatriots', who considered that Saligny had made 'the Mexican question a question of personal pride.' He observed further:

> Je ne crains pas de l'affirmer en toute conscience; le gouvernement de l'Empereur a été trompé, depuis plusieurs années, sur la véritable situation du Mexique; les renseignements de M de Gabriac portaient le cachet de la partialité la plus manifeste, ceux de M de Saligny respiraient la passion et la vengeance.[72]

> [I am not afraid to assert in all honesty that the Emperor's government has been misled, for several years, on the real situation in Mexico. Mr de Gabriac's intelligence was glaringly biased, Mr de Saligny's reports breathed passion and revenge.]

It can be seen that in Mexico, at least, Saligny's behaviour was considered both controversial and misleading before the intervention began, and it was to continue in this vein for two years.

At the same time, Wyke was told that he was to leave Mexico if the demand for control of the customs ports was not agreed to, as continuing negotiations appeared useless.[73] Russell's response to Wyke regarding the July decree, and his correspondence with Zamacona, showed that he accepted without question Wyke's assertion about the Mexican government squandering $6,000,000 in six months. Although his opinion was based solely on Wyke's limited acquaintance with the country, Russell also rejected Zamacona's claim that the government was restoring order and pursuing administrative reorganisation:

> [I]t is notorious that every one of these assertions is directly the reverse of the truth. It is well known that life and property are nowhere safe,

not even in the streets of the capital; that the Administration is as corrupt and as reckless of any interests but their own personal advantage as any that has heretofore governed in Mexico; that great anarchy and disorder prevail in all the departments of the Government.[74]

Her Majesty's government, Russell said, could not accept any of these excuses for what had happened to their subjects in Mexico, so Wyke was again instructed to leave Mexico if the demands in Russell's letter of 21 August were not met. The British and French governments then agreed that they would send naval forces to give them any support they needed.

The Spanish government was also considering taking action against Mexico, on the basis of reports from Saligny of the constant persecution of Spanish nationals. It is strange, though, that it waited until July to consider any action, when its minister, Pacheco, had been expelled the previous December. The Mexican Foreign Minister had written in February to explain that Pacheco had by-passed the Juarez government – the legitimate government – on his arrival at Vera Cruz, and proceeded to Mexico City where he had recognised the rebel, Miramon, as head of the Mexican government. It was claimed that Pacheco's behaviour had in fact prolonged the civil war, and his expulsion for opposing the legitimate government was inevitable. However, the sentiments of the Juarez government were directed only at Pacheco and not towards the Spanish government, with whom they were anxious to resume cordial relations.[75] The Spanish government, though, had only demanded some compensation for Pacheco's expulsion, and had maintained Saligny as their representative.

It was the report of the Spanish Vice-Consul at Cuernavaca that the Mexican government was doing nothing to prevent the persecution of the Spanish, that prompted Collantes to tell the Mexican government that if it did not do something to curtail these persecutions the Spanish government would be obliged to adopt measures to put an end to this state of affairs.[76] Saligny negotiated with the Mexican government to obtain satisfaction for the expulsion of Pacheco, and advised Spain that a special envoy was being sent to offer excuses for Pacheco's expulsion and to discuss Spain's claims against Mexico. This was to be de la Fuente, but, as he made no attempt to see Mon, the Spanish minister in Paris, to obtain an introduction to his government, Mon assumed that he had no intention of approaching the Spanish government.[77] It is, however, possible that the dismissal of de la Fuente by Thouvenel prevented him from approaching Mon.

Although their earlier reports had convinced their governments of the need for firm action, the next reports of Wyke and Saligny would have strengthened that decision. Both wrote at the end of August that coercive action would encourage the Moderate party to form a more creditable government. Wyke advised Russell that the government had imposed a tax of 2 per cent on capital over $2,000 as a further means of raising revenue, because the decree of 17 July had discouraged the merchants from removing their goods from the Custom House at Vera Cruz, thus denying the government the duties. Wyke claimed this had discredited the government even further and resulted in instability within the government itself. He had heard that one of Juarez' generals, Ortega, was plotting to get himself elected president, and that Comonfort was still intriguing with various State governors to head a coalition to overthrow Juarez. Wyke concluded by again asserting that 'the respectable classes' thought a foreign intervention was the only means of saving the country, and that if France or Britain used coercive measures to seek redress:

> then the Moderate party may take courage and be able to form a Government which would afford some hope for the future; but without such moral support and assistance, they are afraid to move, and will remain the victims of the two contending factions, whose dissensions have already caused so much misery and bloodshed.[78]

Saligny also predicted that if the European powers did not intervene, the perpetual civil wars and anarchy would result in an uprising by the Indians, leading to 'a racial war and . . . the destruction of all social order.' He anticipated that Mexico would go the same way as other Central American countries if Europe did not take advantage of the civil war in North America 'to give to this country institutions more in harmony with the aspirations, opinions and needs of nineteen twentieths of the population.'[79] He suggested, further, that in the interests of France's honour, the expenses of the expedition to Mexico, if it were decided upon, should be added to the claims that France already had against Mexico.

By the time these last dispatches from Wyke and Saligny reached Europe, discussions were well under way between the governments of Britain, France and Spain on what might be the aims of an expedition, and how it should be conducted. But it was the claims of Wyke and Saligny that led all three governments to believe that their proposed actions would enable them to recover what was due to them, and, quite probably, see a more reliable government installed – particularly as both had mentioned the existence of a Moderate party waiting for their support. Everything indicated that the three governments were equally anxious to take action against Mexico and see a new, stable government in place. Yet the negotiations over the next few weeks were to reveal subtle differences in their intentions. Most emphasis has been placed on what Napoleon III thought and did, and most blame for the outcome of the expedition laid at his feet. The roles played by the key people in both the Spanish and British governments, however, contributed significantly to the decisions made by Napoleon and need due consideration.

2
The Tripartite Convention

Having decided to take coercive action against Mexico, the French and British governments were about to approach Spain to act with them. However, before they could do so, the Spanish government learned of their intentions and appeared to be overcome with the desire to show it was Spain who had taken the initiative. Despite this, the discussions that ensued between the three governments indicated that they were in agreement on the need for a change of regime in Mexico, but in the final analysis both the Spanish and British ministers were reluctant to put such proposals before their parliaments. Russell's and Palmerston's position was influenced not only by concern over the anticipated reaction of the parliament, but also by discussions with the American minister, who warned against European interference on the American continent. These contradictory behaviours of the Spanish and British, and the early arrival of the Spanish in Mexico, were to have far-reaching effects on the combined expedition. The discussions on the aims of the expedition were protracted, but concluded with all three believing they were in agreement, when they were, in fact, very far from it.

When Alesandro Mon, the Spanish minister in Paris, had learned that the British and French governments intended sending naval support to Mexico, he sent a telegraphic dispatch to Collantes saying the decision seemed to have been taken without regard to Spain.[1] Collantes replied, in apparent disregard of Mon's dispatch, that the Spanish government had resolved to act 'energetically', and was sending a boat with instructions to the Captain-General of Havana, General Serrano, to act against either Vera Cruz or Tampico with all the land and sea forces at his disposal. Naval reinforcements sufficient to maintain the dignity of Spain were also being sent. He went on to suggest that if England and France were agreeable to acting with Spain, the forces of the three powers would join together 'as much to obtain reparation for their injuries as to establish a regular and stable order in Mexico'. If England and France refused, Spain would go alone, as the Spanish government had been waiting for an opportunity, when it could not be accused of purely political motives, to act 'vigorously' against Mexico and make its just reclamations. If the French did wish to act with Spain, Collantes said, similar instructions would be sent to his minister in London.[2] In the Spanish Cortes in 1863 Mon was highly critical of Collantes's apparent intention of claiming credit for initiating the idea of a tripartite expedition. He commented cynically about the decisions conveyed in this dispatch, saying that just a few hours elapsed between the reception of his own dispatch and the resolution of the government, 'which demonstrates the zeal of the Spanish government'.[3]

Regardless of Spain's claim to have taken the initiative, there did seem to be agreement at this stage on what needed to be achieved in Mexico. On receipt of Collantes's dispatch, Mon discussed with Thouvenel the Spanish government's resolutions. Thouvenel told him the Spanish ideas were in complete agreement with those of the Emperor, and suggested the three countries should take control of the customs houses, and that they advise Mexico of the need to establish a new government whose stability could be ensured with the help of the three governments. Thouvenel said he had already written to England with these proposals and had intended writing to Spain as well.[4] Mon then had an informal discussion with the British minister, Lord Cowley, in which a change of government in Mexico was discussed. Mon told Collantes that Cowley thought a monarchy was the most suitable government, with which Mon agreed, adding however that he had no instructions regarding this from his government. When commenting to the Cortes in 1863 on this discussion, Mon said he did not believe anyone had been suggesting imposing a monarchy by force. Everyone believed that all the previous governments in Mexico had been impossible and 'incompatible with a good regime'; that there was no government which had not been offended by Juarez; and that everyone knew that a strong power would have to be represented 'by a person of high standing' who would be morally supported by Europe.[5] The idea that a monarchy was probably the most suitable form of government for Mexico was agreed by the Foreign Ministers of all three governments, but ultimately the Spanish and British ministers were to deny that this was so, and again it was the demands of their internal political situations that dictated their behaviour.

It was clear, though, that the Spanish Foreign Minister was determined that Spain should be in the forefront of any action against

Mexico, and he sent to General Serrano the instructions referred to in his dispatch to Mon. While he said there was absolutely no intention of intervening in the 'internal discussions' of the republic, nor of supporting either of the warring factions, it is not clear whether this excluded giving what Collantes later called 'moral support' to the honest men waiting for that support. He stated that it was the desire of the government to assemble all the resources possible on the coasts of Mexico, and, if necessary on Mexican territory. Serrano was advised that England and France might join their forces with those of Spain, but discussions might take some considerable time. In the meantime, Serrano was to send his forces to the coast of Mexico and demand due reparation. If his demands were not met within twelve days he was to commence 'necessary action to oblige them to submit to his demands'.[6]

When questioned on this action, the Spanish government denied the extent of its proposed actions, so when its forces landed in Mexico before the arrival of the British and French, it was natural that their governments should react with suspicion. Sir John Crampton, the British minister in Madrid, was asked to confirm with Marshal O'Donnell whether orders had been sent to Serrano to occupy Vera Cruz and Tampico, as such an action seemed in conflict with Spain's stated desire to act with England and France. O'Donnell told Crampton that Spain intended to take action alone if England and France declined to join them, but he denied orders had been sent to Serrano to 'take possession of Vera Cruz or Tampico, or to undertake any military operation against Mexico'. Crampton told Russell that O'Donnell assured him 'that no such orders had been given'. All that had been done, O'Donnell claimed, was to make preparations to ensure they were ready to take action when the time came.[7]

These assertions by O'Donnell to the British, and similar ones to the French by Collantes, were later to be disputed, however, by Mon, in his address to the Cortes in 1863. He confirmed that orders had been sent on 11 September 1862, if not to take possession of the ports, at least to take necessary coercive action if demands were not met. The order to suspend the expedition pending negotiations being settled with England and France was not sent until well after Serrano had departed Havana for Mexico. Mon claimed there had been five or six steamers leaving Spain for Havana between 11 September and the date of Serrano's departure, yet even by the time General Prim arrived in Havana to command the expedition, there had been no orders received to suspend the operation.[8]

What was the Spanish government's motivation in all this? Some in Spain thought her ministers were driven purely by the need to prove Spain's greatness, but given the tardiness with which they had reacted to the expulsion of their minister, Pacheco, the explanation seems to be related more to Spain's internal political situation. Barrot, the French minister in Madrid, wrote to Thouvenel that as far as he could judge, the reason Spain seemed to be acting so quickly was not because the question itself was so urgent, or that they hoped to achieve better future relations with Mexico. It was rather to ward off expected serious attacks by Pacheco, in the forthcoming session of the Cortes, over the government's handling of the Mexican situation. Barrot believed then that this haste on the part of Spain was driven by the demands of internal politics more than by the hope of achieving in Mexico *'une œuvre d' avenir'*[9] [a task with prospects].

While Spain was initiating action, discussions had been taking place between France and England to clarify their aims and determine what their combined action should be. Early in September Thouvenel had asked Lord Cowley if Russell would be inclined to take advantage of the United States' preoccupation with her own affairs to recommend 'the rival parties to take unto themselves a sovereign', and Cowley had remarked to Russell: 'No doubt if Mexico would do this of her own free choice, it would be the best chance of restoring herself to a creditable position among the nations of the world.'[10] Thouvenel then expanded the French ideas regarding Mexico in a lengthy dispatch to the Comte de Flahault, now the minister in London. He said that the most important aims were to obtain compensation from Mexico, and then to know that any new government would stay in power long enough to ensure that their demands were met. The experience that both governments had had with the Juarez government since it defeated Miramon proved how powerless Mexico was to overcome, alone, the anarchy resulting from so many years of internal dissension. It was therefore 'chimerical', he said, to hope that another revolution would result in a power strong and sufficiently respected to provide security for the country itself, as well as for foreign nationals and their interests. He argued that as their main objective was the protection of their nationals and of commercial interests in Mexico, they would have more chance of achieving success if they tried to prepare the way for the political reorganisation of Mexico. It was therefore essential that the manner in which France and Great Britain proposed to intervene was determined in advance, and identical instructions given to their agents in Mexico.[11]

Discussion of these suggestions, between Flahault and Russell, seemed to reveal agreement on the need for a better government in Mexico, but also that Russell was anxious about Spain's intentions there. Russell said the French and British governments were in complete agreement on the complaints against the Juarez government and the need for something to be done. He commented to Flahault, though, that even if the three powers agreed on what was to be done, England foresaw one insurmountable difficulty – that Spain would propose the persecution of Protestants in Mexico, and England could not possibly tag along behind a power that would not practise religious tolerance. In summary, they would be more than happy to act with France, but could do so only with the aim of establishing a liberal and tolerant government.[12] In making this latter comment, Russell may only have been wishing to ensure that the Spanish did not exercise their influence to enforce a return to a Conservative Catholic regime in Mexico, but Thouvenel and Napoleon could be forgiven for believing that Russell saw the establishment of a more stable government in Mexico as a principal aim of their proposed action.

Flahault commented on the importance Russell placed on the religious question, saying how careful an English minister had to be in this regard. Any act of intolerance against Protestants by a Catholic in such a situation would elicit cries of condemnation and indignation from all corners of the country and in the parliament. Therefore, they could not expect the least modification of England's views regarding religious tolerance. Cowley also broached this issue of religious tolerance with Mon, who replied that those questions should be left to the Mexican government. He also said Spain had no intention of imposing a 'particular Government on Mexico; all she desired was a Government chosen by the Mexicans, which would make itself respected and would scrupulously fulfil engagements taken with foreign Powers'.[13] Mon saw Thouvenel immediately after this and was assured by Thouvenel that he had told Russell that England's fear of Spain's religious intolerance was a '*puérilité*'. The British ministers, however, were not to be convinced, and their concern about Spain's intentions was to be raised again between Russell and the American minister, in discussions which finally determined Britain's position in relation to Mexico.

Because of O'Donnell's denial that orders had been sent to employ Spanish forces in Mexico, Russell told Cowley there was 'time for deliberation and concert'.[14] But he was not to be allowed that time by the Spanish, who were determined to act promptly. He had sent a telegram to Crampton to ensure Spain postponed any action while France and England conferred, but Crampton replied that the Spanish government would not agree to defer action beyond the beginning of November.

O'Donnell had said that 'he would be unable to justify any delay before the Cortes and country' but he hoped enough time would still be available for the three governments to agree on action 'for the immediate vindication of their respective rights'. He had then added that Spain would be ready at some stage to discuss with England and France measures 'for placing the Government of Mexico in a position to fulfil its international obligations for the future'.[15] Thus Spain's ideas at this point were similar to those expressed by France and England.

In the meantime Russell had responded to comments by Thouvenel regarding action on their arrival in Mexico. Thouvenel had suggested that they should come to 'an early understanding' on 'the measures of coercion to which . . . the two Governments might have recourse', and that 'the two Governments should carry their common understanding still further, and devise means for promoting the political reorganization of Mexico', but that the governments of Spain and the United States should be 'invited to concur in the course to be taken by the two Powers'. Russell agreed with the latter suggestion, and advised Cowley to tell Thouvenel his government was ready to discuss what measures could be taken, although 'it is evident that much must depend on the actual state of affairs at the time when our forces may be ready to act on the shores of Mexico'.[16]

Thouvenel was pleased to see the two governments were basically in agreement, and he decided to broach again the idea of changing the form of government in Mexico. In a letter to Flahault, noted 'not to be given officially to Russell', he said he knew it would be premature in the realm of diplomacy to raise the question of the establishment of a monarchy in Mexico, as England might accuse France of conspiring to hatch a Catholic, monarchical plot with Spain. However, given the proven incapacity of Hispano-Americans to prosper under a republican regime, most could see that the monarchical form was more likely to work there. Flahault should, therefore, at an appropriate time, try to lead Russell to recognise that a change in the institutions of Mexico was surely the only help for Mexico. Mexicans would no doubt ask for this themselves if they felt they were being supported by others. He then suggested that, as Austria had enough Archdukes, it could probably give one to Mexico, which might even help resolve the Italian question.[17] It is interesting to speculate on the delicacy with which Thouvenel wanted this idea brought forward, as the suitability of a monarchy for Mexico had already been discussed openly between Cowley and Thouvenel, Mon and Cowley, and in the Spanish press early in September. He may, though, have anticipated antagonism to the idea of an

Austrian Prince because of concern that France might use this to persuade Austria to cede Venetia to Italy. While many analysts of the intervention have used the unofficial nature of this communication to support the belief that Napoleon was secretly determined to impose a monarchy on Mexico, alternative conclusions can be drawn.

In view of Russell's apparent agreement on the need to see a better government established in Mexico, Thouvenel was surprised to hear him suddenly speaking out strongly against interfering in the internal affairs of Mexico. What precipitated this unexpected and determined opposition was probably a discussion between Russell and the United States Minister, Adams, about proposed loans to Mexico by the United States to cover the interest on its debts to Europe. Russell initially had been alerted to this proposal by Lord Lyons, his minister in Washington, who had advised that Seward, the Secretary of State, had said:

> that if the Convention should be ratified by the United States' Senate, Great Britain and France should engage not to make any demand upon Mexico for the interest, except upon its failing to be punctually paid by the United States.
>
> The inducement to the United States to take upon themselves the payment appeared to be the extreme importance to them of the independence of Mexico.[18]

Cowley mentioned the proposal to Thouvenel, who commented that it 'might not be possible . . . to prevent the United States offering money to Mexico, or to prevent Mexico receiving money from the United States, but neither England nor France ought in any way to recognize the transaction'.[19]

Where Russell may earlier have been prepared to discuss options related to the political situation in Mexico, his meeting with Adams crystallised his concerns about interference in that country. He summarised the American position in a letter to Cowley:

> a direct intervention with a view to organize a new Government in Mexico, and especially the active participation of Spain in such an enterprise, would excite strong feelings in the United States. It would be considered as that kind of direct interference in the internal affairs of America to which the United States had always been opposed. In fact, there was a sort of understanding that so long as European Powers did not interfere in America, the United States might abstain from European alliances; but if a combination of

Powers were to organize a Government in Mexico, the United States would feel themselves compelled to choose their allies in Europe, and take their part in the wars and Treaties of Europe.[20]

This could only be considered as a thinly veiled threat, to which Russell acquiesced, although he did insist that the receipt of payment for outstanding debts would not resolve the problem of protection of 'the persons and property of British subjects', or the fulfilment of Mexico's obligations. But he agreed with Adams that the factions in Mexico were too hostile to each other to be reconciled 'by a small force of Europeans in the name of order and moderation', and he shared the concern of the United States about the reaction in the Americas to any action taken there by Spain. However, he thought a joint venture with Spain, which excluded interference in the internal affairs of Mexico, would be more acceptable than allowing Spain to go alone 'and afterwards opposing the results of her operations'.[21]

Although O'Donnell had said Spain had no aspirations of reconquest in the Indies, to safeguard against this eventuality Russell suggested to Cowley the following clauses on which a combined operation should be founded:

1. The combined Powers of France, Great Britain, Spain, and the United States, feel themselves compelled, by the lawless and flagitious conduct of the authorities of Mexico, to seek from those authorities protection for the persons and property of their subjects and a fulfilment of the obligations contracted by the Republic of Mexico towards their Governments.
2. The said combined Powers hereby declare that they do not seek any augmentation of territory, or any special advantage, and that they will not endeavour to interfere in the internal affairs of Mexico or with the free choice of its form of government by its people.[22]

Cowley was advised to show this dispatch to Thouvenel, and a similar one was written to Crampton, emphasising the futility of interfering by force in Mexican internal affairs, and suggesting that the Mexicans alone could 'put an end to the anarchy and violence which have torn Mexico to pieces during these last years'.[23] Just how they might achieve this, given their singular lack of success in the previous forty years, Russell did not suggest.

He did, however, point out to Cowley the difficulties of any foreign army being able to exert authority over the Mexican factions, which were scattered over a vast territory. Her Majesty's government, he said, was 'on principle' opposed to 'interference in the internal affairs of an independent nation', but it remained 'to be considered' whether Mexico might form 'an exception to the general rule'. He mentioned, though, the 'universal alarm' that would be raised in North America at the idea of a European interference in an American Republic. Further, 'it would be ... unwise to provoke the ill feeling of North America, unless some paramount object were in prospect, and tolerably sure of attainment'. He added that the Spanish government believed the successful enforcement of their just demands

> would induce the Mexicans to institute a government more capable than any which has lately existed to preserve the relations of peace and friendship with foreign powers.
>
> Should such be the indirect effect of naval and military opera-tions, Her Majesty's Government would cordially rejoice; but they think this effect is more likely to follow a conduct studiously observant of the respect due to an independent nation, than to be the result of an attempt to improve by foreign force the domestic institutions of Mexico.[24]

This hardening of Russell's views seriously affected negotiations for the Convention, and they were complicated further by various opinions that a Moderate party was waiting to come forward as soon as the allies arrived. Both Saligny and Wyke, as well as correspond-ents in Mexico, gave credence to the existence of a party awaiting foreign support to form a new government. While the French and Spanish governments were convinced by these reports, the British government did not appear to be influenced by them. On the other hand, perhaps it was, and it therefore thought change would be effected easily, with little or no support from the allies, which might explain Russell's insistence on not using force. A note written in September 1861 by Almonte, the former Mexican representative in Paris, also spoke of the ease with which the allies could convince the government in Mexico City to grant an amnesty to all political prisoners and to convoke a congress to reconstitute the nation. A government organised through such a process, he said, would have the moral support of the three European nations. 'Voilà tout ce qu'il y aurait à faire pour rétablir l'ordre à Mexico et pour assurer l'exist-ence d'un bon gouvernement dans cette malheureuse République'.[25] ['That is all that needs to be done to re-establish order in Mexico

City and to ensure the existence of a good government in this unfortunate republic'.]

The confidence with which such statements were made undoubtedly had an impact on the French government, and Thouvenel told Cowley that though he did not propose influencing by armed force the internal affairs of Mexico, he felt that the 'well-disposed part of the Mexican people' should be supported by the powers if they were encouraged by the allied presence to substitute a new authority. Cowley, however, foresaw possible conflict in what each of the three powers might feel best for Mexico, and his suspicions were aroused about the French and Spanish intentions.[26] In a private letter to Russell, Cowley said he was convinced the French would try 'to establish a monarchical form of Government in Mexico, and of course Spain will be quite ready to assist'. Thouvenel, he said, had suggested 'that an Austrian Prince might be placed on the throne, and that might facilitate an arrangement respecting Venetia! A sop to us no doubt!'[27]

The talks between France and England having reached a stalemate, Napoleon decided the time had come to play an active role and state clearly his position regarding Mexico. He believed that for Europe's sake, and for Mexico's, it was essential that the three powers be prepared to support whoever appeared capable of forming a stable government, and he outlined his views in a lengthy letter to Flahault early in October. This letter has been called the *'pièce justificatif'* [document in proof] for Napoleon's intentions, 'an attempt to "come clean" at the last moment'.[28] It can also be seen as a very open statement of ideas and motivations, which is not at variance with any previously, or later, stated aim. He suggested that the obvious (*ostensible*) aim of a combined intervention should be to obtain redress for their complaints, but added: 'il faut prévoir ce qui peut arriver et ne pas bénévolement se lier les mains pour empêcher une solution qui serait dans l'intérêt de tous'.[29] [We must anticipate what might happen, and not voluntarily tie our hands in such a way as to prevent a solution which would be in all our interests.]

One could argue, as has been done, that this was an attempt to leave himself free to impose a monarchy on Mexico. If this were so, why would he insist that he would only go to Mexico if England and Spain agreed to go, too, and suggest the United States be involved? Could it be that he intended manufacturing a situation whereby France would be left alone in Mexico to impose a monarchy headed by Maximilian? Such accusations have been made, yet how could he possibly guarantee that this would happen, and why go to the trouble of negotiating an entente he intended to break soon afterwards? It is more reasonable to assume that Napoleon believed Spain and England were as committed as he was to seeing a stable and enduring government established in Mexico, and this seemed to be evident in their discussions so far. All three governments had been assured that there was a party of men who would be capable of instituting a new government if given support, and all Thouvenel's and Napoleon's arguments about the content of the Convention were with this in mind. What, in effect, could possibly be achieved if all the allies sought was compensation and redress for the outrages committed against their nationals? Without the establishment of a sound government to ensure that the same difficulties with Mexico did not continue, what was the point in going to Mexico? Nothing in her republican history could instil any confidence in the three governments that such a stable government could emerge of its own accord, and maintain itself for a long period of time without outside support. Therefore, Napoleon's arguments about being prepared to take advantage of events after arrival in Mexico seem plausible.

When discussing the idea of a monarchy, Napoleon told Flahault that after being asked to name a possible candidate for the throne, the initiative had been taken from his own hands by the committee of Mexicans in Europe 'qui prennent naturellement les choses plus vivement que moi et qui sont impatients de voir les événements se précipiter' ['who are naturally pursuing things more eagerly than I am, and who are impatient to see events moving quickly'] and who had already gone to Vienna to approach the Austrian government. Gutierrez de Estrada had in fact spoken with Prince Richard de Metternich, the Austrian minister in Paris, as early as July 1861, of the idea of an Austrian Prince going to Mexico.[30] It would seem he could not contain his impatience once France, England and Spain had agreed to go to Mexico, despite the lukewarm reception he had received from Metternich in July. Napoleon did not condemn the Mexicans' initiative, accepting their act as a *fait accompli* and deciding to work with it. This is not to say he was determined to see Maximilian on the throne of Mexico. On the contrary, he was determined to act according to the desire of the Austrian Cabinet – that the wishes of the Mexican people had to be freely and loyally expressed in favour of Maximilian's nomination – or an alternative government would be accepted.

What is important about this letter is Napoleon's expressed concern for civilisation as a whole, and his ability to look at this question in the context of a world view rather than as a regional issue, or as an isolated incident. He concluded the letter by declaring that his only aim was to see French interests safeguarded for the future by a strong organisation in Mexico, and that helping a nation become prosperous was really working for the prosperity of everyone. He summarised his feelings about the Mexican campaign in his final paragraph:

> En résumé, je ne demande pas mieux que de signer avec l'Angleterre et l'Espagne une convention où le but ostensible de notre intervention sera le redressement de nos griefs, mais il me serait impossible, sans manquer à la bonne foi et connaissant l'état des choses, de m'engager à ne pas appuyer, moralement au moins, un changement que j'appelle de tous mes vœux, parcequ'il est dans l'intérêt de la civilisation tout entière.[31]

> [In summary, I shall be delighted to sign, with England and Spain, a convention with the aim of redressing our grounds for complaint. However, it would be impossible, in all good faith, and knowing the state of affairs, to decide not to support, morally at least, a change which I strongly desire, because it is in the interests of the whole civilisation.]

Was Napoleon trying to justify what he was intending to do regardless, or was he trying to persuade his British and Spanish counterparts to take a different view of the world as a whole? My evidence suggests that the latter course was far more probable than the former. Yet despite his entreaties, Britain was determined to maintain a policy of non-intervention, and Spain was to continue her contradictory behaviour as she responded to pressure from Britain and from Spanish public opinion. While Russell's response to Napoleon's suggestions was reticent, he did remark to Cowley that 'moral influence is not excluded by the terms of the Convention'.[32] But, then, as negotiations continued to draw up the Tripartite Convention for proposed action, none of the three governments ever really defined just what was meant by 'moral influence' nor what constituted 'force'.

Napoleon's letter did not resolve the difficulties between Britain and France, although at first it appeared to have done so. Palmerston agreed entirely that a monarchy was probably the best and most stable form of government for Mexico, and that Maximilian would be a good candidate, but he 'doubted the possibility of any such arrangement'. He told Russell that he had been approached ten or fifteen years earlier by Mexicans proposing a monarchy, but when he asked them 'their views of practicability it came out that they required a Prince of a reigning European family, many millions sterling and 20,000 European troops to give any chance of success'.[33] It would have needed little more than this information to ensure that the pursuit of such an idea was carried no further in Britain. Flahault had already spoken of the influence of public opinion and of political colleagues on the decisions of English ministers, and it is highly unlikely that the prospect of spending millions of pounds on Mexico and sending thousands of troops would engender support in either of those arenas.

This was because Palmerston and Russell had had their initiative in foreign affairs curtailed in recent years, making them even more wary of antagonising the Queen and parliament. As Foreign Minister in the 1850s Palmerston had won few friends, either amongst his colleagues or abroad. Francis Cavendish, who worked in the Foreign Office, observed that 'Lord Palmerston's approval of Liberal principles, and his high-handed way of dealing with the Queen and Foreign Powers, have several times nearly landed us in war, and have made him detested by the Court and his more timorous colleagues'.[34] His manner and his tendency to conduct foreign affairs without guidance from the Queen brought him into conflict with her in 1850 when, with the support of his enemies, she determined that the monarch should have 'a power of review in the field of foreign policy'. Lord John Russell, who was Prime Minister at the time, failed to resist her claims, with the result 'that royal power in the determination of foreign policy was officially recognized in a way which had seemed impossible since the days of George IV and Canning'.[35] In 1851 Palmerston again attracted the anger of the Queen by approving of Louis Napoleon's *coup d'état*, and as a result was dismissed as Foreign Minister at her insistence. In 1859 a similar crisis was narrowly averted. Palmerston, as Prime Minister, and Russell as Foreign Minister supported the position of Italy in the Austro-Italian conflict, while the Queen was 'sympathetic to Austria'. To follow their own policy Palmerston and Russell resorted to 'strategems which left them free of Cabinet control'. The collapse of Austria resolved what could have been another constitutional crisis, but the result was that Palmerston and Russell found that in future the Cabinet would 'support the Queen in preventing' them 'acting on important occasions without the advice of their colleagues'.[36]

These recently imposed constraints undoubtedly had an impact on the way in which Palmerston and Russell dealt with negotiations over intervention in Mexico, for, in the following two weeks, France was to find that Britain's official policy was at odds with the messages that Russell and Palmerston were giving them verbally. Flahault tried to convince them to withdraw their proposed clauses in the Convention that said the parties agreed not to use their forces to overthrow the existing government nor to establish a new one, and that they did not wish to interfere in the internal affairs of Mexico. Thouvenel's main concern was that the insertion of these clauses might discourage Mexicans from coming forward on the allies' arrival for fear of lack of support. Both Palmerston and Russell, however, were convinced that Mexico was in such a state of dissolution that they saw little prospect of the allies' arrival encouraging a party which could form a more worthwhile government, which seems to contradict their earlier position that the Mexicans were the only ones who could bring an end to the years of anarchy. Flahault remarked, though, that overall he had found them both much better disposed towards the Emperor's ideas than he had expected but, 'ils sont convenus, l'un et l'autre, qu'il valait mieux ne pas aborder les questions au conseil qui s'est tenu aujourd'hui'.[37] [they are agreed that it would be better not to broach these questions in the Cabinet which is meeting today]. This inevitably sent confusing messages to Thouvenel and Napoleon but, I am convinced, it was the acceptance of Russell's and Palmerston's *spoken* views that led them to believe Britain and France had similar aims in going to Mexico.

Thouvenel continued to press his argument with Cowley, saying that it was wrong to include a clause in the Convention stating what they would not do when it was in the interests of them all to take advantage of what happened after their arrival if it was to lead to a better government. The only chance for Mexico to resist a take-over by either the United or Confederate States was if it had a strong government supported by Europe. Thouvenel's argument, which was supported by Collantes, was that insisting they did not wish to intervene in the internal affairs of Mexico was in fact giving moral support to the existing order of things about which they had so much to complain. Acting on this premise Flahault suggested to Russell combining the two clauses mentioned above and removing such phrases as: 'and specifically shall not be employed for the purpose of interfering with the internal Government of the Republic' in the first clause, as well as the words: 'in the internal affairs of Mexico' in the second clause. Flahault thought that with these changes the Convention would still indicate that the right of the Mexicans to conserve or change their government would be respected.[38] Flahault found Russell reasonably agreeable to his suggestions, but Russell said he would reserve his final decision till he had read Thouvenel's revised version of the clauses.

In a private letter Flahault told Thouvenel that in preparing the ground for him with Palmerston and Russell he had been surprised at their agreement with the ideas of the Emperor. At the same time he knew the possibility of the institution of a monarchy would not be popular in the British parliament. With this in mind he suggested Thouvenel should be careful in his drafting of the clauses not to deliver *'la pilule trop amère'* [too bitter a pill], because if either Russell or Palmerston felt their political existence might be compromised by agreeing too far with France, they would be far more difficult to deal with than if they enjoyed complete freedom of action.[39] Thouvenel replied with the comment that his counter proposal bound the contracting parties not to act with any aim other than that which had led to their agreement to take action, and respected the sovereignty and independence of Mexico, while showing that they were not indifferent to the restoration of a strong and lasting political regime there.[40] Cowley continued, however, to fuel the accusations that were to be made against Napoleon III that he had just been waiting for the opportunity to impose a monarchy on Mexico. After discussing Napoleon's letter to Flahault with Thouvenel, he had written to Russell:

> More than once His Majesty spoke to me on the subject during the first year of my residence in this country [1852] and has frequently alluded to it since and has always been an advocate for the introduction of a monarchical system as the only one which would save the country from ruin.[41]

Some historians have used Cowley's comment to support accusations that Napoleon was determined to impose a monarchy on Mexico. However, the problems in Mexico were discussed in Europe many times during the 1850s and, as has already been shown, Britain and Spain had also agreed with suggestions that a monarchical system was the most suitable for Mexico.

Spain, while agreeing with France's arguments about the content of the Convention, was, paradoxically, prepared to accept the original clauses if France and Spain could not make their objections prevail. Collantes felt that England was, in fact, paralysing in advance the very measures which they had proposed to adopt, and he understood, like Thouvenel, that it would be 'illogical and impolitic to discourage in advance the men of order, who are in the majority in Mexico', but who would only be strong enough to dominate 'the unpleasant passions of the minority' with the moral support of the combined forces of the three powers.[42] Crampton reported to Russell that Collantes had asked for the inclusion of a clause stating they intended 'to exercise a moral influence on the affairs of Mexico' to effect a suspension of hostilities between contending parties with a view to constituting a new, stable government. While Crampton said that such influence was not excluded by England's proposal, Collantes felt the inclusion of such a clause would demonstrate to the world 'the desire of the Three Powers to ameliorate a state of things which seemed every day to become more at variance with the interests of civilization and humanity'.[43] But again, he was prepared to forego the inclusion of such a reference if England would not change her opinion.

Thouvenel also objected to clauses which clearly specified what the three parties would do on their arrival in Mexico, such as to blockade the ports and to refrain from going to the interior of the country. This latter point Thouvenel saw as particularly important because all three countries had nationals needing protection in all parts of the country. These kinds of stipulations, he believed, would be more appropriately contained in the orders of the commanders, and those orders should provide enough latitude for them to act according to the situation on their arrival. He added that he stood by his counter proposal regarding intervention, saying that it went without saying that they were only seeking redress for wrongs, and that France excluded, with England, any employment of force to impose any form of government on Mexico. At the same time they could not undertake in advance not to give moral support to any attempt by Mexicans to reorganise their administration.[44]

Finally, the Emperor agreed, after discussion, to suppress the words 'partout où elle se trouverait menacée', [everywhere that they find themselves menaced] relating to foreign nationals, from the French counter proposal, hoping that England would agree that their commanders could decide to take necessary action, within the limits of their resources, to protect their nationals.[45] Flahault verified Russell's agreement to this provision and heard that Russell's only objection had been to a prolonged occupation, not to the possible need to go to the interior of the country. With this clarified, Flahault declared he was ready to sign the Convention on behalf of the French government.[46] Russell was perhaps more agreeable at this point because he did not anticipate the need for a prolonged occupation in the light of Wyke's latest dispatch, which had arrived on 30 October. Wyke had advised that the Executive had lost any real authority in Mexico, and that with the moral support of the allied occupation the 'moderate and respectable party' would probably be strong enough to overturn the administration, form a government and treat with the three governments.[47]

The Convention that was signed by Russell, Flahault and Isturiz, the Spanish minister in London, on 31 October 1861, bound the contracting parties not to act with any aim other than that which had led to their agreement to take action. It stated that while they respected the sovereignty and independence of Mexico, they were not indifferent to the restoration of a strong and lasting political regime in Mexico.[48] Despite apparent agreement on the final content of the Convention, the signing of it was by no means an indication of perfect accord among the three powers, and the path from then on was beset by difficulties caused by varying interpretations of the document. From the written and unwritten agreements among the three governments emerged a series of accusations, *malentendues* [misunderstandings], and perhaps disasters, which cannot be laid solely at the feet of Napoleon III.

3
The Venture under Way

The conclusion of the Tripartite Convention was really just the beginning of discussions to reach agreement on the action to be taken in Mexico. Each government had, however, managed to achieve some compromise on the part of the other governments, which laid the groundwork for the ensuing preparations. France and Spain remained convinced of the inadequacy of limiting their actions as the British proposed, and France set about obtaining Britain's agreement, or at least acquiescence, to moving their troops inland. Although Napoleon was accused of being underhand in relation to his intentions in Mexico, it will be seen that, on the contrary, he was open with the other governments about his ideas and plans, although he was, naturally, trying to get them to agree with his perspective. Yet contemporary writers supported the argument about the futility of limiting action to the coast. Charles de Mazade wrote on the impossibility of the powers having any effect on the situation in Mexico if their efforts were limited to the occupation of the coastal customs ports. He remarked that the 'deplorable states' of Mexico were accustomed to acceding to force, and as soon as the foreign forces departed they just resumed their demands and their violence against foreign nationals.[1] An English observer, J.H. Tremenheere, later expressed similar views on the futility of limiting action to the control of the ports, but he was more forceful in his criticism, particularly of the British government, when he said, 'if the objects of the expedition were to be limited only to the seizure and occupation of the ports, a more ineffective and preposterous measure for effecting the expressed purposes of the convention could scarcely be conceived'.[2]

It was precisely with these realisations in mind that Thouvenel advised Barrot, his minister in Madrid, to discuss confidentially with O'Donnell and Collantes the suggestion that instructions to the French and Spanish commanders authorise them to march to Mexico City, if the circumstances seemed favourable to them. In this confidential telegraphic dispatch Thouvenel said that a preliminary agreement in this respect would be impossible with England because of 'the situation of the Cabinet before the parliament'. He felt, though, that if France and Spain together gave the broadest possible interpretation to the article providing for the necessity to protect resident foreigners, it was highly likely that their commanders would not encounter any opposition on the part of the English admiral.[3] O'Donnell immediately agreed and said he would give 'very elastic and discretional instructions' to the commander of the Spanish forces, and that he would give him a personal letter authorising him to act if necessary in the manner outlined by Thouvenel.[4]

Having obtained Spain's agreement, Napoleon and Thouvenel were determined to be as open as possible with England, and Thouvenel wrote to Flahault, saying:

> il était plus franc, en tout cas, de ne pas lui laisser ignorer nos intentions, si éventuelles qu'elles soient. *Le Times*, d'ailleurs, a publié un article reproduit aujourd'hui par les *Débats* et qui prévoit, sans nulle réticence, la nécessité d'aller dicter les conditions d'un arrangement dans la capitale même du Mexique. Demeurer à la Vera-Cruz, en butte aux manœuvres dilatoires du président Juarez et bientôt aux atteintes de la fièvre jaune, ce serait jouer un trop triste rôle![5]

> [it was more honest, in any case, not to leave her ignorant of our intentions, even if they are only contingencies. *The Times*, moreover, has published an article, reprinted today in the *Débats*, which predicts, without reservation, that it will be necessary to go and dictate the conditions of an agreement in the very capital of Mexico. To stay in Vera Cruz, exposed to President Juarez's dilatory schemes, and soon to the attacks of yellow fever, would be too sad a part to play!]

Included in this letter was a copy of the instructions that were to be given to Admiral Jurien de la Gravière, who was to command the French contingent, and this was to be shown to Russell. They expressed the possibility of his having to venture inland, and that it would be left to his discretion to decide that on his arrival. The issue of a possible change of government was also mentioned, in terms that indicated there was no predetermined idea on what might eventuate in this respect. Jurien was advised not to discourage any initiatives taken by any persons or party to try and form a more stable government, and to give his moral support if he thought they had any chance of success. Thouvenel raised the question of whether or not such a party existed with the near certainty of success, and advised Jurien that it would be up to him to determine this on his arrival through his own investigations and discussions with Saligny. But he was not told to proceed, come what may, to support such a party or to ensure a change of government. It was instead suggested that a proclamation should be made prior to a march to the capital to reassure the nation that they had no plans of conquest, or of interfering in their freedom to choose the government, and form of government, they wanted. Thouvenel's instructions were in fact rather circumspect. He wrote:

> Just as it would be generous and useful to aid a nation to leave the abyss, just so it would be rash in itself and contrary to our interests to risk an adventure. Therefore it is to inspire [in] the honest and peace-able portion of the Mexican people [to have] the courage to make its voice known that our efforts must be held out; if the nation remains inert, if it doesn't realize that we offer it an unexpected staff of safety, if it doesn't give a practical sense and morality to our protection, it is evident that there is nothing we can do but remain within the terms of the Convention of 31 October and only occupy ourselves with the specific interests for which it was concluded.[6]

Although Russell at first could see great problems with a march to Mexico City, Flahault convinced him that they would be laying themselves open to the ridicule of the whole world if, after seizing the ports, they were still powerless to obtain reparation. It seemed, though, that Russell's main objection was to the prospect of the Spaniards leading the march, and that the political group encouraged by them would be the most retrograde and intolerant in religious matters. Russell was also concerned at Spain's desire to have the Spanish general in overall command, but was reasonably happy with Flahault's suggestion that if the Spanish troops did march alone to Mexico City they should be accompanied by commissioners from the other two nations. Flahault admitted he had expected Russell to be more 'recalcitrant' regarding going to Mexico City, and although Palmerston had not welcomed the idea with 'great pleasure', he had not completely opposed the idea either. In summary, Flahault felt that Russell's and Palmerston's fears were related more to Spain than to France, and the reputation enjoyed in their country by Admiral Jurien de la Gravière, who was to command the French troops, was enough to inspire confidence there.[7]

In his instructions to Wyke, Russell admitted that originally he had not foreseen the possibility of the Mexicans withdrawing inland and refusing 'to enter into any agreement or negotiation whatever', but now appreciated it might be necessary for the allies to pursue them there.[8] But, in fact, Russell had received a dispatch from Wyke on 30 October advising him precisely of that plan by the Mexicans. Wyke had written that they would 'withdraw the Custom houses further inland, with a view of levying duties on all goods proceeding from the coasts to the capital', but he suggested their lack of organisational ability would prevent them being successful.[9] Russell, however, told him only 700 marines were being sent who could not be employed to go inland, and he was not to direct them to do so even if the opportunity arose. By the same token he had 'nothing to say against this reasoning [of the French] or the measures in contemplation'.[10] In other words, let the French and Spanish go if they like, but Britain will not be involved, an attitude which did not augur well for a combined expedition.

Perhaps Russell was more influenced in his reasoning by another statement in this same dispatch from Wyke, which led him to believe that they would not encounter too many difficulties in the campaign:

> With the moral support given by our occupation to the moderate and respectable party, they will probably be strong enough to turn out the present Administration and form a Government which would be glad to treat with us, and thus re-establish those friendly relations with foreign Powers so necessary to the real welfare of the Republic.[11]

Russell foresaw that it might be necessary to blockade a port, or to prevent 'the establishment of Mexican customs houses between the coast and the upper country of Mexico', or even to send detachments to various points in the country to protect Europeans, but basically he invested Wyke with the power to make whatever decisions he thought were appropriate in the circumstances as the government had 'entire reliance upon [his] judgement and discretion'.

In most respects the instructions of the Spanish government resembled those of the French and British, and provided for the necessity to march inland. Collantes's letter to General Prim emphasised the need for a new, reliable and strong government to be established in Mexico, while stressing that the allies had agreed not to interfere actively in achieving this change. However, he said, it was possible that the presence of the allies would inspire the 'sensible' men of the republic to constitute such a government, and it would be 'supremely unjust and cruel to thwart such a patriotic enterprise'. As Spain had everywhere brought the principles of civilisation, they had a duty to help the Mexicans to regain what they had lost. But, he added, their influence could only ever be 'purely moral'.[12]

Preparations began for the departure of the expeditionary forces, and the constitution of the three contingents is a telling reflection of the attitudes of each of the governments. Of special significance is the fact Napoleon had insisted that the number of French troops be less than those of Spain, which indicates he was not intending this to be a French venture and that an alliance with Spain and Britain was at least as important as the mission itself. He prepared to send 2,000 marines and 600 Zouaves, Algerian soldiers, to be commanded by Admiral Jurien de la Gravière, which also implies he did not anticipate a big military campaign or he would have sent more military personnel and a commander from the army. Britain committed herself to sending only 700 marines, which confirmed her intention to remain on the coast and take limited action. Spain, on the other hand, decided to send 5,000 troops under the command of General Prim, signalling her determination to take decisive action and that she was prepared for war if necessary.

The strange variation in the number and types of troops immediately raises the question of what resistance and difficulties each of the three governments anticipated on their arrival in Mexico. The comments quoted above, however, indicate that the answer to this was very little resistance, and very few difficulties. Charles de Mazade observed that, having provided for the possibility of going inland, the allied forces were to depart singularly unprepared for what they might encounter. They seemed to have had no idea that in an unknown, almost deserted country these soldiers would need means of transport, guaranteed supplies, camping and military equipment. He noted that even the Spanish, who had resources in Havana, were not organised for action, only one battalion having camping gear, and none of the forces had what would be necessary to set up bases inland. He concluded:

Qu'en pouvait-il résulter? C'est qu'une fois l'expédition partie, les gouvernements n'étaient plus maîtres de rien; on allait se trouver à chaque pas en face de l'imprévu, de l'inconnu.[13]

[What could be the result? That once the expedition had departed, the governments were no longer in control; one was going to find at every step the unexpected and the unknown.]

And he was right, for the lack of physical resources and supplies influenced some of the decisions that were later made in Mexico. The impact of this, however, was to be disputed by the various plenipotentiaries and commanders when the Convention was suspended in April 1862.

But already the three governments were 'masters of nothing' in Mexico. While they were negotiating and making preparations, Wyke, Saligny and Serrano were making their own decisions that were to upset their governments' plans. In the first instance, Wyke began to negotiate with the Juarez government in a manner contradictory both to his own earlier views and to his government's instructions. He had decided not to follow Russell's orders of 21 August, which told him to issue an ultimatum to the government to hand over control of the customs houses, or relations with Britain would be suspended. He decided instead to 'reason them into the necessity of complying with the demands which ... would soon be urged in such a manner as to compel the government of the Republic to listen to them with attention'.[14] Although he knew his government was concluding an agreement with France and Spain for a combined expedition, Wyke proceeded to negotiate a settlement of the British claims with Zamacona, the Foreign Minister, who said his government would find it difficult to sanction having interveners in the customs ports, or to accept responsibility for the debts of previous governments. In complete contradiction to his claim a few months earlier that this government was culpable for squandering its resources and should be coerced into paying its debts, Wyke accepted Zamacona's assertion that it was all but impossible for his government to procure resources to comply with the British demands. In answer to this difficulty, Corwin, the United States Ambassador, had come forward recently with the offer of the loan previously mentioned. Wyke told Russell it was impossible for Mexico to pay its debts without such a loan, and Britain should wait for it to be ratified by the American Congress in January.

Wyke's agreement was to find favour nowhere, however. The Juarez government's refusal to ratify it enfuriated Wyke, who immediately announced his departure from Mexico City for Vera Cruz. Russell also refused to approve it, although he was pleased at the precision with which Wyke had drawn up the British claims and felt that it would make future negotiations easier if France and Spain did something similar. He noted, though, that Wyke had not negotiated any security that the terms of this convention would 'be observed any better than former stipulations and engagements', and it was for this reason he disapproved of it.[15] Wyke's actions did not improve his relationship with Saligny either, for in a letter to General Serrano, Saligny referred to 'perfidious Albion', in the guise of Wyke, trying to negotiate a separate agreement for the British claims.[16]

It would seem that Saligny was concerned that if Wyke's negotiations proved successful, the need for an intervention might be obviated. He was also still smarting from the rejection of his accusation of an attempt on his life, and of other claims he had made against the government, so he wrote to Serrano in Havana that if he was going to take strong action he should do so without further delay, especially as there were rumours that the government was in disarray and a change of personnel might be imminent.[17] It is difficult to know if Saligny had any influence on Serrano, but in the absence of precise instructions from his government, Serrano had already made extensive military preparations. Serrano wrote to Collantes that from the bases for the Convention he inferred that he was to wait for the other forces before acting, but as he was not told this formally, he felt the departure should not be delayed because Spain had taken the initiative in this question and could not be seen to arrive in Mexican waters after the others, and, also, that each day of inaction uselessly increased the costs of transport. He was therefore departing on 29 November on the assumption that the other forces would set sail as soon as the Convention was concluded.[18] It is also possible that Serrano cherished ambitions for increasing the prestige of Spain, especially if his relationship with Queen Isabella of Spain was as close as rumoured in England. Francis Cavendish, a member of the Foreign Office, and keen observer of society, politics and diplomacy, commented in 1847 on the 'incompetence' of Queen Isabella's husband, the Duke of Cadiz, and that she was desperately in love with Serrano, who became her lover shortly after her arranged marriage. Cavendish remarked that she had five children, 'though whether the Duke of Cadiz was father of any of the five there are grave doubts'.[19]

It is hard to know what reaction the Spanish government anticipated from the French and British governments to this early departure of the Spanish forces, but there is little doubt that Collantes deliberately delayed sending revised orders to Serrano. On 10 November, he admitted to Mon that it was highly likely that by 'good fortune' Serrano would have left Havana before the arrival of the allied forces. This meant action could be taken without delay by Spain and, in any case, later operations could be agreed among the allied forces. Further, any action taken by the Spanish would be considered as being in the name of all three powers.[20] This proviso of acting for the others was no doubt meant to absolve him from any underhand intent, but the effect of

Spain's action was to alter the approach of the allied representatives on their arrival in Mexico, and to arouse suspicion in the other governments. News of Serrano's departure was sent to Paris by Captain de Challié, captain of the frigate, *La Foudre*, who was most concerned at its probable effects . He believed war between Spain and Mexico would be inevitable and Mexico would refuse to give any satisfaction to the Spanish government. It was also certain that when news arrived of the departure of the Spanish from Havana there would be a popular rising in Mexico against them.[21] When they did arrive in Mexico, de Challié felt they were delighted to have the opportunity to act alone, and that they believed there were Mexicans who would look to the idea of a monarchical reorganisation under a Spanish prince to rescue them from 'the edge of the abyss'.[22]

The response of the Mexican government to the arrival of the Spanish was swift, Juarez making certain that there would be no resources in the vicinity of Vera Cruz to help the Spanish and their allies to move inland. A decree was issued forbidding any communication by Mexicans with the enemy forces, on pain of confiscation of their property and of being charged with treason. Anyone who provided them with supplies would be treated similarly, and any cattle, horses or mules found within a radius of eight leagues of the area occupied by the enemy would be declared public property. Juarez followed this decree with the announcement of a complete and general amnesty for all political offences committed since 17 December 1857, no doubt, de Challié said, hoping by this to rally around him 'the liberals, reactionaries, clericals, independents, highwaymen and *tutti quanti*' [all the people of that kind].[23] It can be seen, though, that Juarez was not intending to succumb easily to pressure from the allies.

Wyke, too, was concerned by the precipitate move of the Spanish and at the Mexican reaction to perceived Spanish ambition. This contributed to a change in his stance regarding determined action against the Mexican government, and led in turn to the decision of the plenipotentiaries to negotiate with Juarez instead of demanding retribution, as they had been instructed. He wrote to Russell that the hatred of the Spanish was intense, and he feared hostilities between the Mexicans and Spanish would result in a war requiring three times the number of troops being sent. He added:

> The Government as such is nearly powerless for defence but from the nature of the climate and the guerrilla habits of an armed people accustomed to war and strife for the last thirty years, it will be difficult

to subdue them by force of arms when their national pride is aroused and they imagine that they are fighting against Spanish ambition to reduce them to their ancient servitude.[24]

This change in Wyke's attitude was also influenced by the reported reorganisation of the Juarez government, which had resulted in the increased power of General Doblado, the Governor of the state of Guanaxuato, and now Minister of Foreign Affairs. Wyke attributed the changes within the government to the disagreements which arose over the Congress's rejection of his Convention with Zamacona. He told Russell that Doblado had now been endowed with the authority

> to settle pending questions with the three Powers as he deemed best . . . He is a man of such talent and influence in the country that the Reactionary Chiefs began to lay down their arms and give in their adhesion on his appointment becoming known, and he is now engaged in forming his Cabinet from the best men he could find, irrespective of their political opinions.[25]

Doblado apparently offered to conclude an arrangement with Wyke that would give Britain guarantees that Mexico's engagements towards them would be fulfilled, but having received news of the joint Convention being concluded, Wyke was unable to take advantage of this 'overture'.

In the meantime the allied commanders had met in Havana and were beginning to make their plans based on their instructions, their own preconceptions of the situation, and the news that reached them from Mexico. Their first discussions covered the issue of going inland from Vera Cruz, a move now made necessary by the retreat of the Mexicans. Admiral Jurien discussed with General Prim and Commodore Dunlop his intention to march to the interior if necessary as soon as his artillery arrived, and Prim advised he too intended to advance to the interior as soon as he could.[26] Dunlop said that though his orders forbade such a move, he agreed with them that events could modify his government's intentions in this regard.[27] It would seem that everyone except the British government anticipated, and was prepared, at least in principle, for a move to the interior of the country as soon as the forces landed in Mexico.

However, the chance of the British being involved in this move, always remote regardless of the urging of Wyke and others, became even more so when the British postal steamer, the *Trent*, was seized by the United States, and two Confederates, James Mason and John Slidell, who were heading to Europe to represent the Confederate States in London and Paris, were taken off. When the United States refused to release the Confederates and return the *Trent* to British control, the prospect of war became distinctly possible. Napoleon immediately joined his protest to that of Britain in the desire to prevent a conflict, and by so doing gave a further indication that he was intent on cementing his relationship with Britain rather than breaking it, as some have claimed. He had Thouvenel write to Mercier, his minister in Washington, to protest that by international law the only thing that could be seized from another vessel was war contraband. Thouvenel added:

> Voulait-on ne voir dans les envoyés que des traîtres, l'arrestation serait encore moins justifiable, car un navire est une portion du territoire de la nation dont il porte le pavillon et par conséquent un souverain étranger ne peut y exercer aucune juridiction.[28]

> [Even if we had grounds to regard the envoys as traitors, to arrest them could not be justified, because a vessel is a portion of the national territory whose flag is displayed, and as a consequence a foreign monarch cannot exercise any jurisdiction over it.]

Thouvenel also suggested that as the United States had at other times protested more strongly than other nations at breaches of this law, they should defer to the demands of Great Britain, and release the two prisoners. Apparently President Lincoln, the Congress and the Cabinet were not disposed to make any concessions to Britain, so Secretary of State Seward hoped that France would help him bring his colleagues to see reason.[29] When the protest from France arrived and was discussed by the Congress, it was agreed that Mason and Slidell be released, and it was recognised that it was the intervention of France that had helped resolve the conflict. The British minister in Washington, Lord Lyons, could not speak highly enough of the part played by Mercier in convincing America that France would stick by Britain in the *Trent* affair, and that there was no intention of leaving Britain to fight the United States while France made war in Europe.[30] Even Palmerston, 'who could rarely judge an act of Napoleon without suspecting some hidden treachery', was grateful to Napoleon for his intervention.[31]

In the light of this major incident there can be no doubt that the attention of the British ministers was diverted from Mexico, which would have been unimportant by comparison. Always reticent to take strong action there, the British government would now be even more wary of antagonising the United States by too active an involvement in Mexico. To resolve the *Trent* affair, Admiral Milne was directed to go to Bermuda, where his presence was considered 'more useful', instead of to Mexico, and reports quickly reached Havana that the British anticipated war with the United States and 'attached no more than a mediocre interest to the Mexican expedition'.[32] This view is confirmed by the fact that reinforcements were ordered for Milne on 6 December, and that in a letter to Lord Cowley in Paris at the end of December regarding the situation in Mexico, Russell added a postscript saying: 'There is no hurry about this Mexican affair'.[33]

Shortly after this, news reached Europe of the arrival of the Spanish forces in Mexico, with the result that the expedition had hardly begun before the three governments, faced with the unknown, found themselves no longer 'master of their resolutions'.[34] Russell made an observation in this respect to Crampton in Madrid when advising him of the British government's response to Spain's explanations of their early arrival in Mexico and the occupation of Vera Cruz. These actions, he said,

> demonstrate that a combined expedition, at a great distance from Europe, is subject to the discretion at all times, to the rashness some-times, of the separate Commanders and Diplomatic Agents... [C]ommanders acting at a distance require to be closely watched, lest they should commit their principals to unwarrantable proceedings.[35]

A sober realisation which was not going to prevent the venture taking a very different turn to the expectations of all three governments.

Surprised by Spain's actions, and believing that the Spanish had some personal plan in hastening the departure of the expedition, Napoleon decided to increase the number of French troops to approximately the same as the Spanish. In justifying this increase Thouvenel advised Flahault that the government was prepared to accept that the Spanish had not intended to take separate action, but it was evident that their arrival alone had aggravated the 'passions' of the Mexicans much more than the simultaneous arrival of the allied forces would have done. Moreover, the withdrawal of the Mexicans from the ports justified the foresight of the government in anticipating the need to go inland, for which purpose they needed to have the appropriate means available. Thouvenel asked Flahault to emphasise to Russell that the Emperor's decision to increase the French contingent did not imply any modifica-tion in the instructions of the French Commander-in-Chief, as will be seen in the orders given to the general in command of this new contingent.[36] Russell accepted the Emperor's motives, but remarked that it was not possible for the British government to send more troops.[37]

In discussions with Cowley, Thouvenel also raised the idea of the advantage of a change in the form of government in Mexico, based on the argument that France and England had 'a real political interest' in preventing Mexico from falling under the influence of the North American States, either united or divided. He suggested that if a monarchy headed by Maximilian eventuated, surely the result would be welcomed in London. He added that he hoped that even if the English ministers could not show themselves to be openly supportive of the idea in the face of parliamentary opposition, France could ask nothing more than that they 'apply the doctrine of "laissez-faire, laissez-passer"'.[38] Cowley, however, reported to Russell that he had told Thouvenel he thought the Emperor

> was preparing unnecessary difficulties for himself, for that if all I heard was true, the Emperor was quite deceived as to the state of public opinion in Mexico ... Any attempts to interfere with the free choice of the Mexicans themselves would, I was convinced, not succeed in the long run. Thouvenel made a number of protestations that there was no intention to coerce, and this may be so, but there is evidently an intention to *advise*, and French advice sometimes resembles coercion.[39]

Russell's response showed that Thouvenel was correct in assessing the English minister's reticence before parliament. He wrote:

> This attempt to set up a monarchy in Mexico will never do – let the French have an equal number of men with the Spaniards, but let them keep to the Convention. If they act otherwise we shall not be able to defend our Convention in Parliament.[40]

Palmerston, on the other hand, told Russell he thought that the 'monarchy scheme ... would be a great blessing for Mexico and a godsend to all countries having anything to do with Mexico'. He saw it as a chance to stop the advance of North America, and therefore as being an advantage to Europe. His only concern was that they should not take part in the project, but he had no complaint if France and Spain wished to support such a proposition.[41] Flahault then had a long conversation with Russell in which he felt he had convinced him that by increasing the number of French troops there would be less chance of the Spanish being able to support the 'ultra Catholic party', and more chance of liberal and enlightened opinions prevailing, especially if a monarchy were established. Although Russell was not opposed in principle to the idea of Maximilian being proposed for a throne in Mexico, he doubted the chances of its success. He hoped that if such a proposal did eventuate it would only be obtained by the free vote of the Mexicans.[42]

When the subject became more open, however, the reactions of both the British and the Spanish governments were to surprise Napoleon. Although the French had always said the decision must ultimately rest with the Mexicans, the English, particularly Cowley, were still concerned that France might try to impose a monarchy. The instructions of Napoleon to General de Lorencez, who was to take command of the armed forces, show that this was not Napoleon's intention, and that his aims had not changed from those expressed the previous October:

> Il est contraire à mes intérêts, à mon origine et à mes principes, d'imposer un gouvernement quelconque au peuple mexicain: qu'il choisisse en toute liberté la forme qui lui convient; je ne lui demande que la sincérité dans ses relations extérieures, et je ne désire qu'une chose, c'est le bonheur et l'indépendance de ce beau pays sous un gouvernement stable et régulier.[43]

> [It is contrary to my interests, my origin and my principles, to impose any government on the Mexican people; let them choose, in complete freedom, the form that is the most suitable for them; I ask them only for sincerity in their foreign relations, and I desire only one thing, that is the happiness and independence of this beautiful country under a stable and legitimate government.]

Napoleon was to emphasise these sentiments many times in the next two years, particularly in his instructions to his commanders and in his negotiations with Maximilian.

Despite Napoleon's declarations, rumours that he did intend to impose a monarchy were fuelled by reports such as that of a conversation between a British Colonel Claremont and Colonel Valazé, who was to accompany General de Lorencez. Claremont wrote to Cowley:

> Although Colonel Valazé made no secret of the object of the expedition, yet it might injure him if it were known that he had made me acquainted with it. He distinctly told me that the Emperor had

informed him they were going for the purpose of proclaiming the Archduke Maximilian of Austria King of Mexico, and he is under the impression that this has been agreed upon with Her Majesty's Government who are to furnish a proportionate contingent of troops.[44]

The British government had of course no intention of sending more troops to Mexico, so this part of Valazé's 'revelation' can be discredited as rumour, and there is no available evidence to show that Napoleon had given instructions to de Lorencez that were contradictory to those cited above. It is also highly doubtful that Napoleon would have confided his intention, if it were true, to a subordinate officer.

Accounts such as this, however, led both the Spanish and British governments to deny prior knowledge of the suggestion of a monarchy and of Maximilian, and although they were motivated to do this by their internal political situations, they justified their denial on the ground that the discussions that had taken place in the previous months had been 'secret' or informal. Russell wrote to Crampton:

> I do not understand that the French Government have proposed the Archduke Maximilian as a candidate for the Throne of Mexico. They have not made any such proposal to the British Government. They have asked whether in case the Mexican people should choose the Archduke for their King Great Britain would oppose such a settlement. Her Majesty's Government said they would not oppose the wish of the Mexican people but they should not take any part in promoting such an arrangement.[45]

Palmerston was quick to reassure his parliament that Britain would limit her operations to obtaining reparation for the outrages committed against them, and that the allied intervention would not degenerate into an opportunity to impose a particular form of government that the Mexicans did not want. He then commented on the stories that some Mexicans wanted to change the republic to a monarchy, saying,

> I am unable to judge how far those reports are well grounded, or how far there is any party in Mexico of sufficient strength and numbers to give effect to such wishes. But what Her Majesty's Government desire is, that there shall be established some form of Government in Mexico with which foreign nations may treat . . . some form of Government with which relations of peace and amity may be maintained with confidence in their continuance.[46]

These comments are remarkably similar to those expressed by Napoleon in his instructions to General de Lorencez, seen above. Comments such as this, then, continued to encourage Napoleon that France and Britain were united in their aims for the campaign in Mexico, despite the alarm caused in Britain by the assertions of people such as Colonel Valazé.

Collantes also denied knowledge of the proposal of a monarchy and of Maximilian as a suitable candidate, but Mon was to challenge him over this in the Spanish Cortes a year later, and accuse him of jeopardising the expedition by his action. Collantes justified his behaviour on the grounds that the initial discussions were secret, but observers such as Crampton, and Mazade, who followed Spanish political events closely, commented that his behaviour was more to do with protecting the government from attack by the Cortes. Collantes wrote to Prim that the proposal of establishing a monarchy in Mexico was gaining ground, but the French government had made no formal proposals in this regard to the Spanish government. Besides, he added, Spain had no intention of disregarding the fundamental principle of Spanish politics in America; that of leaving the Americans complete freedom to choose the government most suited to their needs and opinions.[47]

Mon reminded Collantes that he had been told of the proposal of Maximilian as Emperor the previous October, but in all his responses to Mon's private letters between October and December 1861, which had mentioned both these proposals, Collantes had cleverly refrained from acknowledging any mention of Maximilian. He had, instead, remarked after one of Mon's letters that the Mexicans should be free to choose whomever they pleased for a monarch, if that was what they wanted, but Spain felt a Bourbon prince would be an appropriate choice given its historic ties with Mexico.[48] Charles de Mazade commented at this time that, 'Le nom de l'Archeduc Maximilien est accueilli à Madrid avec une amertume mal déguisée, qui laisserait croire à quelque espérance trompée'.[49] [The name of the Archduke Maximilian is welcomed in Madrid with badly disguised bitterness, which gives one cause to believe that some hopes have been deceived.] Crampton commented similarly when responding to Russell's request to know Spain's views about the French idea. He said of the Spanish Government:

They feared that if that plan went forward the opposition here would fall upon them as having been duped and made a cat's paw of to place a German Prince upon a throne, which if erected for anybody, Spaniards think ought to be given to a Spaniard.[50]

Collantes, it appeared, was protecting himself and his government against attack from the opposition, and he maintained his silence until forced to do otherwise when challenged in the Senate in January 1863. He was compelled then to reveal four letters Mon had written to him, each of which spoke of Maximilian and each of which had been edited before presentation to the Cortes in June 1862, or had been suppressed altogether. He did so with the comment:

> Si je n'ai pas fait ces révélations plus tôt, c'est que le secret m'avait été demandé, et il n'est pas dans mon habitude de trahir les secrets qui me sont confiés.[51]

> [If I have not disclosed this earlier, it is because I was asked to keep it a secret and it is not my habit to betray secrets which have been confided to me.]

The reason he claimed these revelations as a secret was the fact that Mon had written confidentially to him on the subject, which, as Mon reminded him was the normal practice when it was not desirable to make something public knowledge, but the confidentiality of the letters was not a justification for denial of his knowledge. Collantes also used a statement of the French minister, Billault, to the *Corps législatif* in June 1862, to defend his silence. Billault had said that the idea of the candidature of the prince Maximilian had only been indicated in a diplomatic conversation and as a possible outcome of the expedition. According to Collantes, the Spanish government had considered the idea purely from this point of view and not taken it too seriously.[52]

How, then, had Napoleon got himself into this situation where his motives relating to Maximilian created suspicion among his neighbours? And why was secrecy maintained for so long? There were reasonable explanations for both of these questions, but there was also a fair measure of phobia, jealousy and mistrust on the part of his opponents. As Billault also said to the *Corps législatif* in June 1862, Napoleon did not suggest a likely prince for Mexico until he had obtained agreement from the other governments that none of them was seeking advantage for itself in Mexico. A prince from an unrelated family would prevent any rivalry among the three nations, but would only be proposed if Mexico voted in favour of a monarchy and a foreign prince.[53] In his letter to Flahault in October 1861, Napoleon had mentioned Maximilian and said the Mexican emigrants, in their eagerness, had already approached Austria with a request to Maximilian. This, I believe, put Napoleon in a difficult position because he wanted to keep all negotiations quiet until agreement was obtained from Austria, and until the situation in Mexico was ascertained. This view is supported by a conversation between the Duc de Gramont, the French Ambassador in Vienna, and Hammond, the British Under-Secretary of State for Foreign Affairs. Gramont told Hammond that he had been the 'indirect organ' with whom the Austrian government had been communicating regarding Maximilian, 'but that all had passed quite unofficially, and in fact...the Emigrants in Paris were the prime [movers] of the whole affair'.[54] Russell also accepted that it had been the Mexicans who had put the process in train, and observed that 'this class of people are notorious for unfounded calculation of the strength of their partizans in their native country, and for the extravagance of their expectations of support'.[55] But this did not stop him from believing that Napoleon wanted to impose Maximilian on the Mexicans.

Napoleon was motivated also by concern that the Austrian government not be compromised by the open discussion of the proposal of Maximilian before the situation in Mexico became clear. In a conversation with Metternich the previous November, Napoleon had acknowledged there was a possibility that a monarchy would be rejected. He had wanted to ensure that the name of Maximilian was not put forward before the right moment, and that the Austrian government not be seen to be involved in the negotiation of the proposal. By keeping negotiations with them quiet they would be protected from criticism if the proposal was rejected. Because of his efforts in this respect, and in spite of discussions with the other governments on the subject, Napoleon was accused of misleading his allies and intending to impose a monarchy come what may.

In the wake of the open discussion of a monarchy, widely diverse opinions were expressed regarding its feasibility and its suitability for Mexico. The British ministers were, of course, among the most sceptical, and Russell remarked to Bloomfield, his Ambassador in Vienna, that if 'our estimate of the disorganization of Mexico is correct, the Archduke, if he were to assume the Crown, would have to rely wholly on the support of the French troops'. He also said that O'Donnell was in agreement with him that the idea of establishing a monarchy by foreign intervention was 'chimerical' as it would simply collapse as soon as foreign supporting troops were withdrawn.[56] Yet while Russell was saying this, *The Times* was publishing letters from its correspondent in Mexico claiming that it was impossible for a republican form of government to prosper in such a country and that they needed an 'enlightened despot-ism'. The correspondent added that 'although there might be prejudices to overcome at the outset, the educated and respectable portion of the inhabitants will soon be able to appreciate the advantages of a firm, paternal government'.[57] Three weeks later he propounded that a mon-archy supported by the three European governments was the only form of government that could effectively resist the encroachment of the Northern Republics. To be successful, though, it needed to 'blend the influential and respectable of all parties', who 'almost without exception are in favour of a monarchy'.[58]

The opinions being expressed in the French press, however, were somewhat different. *Le Temps* commented that although the three powers had declared that they only wanted to obtain compensation for wrongs and did not intend to impose a government contrary to the wishes of the Mexican people, public opinion was not without some concern in that respect, despite the support given to the idea of a monarchy by some French and foreign newspapers. The article claimed that the idea that a monarchy was best for Mexico was based mainly on stories of the anarchy that had resulted in over fifty governments being formed in forty years. But the European public did not really know or understand Latin America, and the reality was that to the 'peoples of these countries' the form of government did not really matter if they could get on with their lives and make a living.[59] Charles de Mazade was also sceptical of the possibility of success, not so much in establishing a monarchy, but in making it last in such a 'tormented' country. The presence of their troops in Mexico would easily lead the people to pronounce in favour of a more stable regime, and it would not be difficult to obtain a vote in favour of a monarchy, especially with a candidate to propose, he said. But an occupation of indeterminate duration would be inevitable in such an unstable country, and European politics would be involved in an enterprise the dangers and proportions of which they could not predict.[60]

While opinion in Europe was fundamentally divided on the issue of the establishment of a monarchy in Mexico, the opposition of both the Spanish and British governments was still couched in terms that led Napoleon to believe they would support a monarchy as long as it was the free wish of the people – which was exactly what Napoleon was pro-posing. But already control of events in Mexico had slipped from the hands of the governments, and even greater differences than those among the governments themselves were to emerge among their rep-resentatives in Mexico. These differences encompassed not only each one's interpretation of his own government's wishes, but also their individual assessments of the situation in Mexico and the appropriate actions to take. The suspicions each had of the others, as well as their individual ambitions, were to lead the expedition in a direction that would have been impossible for Napoleon, or anyone else, to predict or plan for. In addition there was the problem, impossible to overcome, of the time needed for correspondence to travel between Europe and Mexico, which could mean a lapse of at least two months between sending a report or instructions and receiving a reply at either end. So, while Europe was responding to the early arrival of the Spanish forces and issuing appropriate instructions, the allied commanders had arrived in Mexico, made decisions of their own and begun action which was to disturb their governments.

4
A Life of its Own

While the guidelines and basic principles of the instructions given to the allied commanders were fairly clear, the instructions themselves were rather elastic. All three governments were aware of the difficulty of controlling a campaign at such a distance, but they also recognised that local circumstances would dictate some of their commanders' actions. The roles played by those envoys, therefore, became very important, and their first moves determined how the joint venture proceeded. Previously, most emphasis has been placed on the actions of the French representatives, who will be seen to be responsible for many of the accusations levelled against Napoleon, but Wyke and Prim also acted against their governments' wishes. Their very first decision, on the arrival of Jurien and Prim, was to astound all three governments.

On 9 January 1862, Prim and Jurien met with Wyke in Vera Cruz to discuss 'the best means to be adopted for carrying out the intentions of the allies', and Wyke was pleased to find Prim agreed with him that they should try 'every measure of conciliation' before resorting to force. In reporting this meeting to Russell, Wyke said that both Prim and Jurien agreed

> that our first duty was to aid and assist the Mexicans in obtaining such a Government as was likely to afford more efficient protection to the lives and properties of foreigners resident in the Republic, before exacting from such a Government the execution of those engagements towards foreign Powers which their present penury and hopeless state of disorganization does not permit them to fulfil.[1]

This was, of course, a complete reversal of the priorities expressed in the Convention, and the proclamation issued following these discussions stated that, while they had come to demand retribution for debts and other wrongs, the three nations had a higher motive – to help bring an end to the perpetual civil wars. The presence of the allies was their chance for salvation, it said, and the Mexicans were asked to trust their good faith and generous intentions, as their only aim was to assist in the regeneration of the country.[2]

While Wyke and Prim thought Jurien and Saligny agreed with the terms of the proclamation, they actually silently disagreed. Jurien expressed his opinion immediately in a letter to Thouvenel, saying that Prim had written the proclamation because he was the only one who spoke Spanish. When it was translated, however, Jurien objected to some aspects as they did not really reflect French views. He commented that in any meeting where people express the desire to agree it is always the one who holds the pen who succeeds in having his ideas prevail. For his own part, Jurien let Prim expose his ideas to discover what they were and, as a result, the proclamation was entirely Prim's work.[3] On the surface, Jurien's behaviour seems quite strange, but before leaving Havana, he had written a coded message to the Minister of Marine suggesting Prim had different aims from those of France, but that he, Jurien, had his reasons for maintaining good relations with him.[4] This is not self-explanatory, but it appears that Jurien was somewhat piqued at having to submit to the orders of a foreign general, Prim having been given the role of overall commander. According to Mon, the Spanish minister in Paris, this was why Napoleon had insisted that the Spanish contingent be larger than the French, to justify Prim's position, in the same way as relations among the various generals had been regulated in the Crimea.[5] The Emperor had been anxious that Jurien and Prim work well together, so perhaps Jurien kept his objections from Prim so he could show that Prim was not serving the Emperor's interests as Jurien saw them.

Having stated their intentions to the people, the allies awaited an escort to take them to Mexico City to deliver a collective note to Juarez. Discussions then proceeded on the content of that note, and the differences that emerged in those discussions were profound, and reveal a startling array of individual aims and motives. All agreed that stability was needed so that the country could recover, but Jurien believed a monarchy was the only solution, whereas Prim and Wyke thought they should instead support Juarez. Jurien's confidential instructions, however, had suggested that though a monarchy was a preferred option, assistance could only be given if 'a considerable party appears' looking for their help.[6] However, Jurien told his allies that they all recognised that the amount of the reclamations they had to present to Mexico would for a long time absorb the major part of the country's resources. It was also likely that their demands would be treated no better by this government than previous governments had treated earlier treaties. What was needed, therefore, was a more stable government that would be able to guarantee that their conventions would be satisfied. Their first objective, then, had to be to found a better state of things in this country, for they had no other means of preventing the periodic return of costly expeditions to Mexico.

Prim replied that the Mexicans would never want a monarchy, and that it was his belief that Juarez's Liberal party had more support in Mexico and was the only one that could gain the sympathies of the people. Consequently, it was the only one he was interested in sustaining and consolidating. Jurien concluded his report of these discussions with the following comment:

> Je me trouve donc en présence de difficultés que Votre Excellence n'avait pu prévoir. Prêt à marcher d'accord avec l'Espagne, je ne soupçonnais pas que l'Espagne ne marcherait pas d'accord avec elle-même. Il faut bien le dire, cependant, tout avait été disposé pour rendre ici le Général espagnol l'arbitre de la situation en lui laissant le contingent de beaucoup le plus considérable, le grade le plus élévé entre les Commandants alliés.[7]

> [So I find myself faced with difficulties which Your Excellency could not have foreseen. Ready to walk in agreement with Spain, I could not suspect that Spain would not be in agreement with herself. It must be said, though, that everything had been laid out here to make the Spanish general the arbiter of the situation by giving him the largest contingent and the highest rank among the allied officers.]

Jurien's reports, however, continued to show that he disagreed silently with the others while making independent decisions about action to be taken by the French troops.

It seemed that the early Spanish vigour was to dissipate under Prim's leadership. As Jurien noted above, he was amazed to find 'Spain was not acting in agreement with herself', which suggests that Prim may have had motives different to those of his Foreign Minister. Charles de Mazade, who had observed Prim in Spain and took a keen interest in the Spanish political situation, saw him as totally ambitious and suggested he had to have a motive for asking for the command in Mexico. He thought Prim aspired to becoming dictator or king of Mexico himself, a view supported by rumours in Havana and in Mexico.[8] A report from the captain of the French frigate, *Lavoisier*, gave an account of the welcome given to Prim on his arrival in Havana, in which triumphal arches were erected and the general was crowned in effigy in some streets, amid cries of 'Viva el Vice-Roy de Mexico! El Nuevo Hernan-Cortez'.[9] In Mexico he and his wife, whose uncle had recently been appointed Minister of Finance in Juarez's government, were treated as royalty, and one of the newspapers had even voiced the idea of Prim as Emperor. Prim denied such claims, saying his ambition was related purely to Spain. Crampton, the British minister in Spain, agreed with this when he wrote to Russell that Prim was perhaps O'Donnell's 'most formidable rival', and O'Donnell had sent him to Mexico to get him out of the way.[10] It was also suggested that his family ties with the Mexican government persuaded him to negotiate with Juarez instead of following his instructions. Whatever his reasons, it was obvious that Prim intended to follow a different path to that advocated by his government. It may have been that he saw his relationship with a member of the Juarez government as an opportunity to resolve the question without resorting to war, and to gain prestige with his own government by doing so. If he did have personal ambitions in Mexico, however, they were not to be realised.

In the second allied conference further disagreement arose when Saligny presented the French claims. The British and Spanish representatives rejected them, mainly because of the inclusion of claims on behalf of the Swiss banker, Jecker and Company. Wyke and Dunlop reacted angrily to their inclusion, saying they were inadmissible because they had been contracted by Miramon's government, and would never be accepted by Juarez or any other government. In 1859, the Miramon government had issued bonds totalling fifteen million pesos, to be underwritten by the bank, Jecker Torre and Company, one of the leading banks in Mexico, and guaranteed by the government. Foreigners were offered incentives to invest in the bonds, but when Jecker and Company collapsed in Paris in May 1860 only 700,450 pesos worth of bonds had been sold. After Juarez defeated Miramon his government refused to recognise the bonds and pay the interest on them. When Saligny included the claims of the bondholders in the French demands, he nominated an amount far in excess of the value of the bonds sold, which was bound to incite a reaction from his colleagues.[11]

Much discussion and debate has surrounded Saligny's inclusion of the Jecker bonds in the French claims, many commentators being convinced that Napoleon insisted on their inclusion to give him a pretext for going to Mexico and imposing a monarchy.[12] This conclusion, though, is based on very tenuous evidence, mostly concerning the involvement of the Duc de Morny, half-brother of Napoleon, with the Jecker company. Saligny's dubious character and his mission to pursue the Jecker claims on behalf of business and personal acquaintances, including the former minister in Mexico, de Gabriac, was mentioned in Chapter 1. There is no available evidence to show that there was pressure from Napoleon or Thouvenel to pursue the Jecker claims, nor to inflate them. In fact, Saligny was instructed to modify all claims if relations with their allies were to be affected by their pursuit.

As their differences could not be resolved in the meeting of 14 January 1862, Prim suggested that in the note they were to address to Juarez they state that though they had to demand full reparation for past wrongs, the first thing to do was to help the republic constitute itself in a stable manner to enable it to meet its engagements. In reporting this meeting to Collantes, Prim declared that the English and French commissioners agreed that this was the only action to adopt in spite of their formal orders. To justify the decision, Prim outlined the alternatives that had been open to them:

> Nous nous trouvions dans l'alternative de ne pas envoyer nos commissaires à Mexico, après avoir demandé une escorte qui depuis ce matin les attendait à nos postes avancés de la Tejeria, ce qui nous aurait enlevé tout prestige et aurait donné à entendre qu'il avait surgi entre nous un grand désaccord, ou bien d'envoyer nos commissaires sans modifier l'ultimatum français.
>
> Sir Charles Wyke s'opposa de toutes ses forces à ce dernier parti, et je confesse que, pour ma part, je ne pouvais me résigner à ce que l'influence de notre noble et généreuse nation et le sang de nos soldats fussent employés à précipiter dans une ruine totale ce malheureux pays en soutenant des réclamations aussi injustes.[13]

[We found ourselves faced with the alternative of not sending our commissioners to Mexico City, when the escort we asked for had been waiting since this morning at our advanced post of la Tejeria. But this would have stripped us of all prestige and would have suggested that a major disagreement had arisen between us. The other alternative was to send our commissioners without modifying the French ultimatum.

Sir Charles Wyke opposed this latter alternative with all his strength. And I must confess that, as for me, I could not resign myself to letting the influence of our noble and generous nation, and the blood of our soldiers, be used to precipitate this unfortunate country into total ruin, by giving support to such unjust demands.]

The collective note to Juarez was thus composed along the lines suggested by Prim, stating that the role they had been given by their governments was to demand reclamation for the past and obtain guarantees for the future. The representatives, however, did not believe this was enough, considering the actual state of Mexico. They believed their mission could have 'a higher aim and a more generous result', and that these three great nations were there to be witness to, and if need be, protectors of the regeneration of Mexico, and to assist its organisation without interfering in the form of its government or of its internal administration.[14]

Juarez, though, rejected their opinion of the situation, saying that as all the states of the confederation were behind his government, Mexico had no need of regeneration and that he was not going to dissolve his government. He then effectively quashed any likely movement of a group wanting to overturn the government by issuing a decree imposing the death penalty on any Mexicans who assisted the intervention in any way, be it military, political or economic. In his reply to the allies he said he was prepared to satisfy just demands, and that respect for its engagements would be one of the invariable rules of the Liberal administration. The plenipotentiaries were then invited to Orizaba for discussions, but with an escort of only two thousand men. The rest of their troops were to be re-embarked. The allies refused to re-embark any of their troops, announcing they intended to take them to Orizaba and Jalapa to find a more healthy camping site for them while Prim met General Doblado, the Prime Minister. Juarez did not then insist on the re-embarkation of troops but arranged for Doblado to meet with Prim, a meeting that was to result in the conclusion of the controversial Preliminaries of Soledad.[15]

Before the meeting of 14 January Jurien had made his own observations on Mexico and had begun to consider the idea of separating from his allies. He wrote to Chasseloup-Laubat, Minister of Marine and Colonies, describing the difficulties they had already encountered, and suggested that the Emperor and his government 'would probably have to decide whether it was better to conclude the Mexican question quickly, by whatever means, or whether it was preferable to support the hopes they had encouraged by preparing their own small army to do without the Spanish contingent'.[16] Just why Jurien decided so quickly what he intended to do is difficult to say. He had arrived in Mexico only on

9 January, and within a few days he declared a monarchy was best for Mexico and considered separating from the Spanish contingent. It may have been that the Mexicans' fear of Spain's intentions suggested that a satisfactory solution could only be achieved if France acted separately from them, because the Mexicans were relatively happy that France was represented there. Another reason may be that Prim had stated Juarez's Liberal government was the only one able to save Mexico, and he was not likely to support the monarchy that Jurien quickly became convinced would be accepted. The answer may also lie in the character of Jurien himself, as described by Émile Ollivier:

Esprit cultivé, écrivain distingué, doux, poli, conciliant, d'une scrupuleuse loyauté, ne cherchant qu'à s'éclairer, mais courtisan et soldat discipliné, incapable de résister à ce qui ressemblait à un ordre ou même à un désir de son souverain.[17]

[A cultured mind, distinguished writer, gentle, polite, conciliatory, scrupulously loyal, trying only to understand, but a disciplined soldier and courtier, who cannot ignore what resembles an order or even a wish of his monarch.]

Perhaps these qualities made him too eager to achieve what he had been told to pursue with caution, and only if the opportunity was provided by the people.

Ten days after sending their note to Juarez, Jurien wrote to Thouvenel that a monarchy maintained by a foreign army was the only government that could save the country, but they had been misled in the belief that this could be 'the work of a moment of surprise and the result of an intrigue'. He claimed that there were only two parties in Mexico, the friends and the enemies of the clergy, and the idea of a monarchy initially evoked fears that the privileges and power of the clergy would be supported once again. It was hard, though, to believe the Clerical party was likely to regain mastery of Mexico when they had so far given no evidence of their existence, Jurien stated. In the light of these observations he cautioned Thouvenel against expecting an early result:

Vous voyez donc à quel point vous avez besoin de patience et de confiance en votre humble serviteur. Je ne réponds pas de réaliser votre programme dans toutes ses parties. Je le réaliserai certainement dans la plus essentielle, c'est-à-dire que je maintiendrai ici votre influence et que je ne vous engagerai pas malgré vous dans des frais qui seraient un terrible choc pour nos finances. Si mon plan vous agrée, ne négligez pas de me le dire.[18]

[So you can see to what extent you need patience and confidence in your humble servant. I cannot promise that your programme will be achieved in all its parts. I will certainly achieve the most essential, which is that I will maintain your influence here and will not lead you into expenses which would be a great blow to your finances. If you approve of my plan, do not neglect to tell me so.]

He went on to say that he had to feel Thouvenel had complete confidence in him, that he could act as an agent who was supported, approved and appreciated, and that if Thouvenel ever felt he did not deserve such treatment he should recall him. Jurien's correspondence is often punctuated with such pleas for approval, which seems to suggest a measure of insecurity in his position at so great a distance from France.

In the next few days he was supported in his belief in the Mexicans' desire for a monarchy by Captain Thomasset, the French delegate who went to Mexico City to see Juarez. Thomasset claimed he had seen men of all political persuasions, as well as foreigners, who agreed there was no-one, and no single party in Mexico that could rally enough support to dominate. He believed, however, that the 'moderate and honest men' of all persuasions were ready to rally around a monarchy 'supported for some time, some years perhaps, by troops of the allied Powers'. But for this movement to show itself the allies needed to control Mexico City, and show their position was solid and backed by sufficient forces to deter any opposition, and that agreement prevailed among the powers.[19] Jurien seemed not to heed this final statement, for he announced his plan of action to Thouvenel, saying he wanted to go to Jalapa to assemble enough resources to allow for an advance to Mexico City, recognise the current government purely as the *de facto*, but essentially transitory, government, and not discourage any party he encountered. He continued that he would:

laisser le général Prim et Sir Charles Wyke se bercer de l'espoir d'interroger le suffrage universel en lui dictant sa réponse et attendre ainsi que les gouvernements alliés s'expliquent. Je m'arrangerai pour leur en donner le temps.[20]

[let General Prim and Sir Charles Wyke cherish the illusion that they can consult the universal suffrage by dictating the response, and wait while the allied governments explain themselves. I will manage to give them the time.]

From this it would seem that one of his objectives was to expose the duplicity of Prim and Wyke, as well as to separate the French to allow them to pursue what he saw as the Emperor's aims. He wrote to Chasseloup-Laubat:

> Je me crée ici, peu à peu, un rôle isolée et fort important. Toutes les fautes commises par mes collègues tourneront, j'en suis sûr, à notre profit; mais ce serait une grande erreur de croire que l'on puisse agir brusquement sur les esprits et surprendre, par une marche rapide, une solution.[21]

> [I am creating here, little by little, a lonely but very important role for myself. All the mistakes made by my colleagues will turn, I am sure, to our profit; but it would be a grave error to believe that one can act suddenly on the minds and rapidly come upon a solution.]

Unfortunately for Jurien, in Paris they were expecting far more rapid progress than he thought appropriate.

In contrast to Jurien's, Wyke's report was a justification of why they should continue to negotiate with Juarez and support his government. He believed it would be impossible for the country to find enough resources to satisfy French and Spanish claims as well as their own, until it was regenerated, 'and the sooner therefore we set about helping them to effect this regeneration the better'.[22] He also reported that he had prevented Miramon, the former Conservative president, from landing at Vera Cruz, and could obviously see no conflict with the instructions from Russell that he was to show preference to no party in particular. He said:

> The fact of our preventing Miramon's landing here will have the best effect throughout the country, for had we allowed him to organize an invasion under the protection of our flags, it would have been a cruel sarcasm on the friendly offers we have made to help the present Government in reestablishing peace and order in the country so that they may eventually be able to fulfil their engagements to us in the Republick.[23]

Wyke continued to express his confidence in this government, which he believed was gaining solidarity under Doblado, who was using his influence to 'centralize the powers of the government' and was filling 'important posts with persons devoted to his policy'. He concluded that the intervention was therefore indirectly having an effect, and he trusted it would not be long before there was 'a strong and intelligent Government willing to treat with us and able to turn a deaf ear to the clamours of the mob'.[24]

Prim's report was similar to Wyke's, and he declared that his conciliatory actions were bearing fruit with the Mexican people who were beginning to come around to the allies. It would not be long, he told Collantes, before they would be able to exercise their moral influence to obtain 'the establishment of an order of things which was the result of the wish of the majority' and which would offer guarantees for the future.[25] The previous day, however, Prim had written that the Mexican government had imposed a tax on foreigners of two per cent on capital, which hardly implies a readiness to accept the intervention and help of the allies.

On hearing of the proclamation and negotiation with Juarez the three governments were equally astounded at the action taken by their envoys. Napoleon reacted angrily to Jurien's report of 12 January and had Thouvenel communicate that he 'regretted' that instead of immediately pursuing reparation for the wrongs committed by the Mexicans they had addressed a note to the government which gave it time to organise its resistance and to conduct a pretence of consultation of the wishes of the nation. He believed that the question of reorganisation could only be usefully proposed and resolved after the City of Mexico or its environs had been occupied. Napoleon hoped they had not been stopped from moving forward by an evasive and deceptive response from Juarez, and that they would have already marched on the capital as quickly as their means allowed. Jurien was further advised that his concessions to agreement with their allies did not have to go as far as accepting satisfaction for less than what he considered were France's legitimate demands, although this reaction was tempered in Thouvenel's next dispatch. If Spain and England insisted on not supporting French claims, Jurien and Saligny were authorised to leave their colleagues to treat separately, and to pursue alone the reparation due to France, taking into account, however, the needs of their military situation and the general situation in Mexico. At the same time they were cautioned that such a decision was to be taken only as a last resort and after considering the chances of success in acting alone.[26]

Thouvenel wrote to Flahault in London to express his great concern at the actions of their representatives, and to clarify with Russell whether each nation's claims had to be agreed by its allies. He said, in part, of the proclamation:

> Emprunté d'une fâcheuse apparence d'irrésolution, elle donne au Cabinet de Mexico les moyens de gagner du temps et d'organiser la résistance. Il ne manquera pas d'y voir une preuve de faiblesse que lui rendra cette confiance orgueilleuse en lui-même contre laquelle toutes nos tentatives de conciliation ont échoué dans le passé. L'expérience que nous avons acquise de la manière de penser et d'agir ne nous permet pas d'en douter. Nous courons le risque de nous trouver ainsi en présence de difficultés qu'avec plus de décision les commandants de nos forces sauraient prévenir.[27]

> [Having an annoying appearance of uncertainty, it gives the Mexican Cabinet the means to gain time and to organise resistance. The Cabinet will not fail to see this as a proof of weakness which will give it back that arrogant self-confidence against which all our attempts at conciliation have failed in the past. The experience that we have acquired of their manner of thinking and acting leaves us in no doubt about this. We are running the risk of finding ourselves faced with difficulties which the commanders of our forces could avoid by being more decisive.]

Russell agreed entirely with these views, but reserved his final opinion until he had received Wyke's explanations.[28] When he did receive them, surprisingly, Russell was not critical of the prevention of Miramon's landing, but he condemned the unwarranted belief of Dunlop and Wyke that regeneration of Mexico was their primary object.[29] He accused them of attributing to 'Her Majesty's Government views and intentions diametrically opposed' to his instructions, and he believed their actions would adversely affect their future relations with Mexico.[30] In discussions with Flahault, Russell said that he thought each nation had a right to determine the extent of its own claims. Flahault then suggested that after the claims had been accepted in principle by the Mexican government, France would be happy to have a special commissioner determine the exact amount which would satisfy their claims. Russell accepted this idea and said he would 'invite Wyke to withdraw his opposition'.[31] Collantes also agreed with Thouvenel's criticisms, and remarked that by negotiating with Juarez they had recognised his government as legitimate and discouraged the sound part of the population from seeking the allies' assistance.[32] Collantes responded to

Prim that it was time to take decisive action, and that order and confidence would not be restored until they marched inland and occupied Mexico City.[33] He told Prim that the government approved his moderation to this point, but to temporise any longer would only prolong the expedition unnecessarily. It was now time for energetic and decisive action, which should only be stopped when the desired guarantees were given.[34]

Thouvenel wrote again to Jurien and Saligny, authorising Jurien to go inland and to determine with Saligny whether the reparations they had to demand were to be their main concern from now on, and whether those demands could be modified. To Saligny he said that while it had never been suggested that each nation's claims had to be scrutinised and approved by the others, it might be necessary to prioritise some of the French claims and decide the importance of others. Thouvenel felt they had to decide what was more important – having their own demands met, while seeking neither personal advantage nor territorial acquisition, or maintaining the spirit of the Convention. He told Saligny that his department had not assessed the value of France's complaints as highly as he had, although they did not have enough information to dispute them. While he did not necessarily want Saligny to reduce the figure to which Wyke and Prim objected, he might be a little less 'rigorous' on this point if it was an evident cause of disagreement among the representatives of the three Courts. As far as the Jecker bonds were concerned, Thouvenel thought a distinction should be drawn between those that affected French interests directly and those that affected other nationals. As they had been contracted by Miramon it was important to ensure that the present government would accept responsibility for any such claims.[35]

The differences that arose in Mexico between the French representatives on one side and the British and Spanish on the other, were to fuel the suspicions of Napoleon's intentions that had already been evident in the minds of the British ministers before the expedition began. The extravagance of the demands put forward by Saligny, and Jurien's subsequent determination to separate from their allies, led Cowley and Russell, particularly, to assert that Napoleon had intended all along to find an excuse to carry out his plan for a monarchy. Russell wrote to Cowley that he had heard that Saligny was told 'to make a quarrel in Mexico any how and Mathew told me that upon being told on one occasion that Thouvenel would not approve of his conduct said "What care I for Thouvenel, provided I please the Emperor?"'[36] Cowley added to this suspicion when he wrote to Russell three days later recounting 'a very curious conversation with Metternich about the Archduke Maximilian'. When discussing with him the 'preposterous demands of the French', Metternich had commented that 'these demands were made purposely', but Cowley did not reveal a specific explanation of this, other than that Metternich said the Emperor was keen to see Maximilian on the throne of Mexico. Metternich had added, however:

> There is only one thing . . . which I have not been able to ascertain, and that is his reason for taking all this trouble. We have taken care that he shall have no hold upon us and I defy him to find either in his own archives or in those of Vienna one line that can be turned to our detriment.[37]

Cowley, though, saw in Metternich's comments further proof of his own opinion that Napoleon intended to ensure Maximilian was given the Mexican throne to facilitate the annexation of Venetia for Italy. Yet this had been denied earlier by the Duc de Gramont, the French Ambassador in Austria, in a conversation with the British Under Secretary of State for Foreign Affairs. Gramont had said that nothing had passed in the negotiations

> which could be turned into the story which had got into the Viennese newspapers that Mexico was to be considered a set off against Venetia and a compensation to Austria for the cession of their Italian possessions; and that his Government was perfectly well aware that it was useless at present to enter on a discussion of the question of Venetia.[38]

That Napoleon hoped to see Venetia annexed to Italy was well known, but what was not accepted or understood was that he had no intention of seeing this eventuate without full agreement of all those involved. Cowley added to this another reason for Napoleon's 'pertinacity' regarding Mexico, of which he 'had not a doubt', and that was 'to please the Empress. It pays for other sins both of omission and commission, and helps to keep her quiet.'[39] Cowley may not have been alone in thinking this, but there is little to support this other than conjecture and, in the light of all Napoleon's correspondence relating to Mexico, it is difficult to accept he would have undertaken a venture of this nature for such trivial reasons.

Despite Russell's and Cowley's opinions regarding the validity of the French claims and what they saw as deliberate inflation, Thouvenel had shown he was ready to moderate them and to have them examined by a separate commissioner in Mexico.[40] He wrote to Saligny that he had advised the English government it would not be appropriate to make the demands so high that their recovery became impossible, which refutes the claims made by Cowley and Metternich that this was the intention of the French government. He added:

> En ce qui touche l'affaire Jecker, je ne saurais trop insister sur la distinction que je vous recommandais de ne pas manquer de faire entre ce qui, dans cette affaire, réclamerait bien légitimement notre protection, et les intérêts étrangers que nous n'avons pas, au contraire, mission de sauvegarder.[41]

> [As far as the Jecker affair is concerned, I cannot insist too much on the distinction which I had advised you to make between what, in this affair, rightfully should have our protection, and the foreign interests that, on the contrary, are not our business to protect.]

Any mention of the Jecker bonds in the French or British archives reveals that Thouvenel lacked detailed knowledge of them, and was determined that Saligny should support only those that affected French interests. There is insufficient evidence to support the accusations that the Jecker bonds were to be used deliberately to inflate the French claims.

Concern over French aims was not confined to Britain, for the question was debated in the *Corps législatif* in March 1862 in the discussion on the Emperor's address to the Chambers. The discussion on Mexico was opened by a little known deputy, Achille Jubinal, who was a member of 'the majority', but Ollivier described him as 'worthy on this day to be one of the Five'.[42] Jubinal demanded to know if the rumours that France had gone to Mexico to overthrow the republican government and establish a monarchy were correct. If this were so, he asked, what had happened to the great principle of non-intervention that France had proclaimed and defended elsewhere, and on what basis could they attack a country that was motivated by the same principles as those on which their own 'great nationality' was based.[43] Jules Favre, one of Napoleon's most outspoken opponents, followed this with a proposed amendment 'expressing regret that the Mexican expedition seemed to have as its object an intervention in the internal affairs of Mexico, and praying the Government to reconsider its plans and stay within the limits officially announced, and thus pursue only the reparation of its griefs'.[44] It is ironic that some of those who so strongly criticised Napoleon's government for intervening in Mexico were prominent members of the succeeding government that had few qualms about intervening in Tunisia, Tonkin, Madagascar and Morocco and supported similar interventions by the United States and Britain.[45]

Favre accused the government of going to Mexico, not as creditors but as invaders to enthrone Maximilian. He added that the claims of officers departing for Mexico that this was so, was the proof. Billault, Minister without portfolio, responded on behalf of the government that the idea of enthroning Maximilian had nothing to do with the expedition, and it was hardly likely that 'if such were the solemn and secret intention of French diplomacy it would be handed to troops for broadcasting'.[46] He stated that they were going only to impose respect for their nationals and fulfilment of Mexico's engagements towards France, in pursuit of which it was essential to march to the capital. He then made an emotional appeal to the Chamber:

> Est-il bien opportun, tandis que nos soldats marchent sur Mexico, de tenter de démontrer ici qu'ils ne sont que les instruments d'une intrigue et que la guerre dans laquelle ils vont verser leur sang est une guerre illégitime?

> [Is it timely, while our soldiers march towards Mexico City, to attempt to demonstrate here that they are only the instruments of a plot, and that the war in which their blood will be shed is an illegitimate war?]

Billault finished his address with 'a superb affirmation of victory: "Nos troupes vont à Mexico; parties le 20 février, elles doivent déjà y être"',[47] ['Our troops are going to Mexico City; having departed the 20 February, they must already be there'] an observation based on a letter from Jurien which notified his intention to begin his march inland on 20 February.[48]

Despite the views of the opposition, the deputies supported Billault and voted in favour of energetically prosecuting the expedition 'till complete satisfaction had been procured for French nationals and interests in Mexico'.[49] This same support was reflected in the reports of the Procureurs Généraux, most of whom commented that, although the aims of the expedition were not completely understood, the people believed it was important to maintain their honour in Mexico. One such report said:

> La guerre du Mexique cause une certain préoccupation; on s'effraye des sacrifices d'hommes et d'argent qu'elle doit nécessairement

entraîner, mais on reconnaît, en même temps, qu'il était impossible de ne pas demander réparation des nombreux griefs de la France contre le Gouvernement Mexicain. Notre drapeau est engagé; au Mexique, comme ailleurs, il faut soutenir l'honneur de nos armes, et l'opinion publique s'est associée, avec énergie, au vote du Pouvoir Législatif.[50]

[The Mexican war causes a certain anxiety; people are frightened of the sacrifices of men and the cost that war will obviously entail. But at the same time it is recognised that it was impossible not to ask amends for the many grievances France has against the Mexican government. Our flag is committed; in Mexico, like anywhere else, we have to maintain the honour of our arms, and public opinion has joined with strength in the vote of the legislative power.]

As a result opposition was briefly silenced as the campaign was not envisaged as a long one. However, the news that was to reach France in the next two weeks, that a preliminary agreement with Juarez had been signed, and that the French troops were not in the capital, was to prompt much speculation.

After several conferences had been held by the plenipotentiaries, Wyke reported that he and Dunlop had convinced their colleagues that they should make a final attempt to achieve a pacific solution by allowing Prim to meet with Doblado.[51] This meeting resulted in the drawing up of the Preliminary Convention of Soledad, which was eventually signed by Prim, Wyke, Dunlop, Saligny, Jurien and Doblado on 19 February 1862. This was an agreement on the intentions of each side, pending negotiations that would be opened at Orizaba on 15 April, by which time the plenipotentiaries would have received instructions from their governments. The Preliminaries included the following statements: (1) that the existing government had informed the allied commissioners that they had no need of their assistance as they had all the resources they needed to bring an end to their internal revolutions. Therefore the allies had only to resort to their treaties to present all their grievances; (2) the allied representatives having said they had no intention of interfering with the sovereignty or integrity of the Mexican Republic, negotiations would begin in the city of Orizaba; (3) while negotiations were taking place the allied forces would occupy the towns of Cordova, Orizaba and Tehuacan; (4) if the talks broke down they would withdraw below the lines of fortification on the road from Vera Cruz. If and when the allies withdrew, their sick and wounded would be cared for by the Mexicans. The final article stated that as soon as the allies began their march to Cordova, Orizaba and Tehuacan the Mexican flag would be raised again in the forts of Vera Cruz and St Jean d'Ulloa.[52]

While Prim, Wyke and Jurien all professed to be pleased with what they had done, their reasons were again quite different. Prim told Collantes he had decided to treat with the Mexican government because they had said they needed time to convince the nation that the allies would not threaten the independence or sovereignty of the country. They also wanted to assure the people that the French had not come to impose a monarchy, and neither did the Spanish intend to re-establish their former domination. If the allies gave them time to influence the opinions of the people, the government would guarantee to do all it could to meet its obligations. The government also claimed they had the wherewithal to establish a firm foundation for a stable government, and as this was one of the aims of the expedition, Prim told Doblado that he and his colleagues had agreed that they did not have the right to reject the government by supporting an opposition party. Any other action, he believed, would be unjust as well as impolitic, as it was evident to those in touch with the situation that the Reactionary party no longer existed, because in two months they had seen no evidence of its presence.

Prim added that the French, who had hoped it would be easy to establish a monarchy, and who believed the monarchical element was strong in Mexico, were misled and now recognised their error. Prim claimed they now realised that it was not the intention of their governments to favour any person or party or to violate the independence, sovereignty and integrity of Mexico, which was why they had treated with the government.[53] Prim concluded his report by assuring Collantes that he would resort to the use of arms only if it were absolutely necessary, because he wished to avoid engaging the Spanish government in an exercise requiring considerable resources, given the current state of affairs in Europe. He added:

> Je crois en conscience que la tournure que nous avons donnée à cette question mérite d'être approuvée par le gouvernement de Sa Majesté. Nous avons été modérés et humains, et s'il arrive un jour où, convaincus de l'inefficacité des moyens pacifiques, nous aurons à recourir à la force, nous prouverons au monde entier que la modération et les sentiments d'humanité ne seront pas incompatibles avec ce que la valeur et le zèle pour l'honneur de notre patrie exigent de nous comme Espagnols et comme soldats.[54]

[In all honesty I believe that the direction we have given to this question deserves to be approved by Her Majesty's government. We have been moderate and humane, but if the day comes when we have to resort to force, because peaceful means have proven to be ineffective, we will prove to the whole world that moderation and humane feelings are not incompatible with what valour and enthusiasm for the honour of our country demand of us as Spaniards and as soldiers.]

Wyke wrote in similar vein to Russell, expressing faith in the combination of Juarez and Doblado to redeem the country from anarchy.

Charles de Mazade, however, later asked what purpose could be served by negotiating with a power which had violated its obligations a hundred times already, and that signing the Preliminaries had conferred a legitimacy on the government that previously all three governments had refused to recognise. Mexicans who wanted to establish a more stable government would be discouraged by this, and to imagine that a solution could be achieved by peaceful means was chimerical, as was the thought that the government would be intimidated by the allies. Having momentarily reduced the allies to inactivity, Juarez had only entrenched himself in power and increased the violence against any opposition.[55]

Jurien was also pleased with the signing of the preliminaries, but for startlingly different reasons. One of them, he told Chasseloup-Laubat, was that history had shown how precarious the existence of governments was in Mexico, and if another revolution occurred they would be released from the Convention. The Mexican government was mistaken, he said, if they thought it was in their interests to draw out the negotiations, because it was really the allies who would profit from this. Access to the interior had been opened up, and having to move back below the designated points if talks broke down was not really a disadvantage, for if they moved forward of their own volition they would be doing so before they had assured means of transport. Under these new conditions, Jurien said, Mexico could not hinder their advance, and if they had to withdraw they could recapture the advanced positions in eight days. He added that he was also pleased that it provided the opportunity to separate the three armies. Although the Preliminaries had not yet been ratified by Juarez, he was going to begin his advance with the French troops, his first step in separating from their allies.[56] He later wrote that he believed the influence of France in Mexico was immense, and he commented that 'the Emperor, protector of nationalities in

Europe, need have only one concern in Mexico and that was that his intentions might be misunderstood'.[57] Unfortunately, it was he and his French colleagues who were to make perhaps the greatest contribution to that misunderstanding.

It was at this time that Jurien heard of the imminent arrival of General de Lorencez and the additional troops, and he was both surprised and concerned that his politics of conciliation might be repudiated by their arrival. He also reacted angrily to the news that he was no longer be in command of the expeditionary forces. From a practical point of view it was logical that Lorencez should be given control of the military operations which were now to be concentrated inland – hardly a role for an admiral of the navy – but Jurien was to remain in command of the political, maritime and commercial aspects of the campaign. His self-esteem, however, was dealt a severe blow by this change, even though he was now appointed Vice-Admiral. Lorencez was of a lower equivalent rank, being only a Brigadier, until he was appointed Major-General at the end of March. Jurien wrote to Thouvenel:

> De tous mes honneurs, il ne me reste que la moitié d'un pouvoir Diplomatique. Mais je suis vice-Amiral![58] C'est bon pour moi. Est-ce aussi bon pour vous? Here is the question. [*sic*]
>
> J'écris une longue lettre très sincère à l'Empereur; mais elle arrivera au mois d'avril et pendant deux mois, on aura peut-être pesté contre moi parceque je n'aime pas les joueurs, même quand ils gagnent. Les honnêtes gens s'abstiennent d'aller à la roulette.
>
> Je vois bien pourquoi vous êtes revenu sur votre première dépêche qui m'investissait de la plénitude des pouvoirs diplomatiques. Ma dépêche du 30 décembre vous a fait craindre que je fusse dupe du général Prim. Je vous garantissais cependant le contraire. Tous ces gens-là avec leurs roueries ne m'ont conduit que jusqu'où je voulais aller.
>
> Vous voulez que j'aie confiance en moi. Soyez satisfait. Je suis parfaitement convaincu d'avoir raison et d'avoir toujours raison.[59]

[Of all my honours, I am left with only half of the diplomatic power. But I am a Vice-Admiral! This is good for me. Is it also good for you? Here is the question.

I am writing a long and very sincere letter to the Emperor; but it will arrive in April and for two months people may have railed against me because I do not like gamblers, even when they win. Honest men refrain from going to play roulette.

I can see why you have gone back on your first dispatch which invested me with full diplomatic powers. My dispatch of 30 December made you fear that I was the dupe of General Prim. I guarantee the contrary, however. All those men, with their trickery have led me only where I wanted to go.

You want me to have confidence in myself. Be satisfied. I am absolutely convinced of being right and of always being right.]

Despite this outburst, Jurien assured Thouvenel his relations with Lorencez would be established on the best foundation. He would continue to work happily towards his goal, but if he was withdrawn from his command he would 'return cheerily aboard his ship' and not be angry because he knew that Thouvenel could not possibly know or understand the real situation in Mexico. In this letter, and in others to Thouvenel, there are times when Jurien sounded almost a little mad as he justified his actions and defended his abilities. Perhaps this contributed to the concern in Paris over his handling of the situation in Mexico. He wrote that while they might lack confidence in him, 'a poor makeshift diplomat', he knew it would not be permissible for him to call them 'men of little faith' in return. If he was recalled, he believed that no matter what the future held for Mexico he would have represented the only ideas that could possibly triumph, and they were the moderate ideas. But he concluded that perhaps, after all, God was on his side because he was bound to succeed in his task:

Ah! Si Vera Cruz n'était pas à deux milles lieues de Paris, que je serais donc tranquille! Mais ici, il faut, comme vous me l'avez très bien dit, que j'aie autant de confiance en moi que vous voulez bien en avoir vous-même. Or, c'est là le point difficile. La suffisance m'a toujours manqué. S'il n'y avait pas un Dieu pour les bonnes gens, je ne réussirais pas. Je réussis, donc, il y a un Dieu.[60]

[Ah! If Vera Cruz was not two thousand leagues from Paris I would be untroubled! But here, it is necessary, as you have said so well, that I have as much confidence in myself as you have in me. But, this is the difficulty. I have always lacked self-conceit. If there was no God for good people I would not be successful. I am successful, therefore there is a God.]

Whatever Jurien's ideas, they did not include the possibility of negotiating further with the Juarez government, and perhaps for good reason. On learning of the arrival of General Almonte, Padre Miranda and other Mexican exiles with Lorencez, the government had declared to the allied plenipotentiaries that they would punish any such dissidents who had come to act against the legal government, and demanded that the allies refuse to offer them any support or protection. The government also reiterated that anyone assisting the allies would be punished. Both Prim and Wyke agreed with this ultimatum and requested Jurien and Saligny to agree as well, being convinced that there was nobody else in the country capable of establishing a stable government and that there was definitely no evidence of support for a monarchy. Jurien, in one of the allied conferences, also had acknowledged this might be so, but the severity of the actions of the Juarez government encouraged him to persist in the pursuit of his goal. All the evidence seemed to support Prim's views, yet Jurien was prepared to act in contradiction to his own observations and those of others, in blind obedience to what he believed the Emperor wanted. Prim commented to Collantes that the French language newspapers had openly stated that the mission of the French army was to install Maximilian on the throne, and this was likely to cause problems not only between the French and Mexican governments but also among the allied governments. He added that the refusal of Jurien and Saligny to agree to the ultimatum issued by Juarez and Doblado was likely to lead to a rupture in relations among the allied representatives.[61]

Jurien in fact saw this ultimatum as the opportunity to reach agreement on the form that the intervention should take, believing it gave the allies the chance to broach again the idea of a general amnesty and to reiterate their refusal to sanction the violent methods proposed by Juarez.[62] He therefore decided to issue his own ultimatum to Doblado and Juarez through their intermediary, Colonel Cautelenne. He declared that if they did not grant an unqualified general amnesty to Almonte and the other Mexican emigrants, he would fulfil the conditions of Soledad by withdrawing his troops below the fortifications of Chiquihuite, and twenty-four hours later begin hostilities against the Mexican government. His decision to do this was based on his earlier instructions that he was not to refuse his support to any party that appeared to have the chance of successfully forming a government, and also on the premise that because the Emperor sanctioned Almonte's return to Mexico, it was his party that he wished to help form a government.[63] Jurien did not have any evidence to support this assumption relating to Almonte. As he had not yet met up with Lorencez and the Mexican contingent, he was acting on his own initiative. He also had no idea whether the majority of the people were prepared to support Almonte, and the Emperor and Thouvenel had intimated that they had no preference for a particular party. Always they had stressed supporting the party that came to them with some chance of success in forming a government, and so far none had done so.

Having issued his ultimatum that would result in the opening of hostilities between France and Mexico, Jurien proceeded to carry out his plan to separate from his allies. He reminded Prim that he had always agreed that it was important not to identify with a minority party, but he had told Prim often that he would always advise any party that establishing a monarchy was the only way to end the dissensions dividing the country. Believing conciliation was the only way to achieve this, he had signed the Preliminaries of Soledad convinced that the respite provided by this document would give them time to influence the people, without pressuring them, and 'to prepare them for the solution that to me seems the most favourable'.[64] He congratulated Prim on the fact that his actions had at least reassured Mexico that they had not come to restore an unwanted domination of the country. However, he also lamented that the expedition had taken on a largely Spanish flavour because of the greater number of their troops, and because of the preponderant role Prim had played in the negotiations. Nevertheless, he respected the fact that Prim was also a politician and not just a soldier, or he might have dragged them into a war which would have had the whole country against them.

The most telling part of this letter, however, is contained in the following statements which indicate quite clearly that Jurien was acting on his own initiative:

Je ne mets pas en doute, quoiqu'on ne m'en ait rien dit, que l'Empereur, lorsqu'il s'est décidé à envoyer ici une nouvelle armée et un général pour commander ses troupes, n'a pu avoir en vue que de dégager l'action de la France et de lui réserver l'entière liberté de ses décisions.

[I have no doubt, though no one has mentioned it, that when the Emperor decided to send a new army and a general to command his troops, he could only have intended to isolate France's action and leave her entirely free to make her own decisions.]

He then quite candidly accepted responsibility for his decisions, telling Prim that he believed the importance of his own command meant he could no longer subordinate his political views to any other plenipotentiary. While he respected Prim and believed they would continue to work in agreement, he intended to separate his army from that of the Spanish and English:

> Je suis décidé, en un mot, à poursuivre, à mes risques et perils, le but que je veux atteindre. Je désire profiter, pour y arriver, de la sympathie très réelle qu'on paraît éprouver ici pour la France. Par conséquence, sans renier nos alliés, sans séparer le moins du monde notre cause de la leur, je tiens à ce qu'il soit bien établi, aux yeux de tous, que notre expédition est une expédition française, et qu'elle n'est sous les ordres de personne.[65]

> [I have decided, in short, to follow up, at my own risk and peril, the objective I wish to achieve. To achieve it, I will take advantage of the very real warmth of feeling that people have here for France. Consequently, without distancing ourselves from our allies, without in the least separating our cause from theirs, I want to make it clear to everyone that our expedition is a French expedition, and that it is under no-one's orders.]

What Jurien had failed to understand was that the alliance with Spain and England, intended to be affirmed by this joint venture, was as important to the Emperor as the constitution of a stable government in Mexico. Prim, who did believe this, could not help but express his disbelief and disappointment that the Emperor might have issued instructions that showed an intention to break the Convention of London:

> Si vous avez reçus des ordres de votre gouvernement à cet égard, j'avoue que je ne reconnais plus la sagesse, la justice, ni la grandeur de la politique impériale, comme je ne reconnais pas non plus le haut esprit de conciliation de l'Empereur envers l'Angleterre et l'Espagne.[66]

> [If you have received orders from your government to that effect, I confess that I fail to see in them the wisdom, the justice and the greatness of the imperial politics, nor can I recognise the Emperor's spirit of conciliation towards England and Spain.]

In Prim's opinion, what Jurien was about to do would not only prove a disaster but would severely damage the friendly relations of England and Spain with France, and, he said, 'nobody would be more upset than

I who have the greatest respect and admiration for the Emperor as well as a love of France and the French people'. However, seeing Jurien was set on his plan of action, Prim realised that all that could be done was to meet and formalise the rupture of the accord in a final statement.

Wyke then tried to persuade Jurien against his decision to withdraw his troops to prepare for hostilities against Mexico, and said that supporting Almonte, the head of the party of Marquez, which was at war with Juarez, was showing partiality to an enemy of the government with whom they were negotiating.[67] Wyke had already learned from Dunlop that although Saligny had told him Almonte was to advance under the protection of the French, on orders of the Emperor, Lorencez had denied that this was so and had offered to send Almonte and the other Mexicans back to Vera Cruz.[68] Jurien later told Wyke it had been without his consent and through a regrettable misunderstanding that the Mexicans had been placed under the protection of the French flag. He agreed with Wyke that it was not appropriate to accept the help of another party whilst negotiating with the government, and said if it had been up to him he would have invited them to return to Vera Cruz. However, the action of the Mexican government in executing a General Dobles, whom they accused of conspiring with General Almonte and others, belied the moderation they claimed to be exercising. Jurien felt in the circumstances he could not send them back to Vera Cruz and had decided instead to ensure they came only as far as Cordova. He then justified his decision to draw his troops back, before the conference at Orizaba, on the grounds that if the talks broke down they would have been stranded in the unhealthy zone at the beginning of the hot season, exposing their troops to disease and death.[69] Wyke accepted Jurien's explanations and pronounced him exonerated of any blame regarding the protection afforded the Mexican exiles, but suggested it would only compromise their cause if he did not send them back to Vera Cruz.[70]

Saligny had been highly indignant when he heard a report that Lorencez intended sending Almonte and his friends back to Vera Cruz, and possibly even to France. He wrote to Jurien that he could not believe he would sanction such a move which he, Saligny, believed would be the greatest blow to the politics of the Emperor. If they had to wait in Vera Cruz they would be exposed to the *vomito*, or yellow fever, so he would not hesitate to bring them inland again, convinced that he was obeying the Emperor's wishes.[71] He then told Jurien his firm opinion was that they could no more treat with Doblado than Juarez, as he was the instigator of the outrages committed against their nationals over the previous three months – outrages that nobody else seemed to have heard about. But while he emphasised the need to protect their nationals, he strangely proceeded to warn Jurien against all Frenchmen in the country:

> Je vous supplie mon cher Amiral, de tenir en grande méfiance tous les français sans aucune exception, de Cordova, Orizaba etc. Ce sont tous d'affreuses canailles, rouge sang de bœuf. Il n'en ait presque pas qui n'aient été obligés de quitter leur Pays pour des raisons peu favorables; et tout naturellement ils détestent la France et son Gouvernement et sont inféodés – je crois corps et âme – s'ils avaient une âme – à cette bande de malfaiteurs qu'on appelle le Gouvernement libéral.[72]

> [I implore you, my dear Admiral, to mistrust all the Frenchmen, without exception, from Cordova, Orizaba etc. They are awful scoundrels, with ox blood in their veins. There are hardly any who have not been obliged to leave their country for some unfavourable reason; and of course they detest France and her government and have given their allegiance – body and soul – if they have a soul – to that band of wrong-doers called the Liberal Government.]

It will be seen in Chapter 6 that the French nationals' opinions of Saligny were little better than his of them, although perhaps they had much more justification for their views than did he. But it seemed Saligny's determination not to deal with the Juarez government knew no bounds, because he continued to plead protection of French nationals despite the above comments.

At a meeting of the allied representatives on 9 April, Jurien justified his decision to act more energetically, saying it was in accordance with his government's intentions, as expressed in a recently received dispatch from Thouvenel. This dispatch was referred to above when discussing Napoleon's reaction to the initial proclamation, but it was not received until after Jurien had made his own decision to act. Thouvenel had written that if Spain and England refused to support the French claims:

> M. l'Amiral Jurien et M. de Saligny, en ayant soin toutefois de se rendre compte exact des nécessités de notre situation militaire et de l'état général des choses au Mexique, seraient autorisés à laisser leurs collègues traiter séparément et à poursuivre seul la réparation due à la France. La gravité même de cette résolution indique qu'elle ne

devrait être prise qu'à la dernière extrémité et après calcul fait des chances du succès de notre action isolée.[73]

[Admiral Jurien and Mr Saligny, being careful to be aware of the exact requirements of our military situation and the overall state of things in Mexico, would be authorised to leave their colleagues to deal separately and follow up alone the compensation due to France. The very seriousness of such a resolution indicates that it should be taken only as a last resort and after taking account of the chances of success of our independent action.]

Although these instructions were later moderated, and Saligny advised to be circumspect in his claims, Jurien saw here support for the decision he had already taken to separate his troops and his actions from those of his allies, despite the cautionary direction that such action should only be taken as a last resort.

Wyke suggested that, regardless of Jurien's instructions, they had all agreed to treat with the Juarez government, so on that basis the French decision to offer protection to Almonte showed partisanship and, therefore, was not in accordance with the Convention of London. Jurien responded that the protection offered was only that of the French flag, and such protection of an exile in no way constituted interference in the internal affairs of the country. Prim disagreed, saying that Almonte and the others were hostile to the established government, with whom the allies were in negotiations. Jurien replied that this was not the case, as Almonte, like everyone in Europe, believed they were at war in Mexico and he had come to conciliate with the different factions, and to reassure them of the kindly views of Europe towards them. He then suggested that the very reasons that Prim advanced to support the impossibility of a monarchy were the same reasons that justified such a dramatic change in the institutions of Mexico, because none of the previous republican regimes had been able to halt the continual revolutions that had led the country to its current deplorable state.[74]

Wyke and Prim continued, however, to maintain they had made the right decision to negotiate with the government, and that representatives of the Mexican government had agreed to withdraw the tax of two per cent on foreign capital, to retract the decree interrupting communications between Vera Cruz and the interior, and made known their intention to satisfy all the claims of the allied governments. If these promises were not kept then it would be time to declare war, not now for 'futile motives which could not be justified before the great tribunal of the civilised world'. Prim asked why the French representatives would not wait six more days until the proposed conference with the Mexicans. Saligny said his reasons were based on the numerous complaints he continued to receive, from both French and Spanish nationals, against the Mexican Government. To Wyke's astonished rejoinder that he knew nothing of these claims, Saligny responded that French subjects were unlikely to take their complaints to the British legation.

This sudden claim precipitated a questioning of Saligny's behaviour since the initial proclamation to the Mexican people. Saligny to this point had remained in the background, absenting himself from a number of the allied conferences, but he was suddenly to reveal that he had objected to the combined actions to which he had given silent assent, or to which he had actually appended his signature. He was asked whether it were true that he had said the Preliminaries were not worth the paper they had been written on. He replied he had never had the least confidence in anything emanating from the Mexican government, whether it was the Preliminaries or any other engagement. When asked by Dunlop why he had signed them, and then, having done so, why he did not feel formally bound by them, Saligny said he did not have to give his reasons for signing them but he did not feel bound by them when the Mexican government had violated them in a thousand ways. Saligny had been heard to say, shortly after the signing of the Preliminaries of Soledad, that he had not agreed with either this document or the original proclamation.[75] An anonymous writer to Thouvenel justified Saligny's behaviour with the argument that he had not wanted to compromise the situation by voicing his opposition, and he had in fact prevented a further useless convention being signed with the Juarez government.[76]

While Jurien and Saligny reiterated they could not support the government of Juarez, which had submitted its people to a reign of terror and continued to exile or execute some of the country's more reasonable leaders, Wyke said that the majority of the people supported the government and that it would be difficult to find many who wanted a monarchy. Jurien brushed aside the project relative to the candidature of Maximilian, saying it was not a question of a monarchy at that point, as this could only be raised after considering the urgent need of the country to gain a moral and respected government, which would not stifle the free expression of the intelligent and moderate section of the nation. He continued, that this majority existed but it was possible it had not shown itself because it had reason to believe the allied representatives were hostile to it, and he concluded:

Ce parti, qui attend notre appui ... nous le trouverons partout le jour où il sera libre de déclarer quels sont ses véritables sentiments. Le gouvernement de l'Empereur, bien informé sur ce point, désire marcher en conséquence sur Mexico, et telle est la détermination du commissaire français.[77]

[This party, which is waiting for our support ... we will find it everywhere the day it is free to declare its true feelings. The Emperor's government, well-informed on this point, therefore wishes to march on to Mexico City, and this is the resolution of the French commissioner.]

Yet the evidence before his eyes seemed to refute what he was saying.

The result of this conference was that the French were determined to act forcefully and alone, thus moving the campaign into a new phase. As the French refused to participate in the proposed Orizaba Conference, it was agreed they had severed relations with their allies, and the Spanish and English had no alternative but to re-embark their forces and leave Mexico.[78] The same day Saligny and Jurien wrote to Doblado that the harassment of their nationals by the Mexican government since the signing of Soledad, and the violent measures adopted to stifle the expression of the wishes of the people, meant the French could no longer negotiate with them. They continued:

Les soussignés demeurent convaincus que s'ils pérséveraient dans la voie où le désir d'éviter l'effusion du sang les a engagés, ils s'exposeraient à méconnaître les intentions de leur gouvernement et à devenir involontairement les complices de cette compression morale sous laquelle gémit aujourd'hui la grande majorité du peuple mexicain.[79]

[The undersigned remain convinced that if they continue to follow the path along which the desire to avoid bloodshed has led them, they would be disregarding their government's intentions, and become unintentional accomplices in that moral oppression from which the great majority of the Mexican people are suffering today.]

They concluded by announcing that they would withdraw beyond the fortified positions of Chiquihuite, and when the last Spanish troops had re-embarked they would take the action they believed necessary.

Doblado replied immediately, questioning why the French representatives had recognised his government as the legitimate administration by signing Soledad, if now they claimed that that administration was only maintained by an oppressive minority. Further, he disclaimed any knowledge of harassment or maltreatment of French nationals since Soledad, as none of the local authorities had reported any notable facts in this respect. This denial probably means nothing in itself, but Doblado added that as the French had both the liberty and the opportunity to address reclamations to the government for any such violation, their silence to this point would lead them to believe that no act worthy of reclamation had been committed. This assertion is supported by the reactions of Wyke and Prim in the allied conference, and by the fact that Saligny was the only one who claimed knowledge of any violations. Doblado concluded that they had been prepared to exhaust every possible means of negotiation, but if the French refused to do this, then, without being the aggressor itself, Mexico would defend to the last its independence and right to instigate reform.[80] He said as much to Wyke and Prim when he replied to the combined note from the allied commissioners, and added that his government was now prepared to negotiate with Great Britain and Spain to satisfy all their reclamations and to give them guarantees for the future.

Saligny's questionable claims added weight to the suggestion that the French were looking for a pretext to suspend the accord with their allies, as did Jurien's comments to his Minister about having been determined to find an excuse to do this. He explained to Chasseloup-Laubat that if he and Saligny had agreed to wait until the conference with the Mexicans on 15 April, one of two things might have happened. The government might have agreed without reservation to all their demands, as seemed likely from all reports, giving them no pretext to break with them. Or, alternatively, 'the well established connivance between our enemies and our allies' would have caused the negotiations to be prolonged so that the retrograde movement imposed by Soledad, if talks broke down, would have to be accomplished in the unhealthy season. If either case had arisen, Jurien said, it would have been necessary to find another incident to justify a break with their allies which had become more than ever necessary. Fortunately, such an incident had presented itself when the Mexican government refused to include Almonte and his companions in the general amnesty demanded by Jurien. As they were under the umbrella of French protection and had made no secret of their intention to overthrow the government, Jurien could now openly declare war.[81]

These comments could only add fuel to the condemnation of Napoleon by analysts of the campaign, who have overlooked some important statements by Jurien. It was in this report to Chasseloup-Laubat that

Jurien made it quite clear that he took responsibility for having given his own interpretation to the Convention of London. He said:

> Je n'en demande pas moins que toute la responsabilité n'en retombe que sur moi. J'ai dû à mes collègues et je l'ai fait constater au procès verbal que si le gouvernement de l'Empereur avait conclu la Convention de Londres, c'étaient ses plénipotentiaires qui, à leurs risques et périls, l'avaient interprétée.[82]

> [I do not ask any less than that the full responsibility should be mine. I have told my colleagues, and I have recorded in the proceedings that if the Emperor's government had concluded the London Convention, it was his plenipotentiaries who, at their own risk, had interpreted it.]

While he anticipated the repercussions in Europe, he believed events justified his conduct since his arrival at Vera Cruz, and that he was the only one who could see the venture successfully concluded. He said he was gaining the respect of the Mexican people, who were getting to know him now he was no longer in the shadow of Prim's strong personality, and he was certain they would believe that he was speaking for the Emperor when he promised the French would not restore former abuses or impose an unwanted Prince.

The Convention, then, was suspended by the representatives of the three governments on the basis of their different interpretations of the political situation, and their varied opinions on the most appropriate action to take. Each of them had been acting in opposition to the initial instructions of their governments, yet the French were blamed for the rupture. While neither Wyke nor Prim was blameless, the contradictory and controversial behaviour of the French representatives did little to alleviate suspicion of Napoleon's intentions, and left France with what Thouvenel described as 'a chaos of difficulties' to resolve. All three governments were to be angry with their representatives, but ultimately Spain and Britain agreed it was the French who had precipitated the breakdown of the accord. At the same time they were united in the belief that it was a good thing that France intended to stay on and carry the burden of intervention alone. France's problems were only just beginning, however, as the campaign took on dimensions the Emperor had no way of predicting, and his commanders continued to cause concern.

5
'A Chaos of Difficulties'

While the plenipotentiaries were formalising their separation, their governments were only just responding to the news of the signing of the Preliminaries of Soledad, illustrating just how much the venture was beyond their control. The reactions of the governments to Soledad were to vary, however, once they received the reports from Mexico, and again when they heard the Convention had been suspended and the French representatives intended to act alone. This, of course, renewed suspicion of Napoleon's intentions, and the blame for the rupture was attributed to the French plenipotentiaries and their support of Almonte.

The initial reaction of all three governments to Soledad was one of anger and disbelief that their representatives were continuing to negotiate with the discredited Juarez government. None of them could accept the idea of the Mexican flag being raised beside their own in the forts of Vera Cruz and St Jean d'Ulloa, which they had occupied, nor the stipulation that the allied troops would withdraw from their advanced positions if talks broke down. But when their envoys' reports reached Europe the Spanish and British governments decided to approve their representatives' actions, even though they would have preferred some of the articles of the Preliminaries to have been worded differently. The British government withdrew their objections relating to the Mexican flag on learning that the two forts would remain 'under the exclusive military authority and control of the allied forces'.[1] To Wyke, Russell wrote: 'This Convention will, it is to be hoped, dispel the fears entertained that the allies intended to interfere in the internal affairs of Mexico, and which, it must be admitted, was too much countenanced by the imprudent language held regarding the "regeneration of Mexico"'.[2] However, he also wrote privately, saying, 'I am very glad to see the first article of General Prim's Convention. The Emigrants at Paris had filled the Emperor's head with the notion of a monarchy, and the Empress's with the hope of seeing the Holy Inquisition in Mexico.'[3] These remarks demonstrate that nothing would dispel the suspicions of Russell, nor of Palmerston, regarding the intentions of Napoleon.

The Emperor, though, was furious at the turn events had taken with Soledad, and his initial reaction was to recall Jurien and publicly repudiate his actions. An article in *Le Moniteur* criticised him, and a member of the *Corps législatif* wrote to Jurien that it seemed to have been authorised by the Emperor, who was not pleased with the results of the mission to Mexico City, 'where, in his impatience he believed you had already arrived'. It appeared, he said, that the Emperor had not been made aware of the practical difficulties they would encounter as far as transport and supplies were concerned. He was preoccupied with the need for their prompt arrival in the capital in the light of recent successes of the Federal armies in America, and the opposition that French politics might encounter from a pacified United States. Jurien was advised that regardless of his original instructions he should reach Mexico City as quickly as possible, 'for in our country, people do not take into account the difficulties, they are only concerned with success'.[4] This advice was to be superfluous, however, as Jurien was instructed to return to his squadron.

The Emperor's anger with Jurien may also have been prompted by a letter which Saligny had written in February to his friend General Rollin, the Adjutant-General of the palace, condemning Jurien and voicing his own disagreement with the decision to negotiate with Juarez. Saligny also blamed Jurien for the fact that their troops had been too poorly equipped to move inland immediately, and he had concluded:

L'amiral, je l'avouerai, m'afflige et m'épouvante par ses irrésolutions, par son aveugle foi en nos adversaires, par sa confiance en lui-même et en sa fortune; confiance que je voudrais voir partagée par ses officiers et ses soldats. La mienne est tout entière dans l'Empereur, dans l'Empereur seul, dont la sollicitude saura, quoi qu'il arrive, aviser à toutes les mesures nécessaires pour sauvegarder l'honneur de notre drapeau.[5]

[The admiral, I must say, distresses and frightens me by his indecision, by his blind faith in our opponents, by his confidence in himself and in his good luck; confidence which I would like to see shared by his officers and soldiers. My confidence is entirely in the Emperor, and only in the Emperor, whose concern will allow him, whatever happens, to advise the measures necessary to safeguard the honour of our flag.]

This letter is quite probably the explanation for Saligny being exonerated of blame at this stage.

Napoleon was determined to redeem as much as he could of his policy, so he decided, in spite of the protests of the Ministry of Marine and Colonies, to reorganise command of the venture. Thouvenel advised Saligny that he now would be responsible for the political direction of the venture and that the Emperor was counting on his prudence as well as his 'zeal' for the good of his service, while Lorencez would control all military operations and questions relating to the health and security of the troops. Saligny was told to maintain the best relations with the general and under no circumstances was he to interfere in the military direction of the campaign. Significantly, Thouvenel reiterated the aims of the venture in the same terms that he and the Emperor had always expressed them:

> Ce que nous demandons aux Mexicains, c'est avant tout le redresse-ment de nos griefs et un Gouvernment qui nous donne des garantis pour l'avenir.
>
> Quant à la forme et du personnel de ce Gouvernement, nous ne prétendons pas l'imposer. Ce qu'il doit ou peut être dépend absolu-ment des circonstances locales et de l'appréciation des hommes sages et amis de leur pays, comme le Général Almonte par exemple.[6]

[What we ask from the Mexicans is, above all, that they address our complaints, and that they put in place a government which will give us guarantees for the future.

As for the form and the personnel of that government, we do not claim the right to impose it. What it must or can be depends com-pletely on the local situation and on the judgement of the prudent men who are friends of their country, such as General Almonte, for example.]

This faith in Almonte was probably encouraged by the lengthy account, referred to in Chapter 2, that Almonte had written the previous Septem-ber on the political traditions in Mexico.

In the following weeks, however, reports reached Europe that the French representatives in Mexico were still pushing for the establishment of a monarchy. Muro, the Spanish chargé in Paris told Thouvenel that in the light of information from the Captain-General of Cuba, he felt the Mexicans in Paris were mistaken in their belief there was a large Monarchical party that would declare itself on the arrival of the allies, for so far they had shown no sign of their existence. Thouvenel accepted that Muro's observation might be correct, but added:

> sans arriver nécessairement à la monarchie, il y avait beaucoup de degrés à parcourir dans les formes de gouvernement et que l'on pouvait bien tâcher de pousser au Mexique à l'établissement d'un pouvoir plus solide et plus fort que celui qui existe aujourd'hui.[7]

> [without necessarily arriving at a monarchy as the solution, there are many levels in the forms of government, and we could well try and urge Mexico towards the establishment of a stronger and more sound power than that which exists today.]

In spite of such comments, suspicions of the French were not to be allayed. The British, particularly, were convinced France wanted a monarchy and Russell told Crampton in Madrid that if the Mexicans 'were spontaneously to proclaim a monarchy' they would recognise it, but failing such a proclamation they were happy to negotiate with the present government.[8] He wrote to Wyke that he was most concerned that 'the French General, anxious for the cause of Monarchy and of Catholic unity, may lend the aid of the French arms to the Reactionary Party in Mexico and thus give fresh life to the civil war, which appears at present to have almost died away'.[9] Thouvenel, however, had already written to Saligny to reinforce what he had told both him and Jurien, that the French government had never proposed supporting one of the parties that divided Mexico. Knowing as they did now the situation in the country, they did not want to lend their support to principles that were not in harmony with their own. Their only hope and desire was that the French presence would provide the Mexicans with the moral support to accomplish their own wishes.[10]

Lord Cowley, however, continued to contribute to the suspicion of Napoleon's policy. When Thouvenel assured him there was no intention to impose a government on Mexico, Cowley advised Russell of Thouvenel's statement, then said:

> But I should deceive your Lordship if I did not record my own conviction that there is a fixed, if unavowed, intention to subvert the

> Government of Juarez, whatever may be the consequences, whether the renewal of the civil war or not.[11]

Russell had a discussion with Flahault after receipt of Cowley's letter, and it is obvious he agreed with Cowley. He criticised the French sanction of Almonte's arrival in Mexico and declared it was well known that his purpose in going was 'to raise a civil war in Mexico, to subvert the existing Government, and to put himself and his partizans in their place'.[12]

Shortly after these discussions, news of the suspension of the Convention of London by the plenipotentiaries in Mexico reached their governments. Both the British and the Spanish immediately blamed Jurien's behaviour and the protection of Almonte for the rupture. But France was able to refute this argument, for although Almonte had gone to Mexico with Napoleon's blessing, it was assumed that by the time he arrived the allied forces would have made their demands of the Mexican government and have reached the city of Mexico. As Billault, Minister without portfolio, said to the *Corps législatif* in June 1862, everyone believed that by March the aims of the three governments would have been achieved and the Mexicans given the freedom to choose their own government. It could not be said, then, he argued, that France had sent Almonte to start a civil war. When he did arrive, Jurien and Lorencez had prevented him from taking any action, and it was not until after the rupture that he had been free to act according to his own political opinions. Therefore, the arrival of General Almonte could not be considered the cause of the rupture between the allies.[13]

It was not only the behaviour of the French representatives that should be questioned. For instance, Wyke was the strongest proponent of decided action against Mexico. Yet once he had set the wheels in motion he began to negotiate an agreement to settle British claims, on the basis that there was now a more reasonable person, Doblado, in control. However, by that time the Convention had been signed and joint action planned. After the breakdown, Wyke insisted that the regime headed by Doblado was different to the one previously headed by Juarez. He wrote to Russell that the French continued to confuse

> the existing government under the absolute direction of Doblado, with that formerly existing before his nomination as Prime Minister, simply because Juarez still remains President.
> Now the two periods are quite distinct, and it is necessary that this should be clearly understood ... Juarez still remains President, but

now he is a cypher, whereas formerly he was mischievous from allowing others to do harm unchecked. As his name is discredited the French constantly speak of the present Government as 'le gouvernement Juarez' thus leading those not accurately acquainted with the subject to suppose that it is the same government which by its acts brought about the intervention of the three Powers.[14]

Wyke seems to have been the only plenipotentiary to have suggested that the justification for negotiating with the Mexican government was because it was then a different government. It is also possible that Wyke was justifying their decision to negotiate, instead of issuing an ultimatum, in response to Russell's criticism of the terms of the proclamation made in January. Be that as it may, there is an underlying issue of whether or not the representatives were correct in their judgement that the best course to follow was negotiation. There is much evidence to suggest that Wyke and Prim were more astute in their assessment of the situation, and of the people in Mexico, than were Saligny and Jurien, but their governments' decision had been based on the premise that the time for negotiation had passed and that firm action was required. And that premise had been founded largely on the information that had been sent to them over the previous months by Wyke and Saligny. Whether Prim and Wyke were right or not, however, has become a rhetorical question in the study of the intervention, for in the final analysis it was the behaviour of the French representatives that had the greatest impact on the campaign and on the credibility of Napoleon III.

No-one had anticipated that the expedition they had prepared so hastily was to get so out of hand. But whatever the reactions of the other governments, France was now left alone 'to sort out this chaos of difficulties', as Thouvenel put it to Flahault. He remarked that from one point of view it was probably not a bad thing that only one nation was left to sort it out, but it also meant that their responsibility was greatly increased, particularly if they had a setback. Thouvenel could only hope that seven thousand French soldiers could get the better of the Mexican guerrillas. He said that Saligny had been formally advised that he was not to introduce the candidature of Maximilian, as France would not support it unless it was genuinely accepted by the country itself. He hoped at this point that Russell and Palmerston, glad to be out of an affair about which they were not happy, would not now accuse France of having violated the London Convention.[15]

While the Emperor was disappointed that the opportunity to accomplish a united action with Spain and Britain had been thwarted, he and his government were in complete agreement that the honour of France could not allow them to withdraw without achieving anything – neither reparation for what was owed them nor the assurance that any agreements made with the Mexican government would be upheld in the future. Although Britain and Spain blamed the French envoys for the breakdown of the Convention, neither raised objections to Napoleon's decision to stay in Mexico, Britain hypocritally saying there would be advantages for them all in his action. After a debate in the House of Lords over the suspension of the Convention, Palmerston advised Russell that he thought it would be an expensive proposition for France, which was one more reason intervention was out of the question for Britain. He added, however, that 'a monarchy supported by the great armies of Imperial France might be a very different matter. Then the scheme would have a better chance of success and, at no cost to Great Britain, be doubly advantageous to her in Europe as well as in America.'[16]

The Spanish government, anxious to maintain good relations with France, made many overtures over the following months regarding reconvening the Convention of London and supporting the Mexicans' efforts to establish a more stable government. Without actually saying it regretted Prim's conduct, its determination to reconvene the Convention and confirm its alliance with France would seem to indicate this. Napoleon assured the Spanish Ambassador that he had always been anxious to maintain good relations with Spain, which was why he had sent an inferior number of troops initially and instructed his commanders to work closely with Prim. He said that he did not regret that his politics had turned out to be different from Spain's in relation to Mexico, but he did regret that he had mistakenly believed they were the same from the discussions prior to the signing of the Convention.[17]

The path for Napoleon was not to be easy, for in the months of May and June 1862, he was confronted with contradictory reports from his representatives in Mexico, which finally made him realise they misunderstood his intentions. First he had to determine the facts of the situation from the differing reports he received from Jurien and Saligny. After Saligny's damning criticism of Jurien, he, in turn, wrote to Thouvenel denouncing Saligny's behaviour and attitude, which he believed would cause the war to degenerate into a personal quarrel between Saligny and the Mexican nation. He remarked that although his own name might discourage the 'exalted conservatives', that of Saligny frightened all the Liberal party. Thouvenel therefore needed to decide which of the two he would support. Jurien then reported that his naval colleague,

Devarenne, was on his way to Paris to brief both the ministers and the Emperor on the situation in Mexico, the problems caused by Saligny, and his own assessment of how the campaign should be conducted.[18]

In his first interview with the Emperor, Devarenne told him that Jurien expected to be in Mexico between the 18 and 20 May, that is, about the time Devarenne was actually speaking with Napoleon. He informed the Emperor of the duplicity of Saligny, who had written to Thouvenel that he disapproved the Preliminaries of Soledad after having congratulated Jurien when he had signed them, and who refused to share his knowledge of the country with Jurien. Devarenne assured Napoleon, however, that Jurien would be in Mexico City, where his skill and patience would be indispensable to the success of the enterprise – 'the changing of the form of the government'.[19]

Although he said nothing to Devarenne, this was probably the first realisation Napoleon had that his representatives had misinterpreted his intentions. A letter from Lorencez to Marshal Randon would have added even more to his concern. Lorencez wrote that because they were 'so superior to the Mexicans in terms of race, organisation, and moral discipline' Randon should tell the Emperor that 'at the head of his 6,000 soldiers I am the master of Mexico'. He added that he hoped the Emperor had not been influenced by letters from Mexico to abandon his projects, or that Maximilian had not been discouraged from accepting 'the crown that His Majesty wanted to put on his head', because he was more convinced than ever that a monarchy was the only suitable form of government for Mexico. He concluded that it was true he was moving slowly towards Mexico City, but he had to take all his supplies with him and did not want his men marching for too long in the extreme heat, 'but I will surely arrive there, the government of Juarez will be overturned and Prince Maximilian will be proclaimed'.[20]

Napoleon immediately had Thouvenel reiterate to Saligny their desire to see Mexico reconstituted under new conditions, but he stressed that the initiative for such a regeneration must come not from the French but from the country itself, which would develop its confidence to undertake such a task from the presence of the French. Saligny was told to observe strictly his previous instructions, and that although the Emperor and the government had confidence in Almonte, Saligny was to confine his own actions to the responsibilities given him and to leave Almonte to act according to his own convictions in appealing to the patriotism of his fellow countrymen.[21]

Napoleon then revealed his reaction to Lorencez's news in an angry letter to Maximilian shortly after the arrival of the report:

I have always . . . gone straight upon my way. Being at war with the Mexican Government I have not been willing to treat with it. I have told my representatives that there was no question whatever of imposing any kind of government upon the Mexicans, but only of supporting a monarchy if it found partisans in the country and a prospect of stability. This course of action was quite simple and straightforward, and yet attempts have been made to distort my intentions and misinterpret the character of the intervention.[22]

To Lorencez he wrote:

Il est contre mon intérêt, mon origine et mes principes, d'imposer un gouvernement quelconque au peuple mexicain. Il peut choisir en toute liberté celui qui lui convient le mieux. Je ne lui demande que de la sincérité dans ses relations avec l'étranger, et je ne désire qu'une chose, la prospérité et l'indépendance de ce beau pays, sous un gouvernement stable et régulier.[23]

[It is contrary to my interest, my origin and my principles, to impose any government on the Mexican people. They can choose in complete freedom the one which suits them best. I only ask them for sincerity in their relations with foreign countries, and the only thing I desire is the prosperity and independence of this beautiful country, under a stable and legitimate government.]

Napoleon's spontaneous and angry response is difficult to dismiss, and although it cannot be denied that Napoleon had anticipated little serious resistance to a change in the regime in Mexico, nor that he thought a monarchy best, he always was open to an alternative result. He had written to Maximilian in January 1862, expressing this belief, and in his reply Maximilian showed that his appointment to the throne of Mexico was not an act that was to be taken for granted. He told the Emperor how proud he would be to hoist the monarchical flag aloft in Mexico 'in case I am called upon to reign', indicating that neither he nor the Emperor treated it as a *fait accompli*.[24] A further letter from Napoleon in March revealed that the information from Mexico, which included correspondence from the Prussian and Belgian representatives, indicated there was much support for a monarchy. Napoleon assured Maximilian that he was doing all he could to see this eventuate, but Maximilian's reply reveals that Napoleon had previously advised him that he should reserve his expectations until the freely expressed desires of the Mexican people were known.[25]

Correspondence between Napoleon and Maximilian, published by Corti, supports the argument that Napoleon's proposal of Maximilian was merely part of his contingency plans, should the people vote in favour of a monarchy. That Napoleon was not opposed in principle to a republican form of government can be seen in the writings of his youth, in which he recognised the virtues of both forms of government, and that neither was, *per se*, the better. In *Des Idées napoléoniennes* he wrote:

il n'y a pas plus de formule gouvernementale pour le bonheur des peuples, qu'il n'y a de panacée universelle qui guérisse de tous les maux ... Tous ont été bons, puisqu'ils ont duré; telle forme a été la meilleure pour tel peuple qui a duré le plus longtemps. Mais, *a priori*, le meilleur gouvernement est celui qui remplit bien sa mission. C'est-à-dire celui qui se formule sur le besoin de l'époque, et qui, en se modelant sur l'état présent de la société, emploie les moyens nécessaires pour frayer une route plane et facile à la civilisation qui s'avance.[26]

[there is no more a governmental formula for the happiness of people than there is a universal panacea to cure all diseases ... All have been good, since they have lasted; the form which has been the best for a particular people has been the one which lasted the longest time. So, *a priori*, the best government is the one which fulfils its mission. That means, the one which is based on the needs at the time, and which, by adjusting to the present state of the society, uses the necessary means to open up a smooth and easy road to advancing civilisation.]

Napoleon's instructions to Jurien and Lorencez confirm he still maintained these ideas of his youth, and they were reiterated in his instructions to General Forey, who was shortly to replace Lorencez as commander of the Expeditionary Forces.

Having been assured that his army would soon reach Mexico City, Napoleon was surprised to learn of its defeat at Puebla in early May. In the debate over involvement in Mexico in the *Corps législatif* towards the end of June, Jules Favre remarked that it was obvious that the government had been misled by inaccurate information and that, in fact, the Juarez regime was not going to be easily overthrown. It was also apparent that the Mexican government had at least enough 'vitality' to unite the population to resist the French, he said, referring to the defeat at Puebla.[27] Billault, for the government, then rejected Favre's suggestions that they should now treat with Juarez and leave Mexico as soon as possible. How could they do that, he asked, when all the promises of the Mexican government had proved worthless, when French blood had already been spilt, and they had suffered a military setback? Withdraw, when at this sad news the patriotism of even the Opposition had been moved to vote in favour of the 15 million francs that had been asked of them? Billault continued to appeal to their patriotism and to the fact that France's honour had now been engaged. In view of its glorious past France would suffer considerable humiliation if the army returned home without achieving any military satisfaction after this setback.[28] This appeal to the deputies succeeded, and because of it they voted in favour of the extra money needed to send reinforcements. Émile Ollivier, however, commented disparagingly:

nous le votâmes et je dis pourquoi: nous sommes unanimes sur ce point, c'est que là où nos soldats sont engagés et souffrent, peu importe pour quelles raisons et dans quelles circonstances, il faut les secourir. En votant ce secours, je le dis à l'avance, nous ne renonçons pas au devoir de rechercher ce que nos soldats sont allés faire au Mexique et quelle attitude il convient que nous imposions ou conseillons au gouvernement (16 juin).'[29]

[we voted for it and I tell you why: we are unanimous on this point, that where our soldiers are engaged and suffer, no matter for what reasons and in which circumstances, we must support them. In advocating this support, I say beforehand, we are not failing in our duty to discover to what purpose our soldiers have gone to Mexico, and what attitude would be appropriate for us to impose or advise the government to take (16 June).]

Overtly the support was there in the form of the vote in favour of the budget for Mexico, but Ollivier maintained that the facts of the situation were altered or deliberately misconstrued by Billault to mislead the country.

The problem was that Napoleon's motives, such as concern over the expansion of the United States and its effect on Europe, were not divulged to either the French parliament or the public, until his instructions to General Forey of July 1862 were published, in part, in 1863 in the *Archives Diplomatiques*. According to General Comte Fleury, an aide to Napoleon, this was a mistake, because the war would not have been so unpopular if Napoleon had revealed all his motives, at least to parliament, much earlier. Unfortunately, he said, discussion was not permitted on diplomatic problems, when in fact it might have lessened the difficulties, and the consequences were grave:

> Cette discretion imposée par la politique n'a pas eu seulement l'inconvénient grave de discréditer les projets mal connus de l'Empereur. Elle a pesé lourdement sur la conduite et la préparation des opérations militaires, parce que, n'osant pas tout dire aux Chambres, on a lésiné dès le principe sur l'envoi des moyens nécessaires pour en assurer le succès.[30]

> [This discretion imposed by politics has not only had the grave disadvantage of discrediting the little known projects of the Emperor. It has heavily influenced the management and preparation of the military operations. Because one did not dare to tell everything to the Chambers, one was compelled to haggle from the start over sending the necessary means to ensure success.]

While there were problems with the material preparations for the campaign, Fleury, writing with hindsight, overlooked the fact that nobody had anticipated a lengthy or difficult campaign.

The Emperor's initial response to Lorencez's report on defeat at Puebla was an acceptance that in war these setbacks occur, and that he should not be discouraged. He wrote that the honour of France had been engaged and General Lorencez could expect all necessary resources to continue his move towards the capital.[31] But his anger was very quickly roused by the ensuing reports that arrived from Lorencez and Saligny criticising, in violent language, each other's behaviour and integrity in the aftermath of the defeat. The first was from Saligny in the form of a personal damnation of Lorencez 'with whom he tried his hardest to get on'. He wrote to Thouvenel:

> esprit craintif, paresseux, endormi, pour ne pas dire éteint, caractère faible, incapable lui-même d'initiative et ne pouvant souffrir celle d'autrui; ne demandant jamais de conseils et prenant ombrage de ceux qu'on lui donne, il joint à tout cela une susceptabilité, maladive, toujours en éveil et que les plus grands ménagements, les déférences les plus empressées ne sauraient rassurer. Il est, en outre, sujet à de fréquentes absences qu'on prendrait parfois pour de l'aberration à des accès d'humeur ivre qui le rendent pendant plusieurs jours inabordable, même pour son entourage, avec le quel [sic] il est d'ailleurs, sur un pied de continuelle méfiance, presque d'hostilité.[32]

[a fearful person, lazy, sluggish, not to say dull, a weak character, incapable of initiative himself and unable to suffer that of others; he never asks for advice and takes offence at that which is given to him. This is compounded by his morbid sensitivity, and his being on constant alert, so much so that even the greatest care and deference cannot reassure him. Moreover, he is subject to frequent absent-mindedness which can be taken at times for the outbursts of a drunken mind which render him unapproachable for several days, even by his entourage, whom he mistrusts and treats almost with hostility.]

This was followed by Lorencez's lengthy report to Randon blaming Saligny and Almonte for the setback, and saying it was they who had misled him as to the support he would receive and the opposition he would encounter. He was amazed at the strength of the defence he encountered when, according to the assertions of Almonte and Saligny, 'a hundred times repeated', he would be welcomed with transport for his journey to Mexico City, and his soldiers would be covered with flowers. He was faced then with three options: to attack the barricades of Puebla directly, a project his officers commanding the engineers and artillery advised against as they would lose at least a thousand men in the attempt; to go around Puebla and head to the capital, which was not feasible because of limited supplies; or, to retreat to Orizaba to await the arrival of supplies and equipment strong enough to destroy the town of Guadaloupe in order to reach the capital. Following advice from Saligny and Almonte that the army of General Marquez was coming to meet him at Amazoc on the route to Orizaba, Lorencez decided on the third option and proceeded to Amazoc where he waited for three days. Marquez failed to appear and when news reached them that the head of the Reactionary Party, Zuloaga, had made a pact with Juarez to neutralise the army of Marquez, Lorencez decided to continue his retreat to Orizaba. On the way he encountered Marquez who said he had come by another route far from the direction of Puebla, and had never been to, nor intended to go to, Amazoc, a statement that contradicted the assertions of Saligny and Almonte.[33]

Lorencez added to this another dispatch condemning Saligny and the reports he believed Saligny had written against him and the army. Information that Saligny was trying to prevent Lorencez's mail leaving the country so only his own reports would reach Paris, led Lorencez to take extraordinary measures to ensure his dispatches reached the boats safely. He told Randon that Saligny was not well thought of in Mexico, and had done nothing for the French there but mislead them. He continued with a condemnation of Saligny similar to Saligny's report of him:

> Il est entièrement inepte en affaires; sans aucun jugement, il n'a d'autre aptitude que la déplorable facilité d'écrire des mensonges; son manque de dignité et ses habitudes d'intempérance, l'ont placé dans l'opinion de l'armée, à un rang de beaucoup au dessous de celui que sa position officielle lui donne. D'un jour à l'autre je me vois dans l'obligation de faire arrêter M. le Ministre de France au Mexique et de le faire embarquer.[34]

> [He is totally inept in his dealings; without any judgement, he has no other aptitude than the deplorable talent for writing lies; his lack of dignity and his habits of intemperance, have placed him, in the opinion of the army, at a much lower rank than his official position has given him. From day to day I see myself being compelled to arrest the French Minister in Mexico and put him on board a ship.]

What was Napoleon to make of events in Mexico, especially when a further report arrived from Saligny at the same time criticising the approach of the army to Puebla, and giving his view of their defeat? Saligny told Thouvenel that if they had marched straight to Mexico City, as he believed the Emperor wanted, without waiting for supplies, all would have been well and Puebla would not have been fortified. Jurien's claims of lack of transport in the early stages were totally false, he said, because a Mexican had offered horses and equipment which Jurien rejected.[35] It is hard to imagine that one Mexican could have had sufficient equipment to meet the needs of the army, but this report was enough to anger Napoleon and cause him to direct Marshal Randon to censure Lorencez for having made an imprudent attack against Puebla, and for criticising Saligny, his representative in Mexico. After carrying out his instructions, Randon wrote to Napoleon and strongly criticised the unfair judgement of Lorencez, which was based on the observations of a person entirely alien to the army. He continued:

> Ce n'est pas seulement le général de Lorencez qu'attaque M. de Saligny; l'amiral Jurien n'est pas épargné, puis le colonel Valazé et l'état major tout entier ... En lisant les dépêches de M. de Saligny, en examinant la valeur de ses appréciations, il est bien permis de sourire et de ne pas prendre au sérieux ses raisonnements pour critiquer les opérations des troupes ... Quel est le général qui consentirait à se charger d'un

commandement si ses moindres actions de guerre devaient avoir pour juge un homme qui, placé près de lui pour une tout autre mission, s'arroge le droit de scruter sa conduite et dénoncer ses actes?[36]

[Mr de Saligny does not only attack General de Lorencez; Admiral Jurien has not been spared, nor Colonel Valazé and all the headquarters staff . . . When reading Mr de Saligny's dispatches, and evaluating his opinions, one can be excused for laughing and for not taking seriously his arguments for criticising the military operations . . . What general would agree to take a command if the least of his military actions are judged by a man who was sent on a completely different mission, but who takes it upon himself to scrutinise his conduct and denounce his actions?]

Napoleon's faith in Saligny's reports has been the subject of wonder and conjecture, which has led frequently to the conclusion that Saligny was carrying out the secret intentions of the Emperor, and that his relations with Morny meant Napoleon was using the Jecker bonds as an excuse to intervene in Mexico. Yet when all the contradictory reports from Mexico are considered, it can be seen that Napoleon had to decide who was the most reliable informant. Saligny had been in Mexico much longer than Jurien or Lorencez, and before their arrival there had been no reason to doubt the veracity or integrity of his reports. His letters to General Rollin, the Adjutant-General of the palace, were no doubt another influencing factor, as they avowed devotion to the Emperor while denouncing Jurien and Lorencez. In addition, the observations of such presumably reliable people as the ministers and consuls of Belgium and Prussia, which agreed with Saligny's views, added more weight to his reports.

The Emperor's use of other agents, both civilian and military, to obtain information about the situation in Mexico was, and is, widely criticised. Émile Ollivier held that it created problems by undermining the authority of Napoleon's commanders, and that while sometimes the results were beneficial, often discipline was impaired, and the commander was disgraced.[37] It also raises the question of how Napoleon was influenced. Randon had criticised the validity of accepting a civilian's judgement of an officer, but perhaps Napoleon thought the unsolicited opinions of those who wrote to him were more disinterested than those of his minister. Without more information one can only speculate. Lorencez was bitter that he had been judged and admonished by the Emperor on the basis of reports from people such as Saligny and a civilian,

Vicomte de Lapierre, an aide-de-camp to Almonte, and he wrote to Randon in anger at the reprimand he had been sent at the command of the Emperor.[38]

Yet was Napoleon wrong to use other sources to obtain as clear a picture as possible of the situation? To Egon Corti he was like 'many crowned heads before and since' who accepted information 'from unauthorised sources for preference, so as to serve as a check upon the responsible persons to whom he ostensibly gave his "confidence"'.[39] Corti commented, however, that the views of these 'unofficial' parties were not necessarily reliable because, being free from responsibility, they were likely to judge things differently than if they did have responsibility. Whether or not the information obtained by Napoleon by these methods was more accurate or any less biased, it must nonetheless have served to broaden his understanding of what was happening in Mexico, even though it took some time for him to appreciate the deception of his agent, Saligny.

Rightly or wrongly Napoleon supported Saligny, but to avoid further complications he decided to send a new commander, General Forey, whom he would invest with both political and military powers. Before that eventuated, however, Napoleon and his Minister, Randon, were besieged with further conflicting reports from Lorencez, Saligny and Almonte. Lorencez wrote that the financial measures taken by the other two were 'deplorable', and there was not enough money to pay the Mexican troops adequately to stop them pillaging and giving the French army a bad reputation.[40] Almonte wrote to Napoleon that Lorencez and his assistant, General Douai, did not understand Mexican warfare and refused to listen to his advice which would have seen them defeat the army of General Zaragoza. There was no other army between Orizaba and Mexico City, Almonte claimed, and he had heard from the capital that there were no more forces to send against them, so if Lorencez listened to him, Juarez could be put down easily.[41] Almonte's confidence in his knowledge of his country, and his belief that he understood the Emperor's politics, were to prove a major cause of the problems that arose in the conduct of the campaign.

Lorencez, however, soon came to the conclusion that there was little support for the French in Mexico, that the Moderate party did not exist, and that the Reactionary party was reduced to nothing and was in any case 'odious'. Most Mexicans, he said, were liberal in their thinking and there was little support for a monarchy, which would only be achieved after years of occupation by the French. As for Almonte, Lorencez thought Saligny had been too enthusiastic about supporting him, in the belief that he was under the protection of the Emperor, and now Almonte was accepting the role of *chef-suprême* instead of helping to form a provisional government. He told Randon that nothing would be possible with Almonte and Saligny in Mexico.[42] Saligny, on the other hand, wrote again to General Rollin saying that the Mexican army was practically non-existent, in spite of claims to the contrary. He added that their only serious enemies were their own military commanders who were fighting their own war against the politics of the Emperor, against his representative and against Almonte. Saligny claimed that General Lorencez, General Douai and Colonel Valazé spoke of each other in insulting terms in front of the soldiers and this was disastrous for morale and had to cease. He awaited anxiously the arrival of General Forey, whom he and Almonte believed could have defeated the Mexican army easily with the forces already in Mexico.[43]

Because the honour of France had been engaged by the defeat at Puebla, the campaign was about to move into another phase. Napoleon hoped it would be better directed as a result of the precise instructions he was to give Forey, which were also intended to clarify his aims. These instructions are important because, in the first place, they explain Napoleon's reasons for accepting Saligny's reports over those of his commanders, and, particularly, because his view of the Mexican situation and his aims for the expedition are so clearly expounded. They have also given rise to much comment and speculation and have been used to support the arguments that the Emperor intended to impose a Latin-Catholic barrier to the advance of the United States into Central and South America; that he was seeking exclusive economic benefits for France; and that he intended to impose a monarchy on Mexico.

The Emperor invested Forey with both political and military powers, making sure that his directions were clear and precise, and even going so far as to detail how he would conduct the military operations if he were in Forey's place. In support of Saligny, Napoleon told Forey that he had seen a report from the Belgian consul in Puebla and received letters himself from that town, which stated that the day after the French had been checked at Puebla the population in the town had been amazed that they had failed to take it. He said he had also seen letters from Mexico City, including reports from the Belgian and Prussian ministers, which said that before 5 May:

> le gouvernement était dans la stupeur et que la population nous attendait avec impatience comme des libérateurs. Ainsi le Général Lorencez, n'a pas été trompé par les rapports de M. de Saligny et du

Général Almonte car s'il avait réussi dans l'attaque de Puebla tout ce que ces messieurs lui avaient annoncé se serait réalisé.

[the government was stupified and that the population was waiting impatiently for us as liberators. Therefore General Lorencez has not been misled by Mr de Saligny's and General Almonte's reports, because if he had succeeded in the attack on Puebla everything these gentlemen had predicted would have been realised.]

These reports, Napoleon said, actually confirmed Saligny's assessment of the situation. He had not claimed that the population was so enthusiastically in favour of their intervention that they would immediately rise up and overthrow their oppressive government, but he had said that once they were in the interior of the country they would find the population sympathetic. He added that although he did not know if Saligny's character left something to be desired, or if he could be reproached for his intemperate language, he believed his despatches had always shown good sense, steadfastness, and a concern for the dignity of France. It was therefore probable that if his advice had been followed, the French flag would already be flying in Mexico City. He impressed upon Forey how important it was that he get along with Saligny, who knew the country and was *au fait* with the claims that were to be redressed. This unity was essential because the earlier disagreements and jealousies had caused everything to be compromised so far.

Napoleon went on to discuss the advantages to be gained from the campaign, saying that Europe could not be indifferent to the prosperity of America because it provided raw materials for their industries and markets for their commerce. It was this aspect of Napoleon's plans that Fleury believed he should have revealed to both parliament and the public when Forey departed for Mexico. The effect of not doing so was that commentary focused on assertions that Napoleon's interests were selfish and that he was intent on imposing a monarchy. The Emperor explained to Forey that although Europe was interested to see the United States powerful and prosperous, they did not wish to see her seize all the Gulf of Mexico from which she could dominate the Antilles and South America, and thence be the sole administrator of the products of the New World. He continued:

Maîtresse du Mexique et par conséquent de l'Amérique centrale et du passage entre les deux mers, il n'y aurait plus désormais d'autre puissance en Amérique que celle des états unis.

Si au contraire le Mexique conquiert son indépendance et main-
tient l'intégrité de son territoire, si un gouvernement stable s'y con-
stitue par les armes de la France, nous aurons posé une digue
infranchissable aux empiètements des états unis, nous aurons main-
tenu l'indépendance de nos colonies des Antilles et de celles de
l'ingrate Espagne; nous aurons établi notre influence bienfaisante au
centre de l'Amérique et cette influence rayonnera au nord comme au
Midi, créera des débouchés immenses à notre commerce et procurera
les matières indispensables à notre industrie.[44]

[Mistress of Mexico and therefore of Central America and the passage between the two oceans, there would be from now on no other
power in America but the United States.

If, on the contrary, Mexico conquers her independence and maintains the integrity of her territory, if a stable government is formed
with French arms, we will have created an impassable barrier to the
encroachments of the United States. We will have maintained the
independence of our colonies in the Antilles and of ungrateful Spain.
We will have established our bountiful influence in Central America,
and that influence will shine to the north as well as to the south, it
will create immense openings for our trade and will procure essential
materials for our industry.]

In an analysis of this letter Alfred and Kathryn Hanna commented
that there was no mention of 'debts, claims, and damages to French
nationals', and claim that this is revealing in the light of 'the almost
hysterical devotion to French "griefs", so much a part of earlier policies'.
They concluded that 'now that they were no longer needed to mislead
England and France [*sic*], they were not even mentioned'.[45] This is not
strictly accurate, as Napoleon did mention them when he wrote of the
aim not being to impose a government but to support the Mexicans to
establish the kind of government they wanted, and one which had some
chance of stability and of guaranteeing to France redress for the 'griefs of
which they had to complain'. This issue was not neglected, but now that
the honour of the country was engaged, Napoleon focused more on
getting the expedition back on track and on the issue of the institution of
a new government as a prerequisite for the settlement of France's claims.

American historians, particularly, have concentrated on what they
call Napoleon's anti-American policy as the principal motive for his
intervention in Mexico, and played down the fact that he was also
highly motivated by the idea of helping Mexico regenerate itself.

Alfred and Kathryn Hanna and Dexter Perkins relied heavily on the writings of Michel Chevalier in their arguments, believing that his close association with the Emperor meant they shared similar ideas.[46] Chevalier, however, gives no indication, implicit or explicit, that what he wrote regarding Mexico and the Americas reflected the Emperor's ideas. He had studied the growth of other Christian powers, including Russia, which embraced the Orthodox religion, the nations rising from the imminent collapse of the Turkish Ottoman Empire that would lean towards the Greek Church, and the growth of the Protestant States of the United States, Canada and the Pacific, and suggested that eventually they would threaten the future of Catholic nations like France. He wrote:

> This comparative exhibit of the progress of Catholic States and those of the Christian peoples that profess other tenets, is of a nature to inspire gloomy reflections in those statesmen who, not without reason, consider that the destinies of France, and the greatness of her authority, are dependent on the chances of the future of the Catholic States in general, and of the Latin races in particular. It is the most powerful argument that can possibly be put forward in support of the expedition to Mexico.[47]

These ideas, in fact, seem to be in opposition to those of Napoleon, who was concerned that those of other religions should be allowed the freedom to worship as they chose. His determination to reduce the power of the Catholic Church both in France and Mexico bear witness to this.

Economic motives for intervention have been strongly supported by many historians and analysts of the campaign and, given the volume of correspondence from adventurers, such as the Count de Raousset-Boulbon, a former soldier, on the potential mineral wealth in the States of Sonora and Chihuahua, during the 1840s and 1850s, the emphasis is understandable.[48] The desperate need for new sources of cotton after the onset of the American Civil War, has also been suggested as a motive for going to Mexico. However, none of the arguments in favour of these motives is strong enough for them to be considered the primary reason for Napoleon's involvement in Mexico. He did ask for reports relating to the potential of mining of silver, particularly, but his main motivation seemed to be that Mexico's resources be developed to help the regeneration of the country, as will be seen in later stages of the expedition.

Cotton, also, could hardly be considered a primary motive, because it was by no means certain that they would get large supplies from Mexico.

Thouvenel approached England with the Emperor's idea of growing cotton there, but, as England had a reasonable stockpile in Liverpool and cotton was beginning to come from India, there seemed no need to pursue a project that might bring them into conflict with the United States.[49] Although attempts were made to grow cotton in Mexico, France also imported cotton from India and Egypt, which helped, at least partly, to make up the deficit. It cannot be denied that Napoleon was looking for economic advantages for France, but this was never to be at the exclusion of other European nations, because free trade, as has been seen, was the core of his foreign policy, and the reason he was concerned to prevent the exclusive influence of the United States in the Americas.[50]

The statement in Forey's instructions about the Prince aided by France being bound to act in their interests, could be used to support the argument that Napoleon intended from the beginning to impose a monarchy. In the same letter, however, there are also two references to the importance of the Mexicans being able to choose the form of government they believed was best for them, whether that be a monarchy or a republic:

> Le but à atteindre n'est pas d'imposer aux Mexicains une forme de gouvernement qui leur serait antipathique, mais de les seconder dans leurs efforts pour établir, selon leur volonté, un gouvernement qui ait des chances de stabilité et puisse garantir à la France le redressement des griefs dont elle a à se plaindre.
>
> Il va sans dire que si les Mexicains préfèrent une monarchie, il est de l'intérêt de la France de les appuyer dans cette voie et en ce cas le Général [Almonte] pourrait indiquer l'Archiduc Maximilien comme le candidat de France.

> [The aim is not to impose on the Mexicans a form of government they would not like, but to assist them in their efforts to establish, according to their will, a government which could be stable and could give France assurances that it will settle her grievances.
>
> It is not necessary to say that if the Mexicans prefer a monarchy, it is in the interest of France to help them in that direction. In this case the general [Almonte] could put forward the Archduke Maximilian as France's candidate.]

Towards the end of the letter he added:

> Ainsi donc aujourd'hui notre honneur militaire engagé, l'exigence de notre politique, l'intérêt de notre industrie et de notre commerce,

tout nous fait un devoir de marcher sur Mexico, d'y planter hardi-
ment notre drapeau, d'y établir soit une monarchie, si elle n'est pas
incompatible avec le sentiment national du pays, soit tout au moins
un gouvernement qui promette quelque stabilité.[51]

[So today, our military honour engaged, the demands of our politics,
the interests of our industry and trade, all of these make it our duty
to march on Mexico City, to daringly plant our flag, and to establish
there a monarchy – if it is not incompatible with the national feeling –
or at least a government which will show promise of some stability.]

Closely tied to the choice of the form of government, of course, was
how that choice was to be made. Whether or not Napoleon intended to
conduct only a 'kind of universal suffrage' has also been one of the
most contentious issues surrounding the intervention, and will be
explored in Chapter 6.

In the light of the controversy surrounding the intervention, both at
the time and in subsequent analyses, it is worth considering just how
much importance Napoleon himself placed on it. One way of determining
this is by examining how the expedition was to be commanded, and by
whom. It was not for some time that Napoleon learned he had been
misled as to the strength of Juarez's opposition, but from the beginning
it can be seen that it was not meant to be a major French campaign. The
Emperor was determined that France's forces would not be superior to
those of his allies, and he also sent an admiral as commander. When he
did send further troops, after Spain's precipitate action, the general he
sent, Lorencez, was only promoted to the rank of Lieutenant-General
on his departure, and had never commanded a division before. Pierre de
la Gorce said of Lorencez:

Le chef même semblait inégal à la táche. Général de division depuis
quelques jours seulement, il n'avait ni l'habitude ni l'autorité des
grands commandements.[52]

[The commander himself did not seem equal to the task. Lieutenant-
General for a few days only, he had neither the bearing nor the
authority of great commanders.]

Although more senior, in that he had been made *Général de Division*
[Lieutenant-General] on 22 December 1851, Forey could not be considered a distinguished commander either. La Gorce wrote of him:

officier de capacités ordinaires, mais ayant de beaux états de service, une longue ancienneté de grade, et recommandé par le souvenir du combat de Montebello.[53]

[officer of average abilities, but who carried out his duties conscientiously, who was of longstanding seniority in his rank, and was recommended because of his service in the battle of Montebello.]

The choice of commanders could be explained by the fact that it was not anticipated to be a lengthy or difficult campaign. Although the setback at Puebla changed the nature of the intervention to a matter of defending France's honour, even this did not seem to change its importance as a military campaign in Napoleon's eyes. At exactly the time he expounded his aims in Mexico to Forey, he replied to requests by two of his generals, obviously to send stronger command there, that he did not think the Mexican expedition was important enough to send a general to command the engineers or one to command the artillery. He did not say he only anticipated a short campaign, or that the war was not big enough to warrant sending generals to command these sections of the expeditionary forces, but he told both General Lebœuf, who asked to be sent with General Forey, and General Frossard, a close aide-de-camp, that it was not important enough to do so. To General Frossard he wrote this note:

Mon cher Général, L'expédition du Mexique n'a pas assez d'importance pour y envoyer un Général du Génie, c'est l'unique raison qui m'empêche de satisfaire le désir que vous m'exprimez.[54]

[My dear General, the Mexican expedition is not important enough to send a general from the Engineers. This is the only reason which stops me from satisfying the wish you have expressed.]

If it was not so important that it needed senior officers to command the artillery and engineers, what did Napoleon really think of the campaign? It is obvious that the maintenance of European influence in Central America was essential to his vision, but these comments show he was not prepared to use excessive force to see that vision materialise. By the same token he had underestimated the strength of Juarez and his support. As Ernest Louet, paymaster of the French forces in Mexico, observed, the intervention had been based on the premise that Juarez would be easily overthrown, and initially hardly anyone doubted the success of the expedition. He added that there were very few 'wise spirits, more prudent, more reflective than others' who realised that Juarez had the advantage of being able to sustain himself and his supporters in some part of the huge country, which enemy forces would find impossible to occupy in its entirety. Juarez, he believed, would always be able to escape his enemies and wait for better times, and could feel secure in the support, direct or indirect, of his northern neighbours.[55] But this was yet to be realised in Paris where it had been decided to pursue the war to redeem France's honour. Despite Napoleon's efforts, however, the campaign was still to demand more time and resources than he could have anticipated. The months ahead revealed even more problems with his representatives, and finally, the realisation that he had, indeed, been badly served.

6
The Will of the People?

Forey arrived in Mexico on 24 September 1862, landing at Vera Cruz where he issued a proclamation to the Mexican people, reassuring them of the Emperor's intentions. In part it stated:

> On a cherché à soulever contre nous le sentiment national, en voulant faire croire que nous arrivions pour imposer à notre gré un Gouvernement au pays; loin de là, le peuple mexicain, affranchi par nos armes, sera entièrement libre de choisir le Gouvernment qui lui conviendra; j'ai mission expresse de le lui déclarer.
>
> Les hommes courageux qui sont venus se joindre à nous méritent notre protection spéciale; mais, au nom de l'Empereur, je fais appel, sans distinction de parti, à tous ceux qui veulent l'indépendance de leur patrie et l'intégrité de son territoire.[1]

> [Some have tried to raise national feeling against us, making you believe that we were coming to impose a government of our choice on your country. Far from this, the Mexican people, liberated by our arms, will be entirely free to choose the government which will be most suitable. My mission is to make this known.
>
> The courageous men who have come to join us, deserve our special protection; but, in the name of the Emperor, I appeal, making no distinction between the parties, to all those who wish for the independence of their country and the integrity of its territory.]

At that point he had no idea how difficult his task would prove to be.

He then proceeded to Orizaba, where he began appealing to the moderates of the different parties, much to Almonte's annoyance. Almonte had previously written to the Emperor suggesting he and Saligny would

133

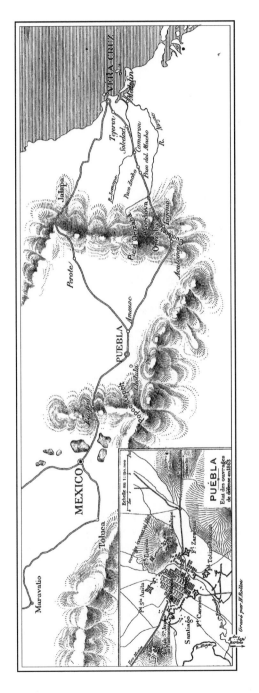

Map 2   Route from Vera Cruz to Mexico

be able to help Forey understand the true political situation of the country. All Forey had to do, he said, was to follow the path they had cleared for him. He continued:

> Le parti conservateur est organisé et se trouve avec nous, et tout ce qu'il y a à faire pour ne pas le décourager, c'est de nous laisser marcher jusqu'à Mexico de la même manière que nous l'avons fait jusqu'ici.[2]

> [The conservative party is organised and is with us, and all that is required not to discourage them, is to let us march to Mexico City in the same manner as we have until now.]

This report must have startled Napoleon, because aligning with any party, let alone the Conservatives, was in complete opposition to the instructions he had given each of his commanders. If the Conservative party came to power again the population feared that the clergy would seize the religious properties that had been sold by Juarez and previous inequities would continue. Fortunately, Forey was not about to support the Conservatives.

Forey reported to Randon that many moderates had returned to the various towns occupied by the French, while he had received reports of other towns that had turned against Juarez and organised counter-guerrillas. He said that an influential liberal from Cordova claimed there was a change of ideas within the Liberal Party and before long the Congress itself was likely to overturn the Juarez government. On the other hand, a letter from Mexico City informed him that some important Mexicans wanted to demonstrate in favour of Juarez and call for the expulsion of French residents in Mexico. Saligny, he said, who is 'well informed of Mexican affairs', believed there was nothing serious in the rumours, however, and that the government would not dare take such steps, even though some expulsions had already been carried out. To reassure the Mexican people Forey issued a further proclamation saying that, with the help of the French army, they could establish a better government, which would be able to develop the country and put an end to the anarchy and suffering that they had endured for so long.[3] He believed his proclamation had made a favourable impression and that it would not be long before the people began to forget their differences and rally to the French in order to establish 'a government capable of ensuring the prosperity, no less than the greatness of Mexico'. [4] This would of course necessitate reciprocal concessions on the part of the extreme parties, but Forey was confident of such an outcome. He even believed that the clergy would resign themselves to the loss of their property and be prepared to make some concessions. To ensure this, though, he had asked Padre Miranda, a Conservative, who had arrived at Orizaba, to give a written undertaking to give complete support to the French conciliatory politics.

Forey was also determined to re-establish good relations between the army and the French legation. Although he took decisive steps in this direction, within a month he realised that Almonte and Saligny were acting in opposition to his instructions from the Emperor, and that he was to be faced with similar difficulties to those of his predecessors. He regretted the association with Almonte and wrote to Napoleon that, despite appearances, Almonte was 'cunning and a rogue who was certainly the representative of the reactionaries that the same part of the population did not want'. More and more he was gathering representatives of the retrograde party around him, Forey added, and it would become more difficult to get these people to compromise with the moderates of other parties, who were the only ones who could help establish a stable and honest government.

He then told Napoleon he had heard that his own position was going to be attacked by someone returning to France, so he assured him that he believed what he was doing was exactly what he had been advised to do, which was 'to rally all the honest men regardless of their opinions; to favour none of the extreme parties, leaning more towards the side of sound liberty and real progress, according to our great principles of '89, than towards the reactionary side'.[5] As the campaign progressed, these elements of Napoleon's politics in France – 'equality before the law, civil and religious liberty, an upright administration, an equitable judicial procedure', amongst others – were to be reiterated as the blueprint for Mexico's new administration, both in Napoleon's instructions to his commanders and in his advice to Maximilian.[6] Some, however, claimed that Juarez and his government also upheld these very principles of liberty and progress, but Juarez had lost credibility, rightly or wrongly, with Napoleon, who would not negotiate with him.

But the task of rallying the 'honest men', and that of maintaining good relations with Saligny was to prove almost impossible for Forey. He told Napoleon that it was very obvious that Saligny was not happy with being subordinated to him, and that Almonte did not like the idea of relinquishing the title of *chef-suprême*. Saligny was alleged to have sent a Spanish general to San Andrès to spread propaganda in favour of Almonte, and that this general had declared that in spite of General

Forey's proclamations Almonte should still be regarded as *chef-suprême* of the country. When confronted, Saligny and Almonte denied this, saying Saligny had given the Spanish general a purely personal mission to undertake for him, while Almonte produced a declaration that he had been going to publish, dated a week earlier, relinquishing the role and title of *chef-suprême* because of the arrival of General Forey.[7]

Based on his experience with them so far, Forey, understandably, was sceptical of their sincerity. To General Fleury, aide-de-camp to Napoleon, he wrote that Saligny did not deserve the Emperor's confidence, because he was disloyal, and lacked the uprightness of character one would expect from a person in his position. He had been unable to get on with Admiral Jurien, who was 'honour itself', and Forey was convinced his problems with Lorencez were not the fault of the latter. Forey himself was not going to give Saligny any opportunity to make him the third victim, knowing how distressed the Emperor would be at another breakdown within the command.[8] Captain Gallifet, a former military aide-de-camp to the Emperor, supported Forey's criticism of Saligny and condemned him for his habit of denouncing both Jurien and Lorencez in front of the officers, particularly as the army regretted the departure of Lorencez, who was regarded with affection in spite of the defeat at Puebla. Almonte, he said, was not well respected, either, because of his 'inactivity'.[9]

Although the actions of Saligny and Almonte disturbed him greatly and made his task extremely difficult, Forey's greatest concern was how to get the people of Mexico to vote, by universal suffrage, on the form of government they wanted. This issue of Napoleon's intentions regarding a vote by universal suffrage has given rise to perhaps even more debate than other aspects of the campaign. The difficulties, Forey wrote to Napoleon, were insurmountable, and the nature of the Indians was such that they should not be consulted at all. In France, he said, it was easy, but in Mexico there was no centralisation, each province being independent of the capital in reality, if not legally; there was no regular administration or rapid means of communication; and the population consisted of one or two million Mexicans, and six or seven million Indians, who had no bond with the government, and whose form mattered little to them. He continued with his description of the Indians:

> d'une ignorance absolue, espèce de bêtes brutes vivant presque à l'état sauvage et chez qui n'existe même pas d'état civil, je me demande comment il sera possible de receuillir les votes; et d'un autre côté, à supposer que l'on ne tienne aucun compte de cette partie

de la population qui est cependant la plus considérable de beaucoup et de beaucoup enfin la plus intéressante parce qu'elle est laborieuse, de mœurs douces et très facile à gouverner; l'autre partie se composant de la masse des mexicains qui tremblent devant quelques centaines de mille d'individus audacieux ne vivant que d'exactions, de rapines, de meurtres et qui dirigeront les votes des premiers par la terreur qu'ils inspirent, je me demande encore si la résultat de ce vote pourra être considéré comme l'expression de la volonté nationale. La difficulté sera grande, n'en doutez pas, Sire, enfin j'espère que vos conseils en cette circonstances ne me feront pas défaut.[10]

[totally ignorant, like wild beasts living almost like savages and who do not even have civil status, I ask myself how it will be possible to collect the votes. At the same time, let us suppose that we do not take into account this part of the population, which after all constitutes the majority of the population and ultimately the most interesting group because they are hardworking, softly mannered and easy to govern; the other part comprising the mass of Mexicans, who live in fear of some hundreds of thousands of audacious individuals who thrive on extortion, pillage and murder, and who will direct the votes of the former using the terror they inspire. I ask again whether the result of this vote could be considered as the expression of the national will. The difficulty will be great, have no doubt about this, Sire, so I hope you will not fail to give me your advice on this situation.]

To a certain extent Forey's assessment of the population of Mexico was correct. By the 1860s the Indians probably formed more than half of the population, but, as seen in Chapter 1, they had occupied a position of inferiority for centuries under the Spanish occupation. The Creoles, Spanish people born in Mexico, considered coloured races inferior and that the Indians were 'by nature, lazy, drunken and stupid'. If they appeared this way it was not because it was their nature, but more likely the result of oppression ever since the conquest by Cortez. They had not been educated by the Spanish and were mostly kept in farming and labouring positions before independence opened opportunities, at least for education. Juarez benefited from this, and qualified as a lawyer. But the new race, the *mestizos*, who were a result of Creole and Indian intermarriage, became the Mexicans, the revolutionaries who resented the Creoles and were not accepted as Indians either.[11] The Indians had generally been excluded from involvement in the choice of government, so

Forey was correct in his realisation that this task would be new to them. But it would also be new to a large proportion of the population, for despite a limited franchise, most elections had been heavily controlled. The franchise had only been extended to all males aged eighteen if married, and twenty-one if not, by the Constitution of 1857, and because of the civil war that broke out almost immediately, it had never really been in effect.[12]

It was only in response to this letter from Forey that Napoleon suggested that if necessary he should conduct 'a kind of universal suffrage, or even a vote of a Congress named by the traditional and usual revolutionary means used in Mexico'.[13] Émile Ollivier commented on this, but failed to show that it was in response to the letter Forey had written in January, although he may not have known of it. He probably added fuel to the arguments of later analysts that Napoleon had no intention of conducting a genuine vote by universal suffrage. Ollivier also commented on a later letter from Napoleon which suggested that Forey should consult the nation in the way he thought most suitable, and he claimed Napoleon was telling Forey to arrange matters to give him 'something that resembled a vote of the nation'.

Corti had a similar opinion, and said that Napoleon's instructions to Forey implied:

it must appear as if the Mexicans were being allowed a free choice, while in reality the plan long since hatched in Paris was to be carried out in its entirety: namely, the monarchy and the Archduke Ferdinand Max! Napoleon attached the greatest importance to 'keeping up appearances'. The world must believe in all seriousness that it was far from being the liberal Napoleon's intention to impose an alien domination upon the Mexicans. And so everything must be skilfully led up to in a manner befitting the Emperor's plans.[14]

In making this claim Corti referred only to the content of Napoleon's letter of 14 February 1863, as had Ollivier, although he did not mention the date of the letter. Neither did he refer to Forey's letter of 11 January 1863, which had prompted Napoleon's statement, but it is quite possible he did not know of this letter, either. His source for the former letter was Gaulot, but he did not refer to the two other letters from the Emperor quoted by Gaulot at the same reference, both of which said in similar terms:

La seule politique à suivre est de marcher sur Mexico, d'y installer un gouvernement des hommes les plus honorables que vous choisirez

vous-même, et ensuite, de faire voter par le suffrage universel, le peuple mexicain, sur la forme du gouvernment à établir.[15]

[The only policy to follow is to march to Mexico City, establish a
government with the most honourable men, whom you will choose
yourself, and then to get the Mexican people to vote by universal
suffrage on the form of government to establish.]

Nor did Corti mention the following comments made by Gaulot, based
on the notes of Ernest Louet, the chief paymaster in Mexico, to explain
this apparent change in Napoleon's instructions, perhaps because Corti
decided that Napoleon had intended all along to conduct 'a kind of
universal suffrage'. Gaulot's words are worth quoting at length:

> Issu du suffrage universel, Napoléon III se montrait ici fidèle à son
> origine en recommandant d'en appeler au suffrage universel. S'il
> ajoutait un correctif en disant 'une espèce de suffrage universel', il y
> avait là, non point un abandon du principe, mais une concession
> faite à des impossibilités matérielles. Les registres de l'état civil
> étaient fort mal tenus au Mexique, par conséquent, des difficultés
> insurmontables s'opposaient à ce que l'on fabriquát une liste
> générale des électeurs. En outre, on n'occupait encore qu'une partie
> du pays. Mais l'Empereur répète sans cesse le mot de nation: c'était
> donc la nation qu'il fallait consulter et non point seulement
> quelques notabilités choisies uniquement dans la capitale.
>
> De plus, la pensée de l'Empereur était bien claire: il ne voulait pas
> de précipitation, pas de vote 'escamoté' à quelques individualités,
> groupées sous un nom pompeux, et réunis à la háte en quelques
> jours. Il tenait à ce qu'un gouvernement provisoire commençát par
> rendre au peuple mexicain l'apparence de son autonomie et de la
> liberté; puis, à l'abri de cet ordre de choses, on devait faire peu à
> peu pénétrer dans le pays entier ses intentions, c'est-à-dire son désir
> de voir la nation mexicaine recouvrer son indépendance sous un
> gouvernement qu'elle choisirait elle-même.

[Elected by universal suffrage, Napoleon III showed himself faithful
to his origin by recommending an appeal to universal suffrage. If he
qualified this by saying 'a kind of universal suffrage', he was not
abandoning the principle, but making a concession to the practical
difficulties. The registers of births, deaths, and marriages were very
poorly kept in Mexico, and consequently there were insurmountable
difficulties to making a general list of voters. Besides, at this stage we

only occupied a part of the country. But the Emperor continually repeats the word 'nation': thus it was the nation that had to be consulted and not only some leading citizens chosen from just the capital.

Moreover, the Emperor's thought was quite clear: he did not want things to be rushed, no 'phoney' votes for some individuals, who had grouped themselves in just a few days under a pompous name. He insisted that a provisional government begin by giving back to the Mexican people the appearance of autonomy and liberty. Then with this in place, his intentions were to be made known gradually throughout the entire country – that is, his desire to see the Mexican nation recover its independence under a government that it would choose itself.]

Opinions similar to Corti's, however, have been generally more widely shared by both contemporaries and historians, but I am convinced there is more to support Paul Gaulot's views than there is to support Corti.

While Forey was pondering these difficulties, his delay in reaching Mexico City began to be questioned in Paris, although Napoleon himself was quite understanding of the problems caused by lack of supplies or equipment. Marshal Randon, however, was not, and strongly criticised Forey. Gallifet, though, supported Forey, and told Napoleon that he had many difficulties to surmount and that all sections of the army complained of the 'parsimony' with which Saligny had estimated the equipment and provisions they would need.[16] But he also wrote that the other officers were critical of Forey's slow progress towards Puebla, although, he assured Napoleon, they still had confidence in him. While they recognised in principle that it was better not to attack the town until he had all that he needed to do so, they disagreed with his prolonged stay at Orizaba, saying he could have made better use of the available transport and would have been able to get provisions along the way. Tactically, Gallifet said, it would have been better to move on to towns such as Amazoc which were closer to Puebla, to await the extra equipment.[17]

Napoleon was not concerned at these strategic delays, but when he heard Forey had stopped again a few days from Orizaba to wait a further five days for money to arrive to pay the soldiers, he was incensed. The paymaster had apparently been concerned there was not enough money left to pay for essential services or to pay the Mexicans who were helping with the transport, and it was fear of them abandoning the convoys that had made Forey wait for the arrival of extra money from Havana. But Napoleon wrote:

J'ai reçu votre dernière lettre qui va jusqu'au 28 février. C'est la première, je l'avoue, qui m'ait fait éprouver une grande déception. Je conçois qu'un général d'armée se trouve entravé dans ses opérations par le défaut de vivier ou de munitions, mais retarder sa marche devant l'ennemi pour attendre un convoi d'argent, c'est ce qui me passe et que je ne puis admettre. J'espère que les premiers courriers qui m'arriveront m'apporteront des nouvelles qui me feront oublier ce fâcheux contre temps.[18]

[I have received your last letter which is up to 28 February. It is the first, I declare, which has given me a great disappointment. I can understand that an army general could find himself hampered in his operations by a lack of provisions or ammunition, but to hold up his march before the enemy to await a convoy of money, it is that which is beyond me and which I cannot accept. I hope that the first mail that arrives will bring me news which will make me forget this untoward delay.]

The remainder of this letter was devoted to detailed instructions to Forey on what to do after his arrival in the capital, instructions that were modified by Forey under the influence of Almonte and Saligny. He was instructed to form a provisional government composed of the most commendable men, but to appoint their own M. Budin as provisional administrator of finances so that they could control the financial resources of the country to help 'introduce the politics of order and integrity'. The provisional government could be assisted by a junta of notables composed as far as possible of men chosen by Forey from the 'rich classes' of the country. While this provisional government was to 'function nominally with independence', it was to remain in fact under Forey's command. This, he said, was to allow time for the people to become confident that France really intended to help them, and did not intend to impose an unwelcome government.

The Emperor outlined a number of tasks that the provisional government was to undertake, but the provisional government was in many respects to take action almost diametrically opposed to Napoleon's ideas. Their first duty would be to disband the reactionary or other groups of soldiers and organise an auxiliary army of the best elements of the Mexican troops, the first step in Napoleon's plan to reduce

French involvement. The people were to be assured that church and state property bought legitimately would not be taken from those who had bought it, and while the Catholic religion would be protected, freedom of other religions would be established. But when the provisional government began courting the Conservative party, this became another promise of Napoleon's that was in danger of being broken.

This letter reveals not only Napoleon's ideas on the formation of the government, but also his intentions to improve the administrative and social aspects of the country, which included developing the roads and railways and improving the cleanliness of the waterways. Forey was directed to deliver a manifesto to the people describing his proposals, which also included the removal of exacting taxes and other burdens on the poorer classes. Napoleon concluded his instructions with the following direction:

> Lorsque ses mesures et d'autres semblables auront pu être prises et qu'on aura répandu dans le pays mes intentions, et fait connaître le but de l'intervention, on pourra alors consulter la nation, de la manière que vous jugerez le plus convenable.

> [When these and other similar measures have been taken, and news of my intentions has been spread throughout the country, as well as the aim of the intervention, one can then consult the nation in the manner that you think most advisable.]

This latter instruction was referred to by Ollivier to shed doubt on Napoleon's intentions relating to the system of voting. But, seen as a response to Forey's request for advice after he had described the difficulties he foresaw in this regard, it does not imply a reversal of Napoleon's intention to consult the nation on its choice of government. Nor does it reveal that he had never intended to consult the people.

In April the army suffered another setback, which concerned Marshal Randon, while the slow progress and continued requests for more men and equipment evoked steady opposition in the *conseil* and among the population. Randon opposed the Mexican campaign, but recognised that France's military honour had been engaged and it was important to conclude a solid victory and then leave. He therefore suggested to the Emperor that he should send a trusted aide to Mexico to gain more accurate information on the situation, the condition of the troops, and what was needed to complete the campaign. Unfortunately, news of victory at Puebla shortly reached Paris and Napoleon decided not to follow Randon's advice. It was to be another three years before he did decide to send an aide to assess the situation for him.

When Puebla fell to the French in May 1863, Napoleon wrote to Forey and congratulated him and the army on their achievement, revealing his respect for the general and his appreciation of the difficulties that had confronted him. He recognised that the enemy had been far more stubborn than he had been led to believe, and that as a result the army must have felt they had been misled about his intentions in Mexico. To reassure them, he concluded his letter:

> Je déplore amèrement la perte probable de tant de braves, mais j'ai la consolante pensée que leur mort n'a été inutile ni aux intérêts, ni à l'honneur de la France, ni à la civilisation. Notre but, vous le savez, n'est pas d'imposer aux Mexicains un gouvernement contre leur gré, ni de faire servir nos succès au triomphe d'un parti quelconque. Je désire que le Mexique renaisse à une vie nouvelle et que bientôt régenéré par un gouvernement fondé sur la volonté nationale, sur les principes d'ordre et de progrès, sur le respect du droit des gens, il reconnaisse par des relations amicales, devoir à la France son repos et sa prospérité.[19]

> [I bitterly deplore the probable loss of so many courageous men, but I am comforted that their death has not been unprofitable for our interests, the honour of France or for civilisation. Our aim, as you know, is not to impose on the Mexicans a government which is against their wishes, nor to use our success to assist the triumph of any particular party. I am anxious that Mexico take on a new lease of life, and that when she is regenerated by a government founded on the national will, on principles of order and progress, on respect for the rights of men, she will acknowledge through friendly relations, that she owes her peace and prosperity to France.]

His optimism, though, was not to be rewarded by events following the occupation of Mexico City.

However, it would seem that after the fall of Puebla Napoleon finally found that the views of his commanding officer and those of his former aide, Captain Gallifet, coincided, and he realised that it was his minister, Saligny, and Almonte who had been misrepresenting his intentions and acting against his policy. At the same time as he wrote to Forey he also ordered the recall of Saligny, whom he now knew had misled him over the difficulty of the situation his army would encounter. But in the meantime, Saligny and Almonte continued directing events in their conviction that they alone knew and understood Mexico and that they were fulfilling the Emperor's wishes. Almonte, in his confidence in his relationship with the Emperor, told him that if Forey followed his advice he could pursue Juarez, who had abandoned the capital in the face of the imminent arrival of the French, and within two months he and his followers would have left the republic. He then proceeded to say how he regretted that the direction of political affairs was no longer in Saligny's hands, and he advised Napoleon of the problems that would result from Forey's continued direction, and suggested how the campaign should henceforth be directed:

> tant qu'il [Saligny] sera subalterné au Général en Chef, la pensée de Votre Majesté restera exposée à être souvent contrariée à cause du manque d'intelligence du Général et du peu de connaissances qu'il a des affaires et des hommes de mon pauvre pays. Je crois, sire, que tout pourrait se remédier politique [*sic*] et militairement parlant, et Votre Majesté pourrait se rassurer sur la marche favorable des affaires de l'entreprise, si elle se décidait à nommer le général Bazaine, Général en Chef du Corps Expéditionnaire, et M. de Saligny, directeur exclusive de la politique. Votre Majesté pourrait accorder pour cela au Général Forey la recompense qu'elle jugerait convenable et il rentrerait en France en laissant les choses ici prendre leur marche naturelle.[20]

> [as long as he [Saligny] is subordinated to the General-in-Chief, Your Majesty's intention will remain exposed to the likelihood of being thwarted because of the general's lack of intelligence and the limited knowledge he has of the affairs and of the people of my poor country. I believe, Sire, that everything will be put right, politically and militarily speaking, and Your Majesty could be assured of the favourable progress of the details of the enterprise, if He decided to nominate General Bazaine as Chief of the expeditionary corps, and Mr de Saligny exclusive director of politics. Your Majesty could reward General Forey as He considers appropriate and he would return to France leaving things here to take their natural course.]

There is no record of Napoleon's reaction to what seems very impertinent advice, but it is probable that it was not favourable, as might be judged from his reaction to Almonte's suggestion, later that same month, of a reward for Saligny.

Saligny and Almonte wasted no time in preventing Forey from using his own initiative after the occupation of Mexico City. Saligny advised him on the method to use to convoke a provisional government, presenting him with a manifesto, already prepared for his signature, to advise the people of the procedure that was to be adopted. He suggested that the 'triumphal march' of the army into the capital and their rapturous greeting by the people, was sufficient proof of 'the sentiments of the vast majority towards the liberators of Mexico'. The perfect order which had persisted in the capital since the flight of the defeated government indicated without doubt that the people were ready, with France's help, to begin the regeneration of their country. They could not therefore afford to disappoint the people or fail to fulfil the benevolent thoughts of the Emperor. He then suggested how the wishes of the people should be determined:

> Je viens vous apporter la fruit de l'étude approfondie que j'ai faite sur la situation du pays, de ses besoins, et des mesures que me paraissent propres à remplir le but que la France se propose, c'est à dire la réorganisation des pouvoirs publics, afin que la nation rendue à elle-même, puisse dans toute son indépendance, et par l'organe de ses citoyens les plus intelligents et les plus considérables, faire connaître la forme définitive du gouvernement qui lui conviendra le mieux.[21]

> [I bring you the product of the extensive study I have made of the country, its needs, and the measures which seem to me proper to achieve the aims that France proposes, that is to say, the reorganisation of public powers, in order that the nation, left to itself, can, in complete independence, and through the organ of its most intelligent and eminent citizens, make known the definitive form of the government which is most suitable for it.]

Saligny then proceeded to justify his proposal for a limited suffrage by advising Forey that it was impossible to convoke a general congress to decide the important questions facing the country because the state of the country would not permit the representatives of the large cities and distant provinces to respond to their appeal. Neither could Saligny consider including the Indian masses 'in this important act of the Mexican nation'. 'This population', he said, 'so worthy of interest in many respects, until now has been kept outside public affairs, so would not understand the gravity or the consequences of a vote'. Having dismissed these sections of the population from the suffrage, Saligny persuaded Forey that representatives from Mexico City were sufficient to obtain the vote of the nation:

> La capitale, où il n'est pas un seul état qui ne se trouve représenté par des citoyens illustres, compte près de 200,000 habitants. Elle renferme un nombre considérable d'intelligences, d'élite habitué à la vie publique et aux affaires politiques. C'est d'ailleurs dans la capitale qu'a pesé la plus lourdement le gouvernement qui vient de tomber. A cette grande population doit appartenir par conséquent, dans les circonstances actuelles, le soin de faire connaître le meilleur moyen de fermer l'ère des révolutions périodiques dont le Mexique est le théátre, depuis près d'un demi-siècle.[22]

> [The capital, where there is not a state which is not represented by renowned citizens, consists of nearly 200,000 inhabitants. It includes a considerable number of intelligent men, of elite citizens used to public life and political affairs. It is, moreover, in the capital that people have felt more heavily the hand of the government which has just fallen. Consequently, in the current circumstances, it is this great population that should have the responsibility of deciding the best means of ending the era of periodic revolutions of which Mexico has been the stage for nearly half a century.]

With the path cleared for a limited suffrage, Saligny proposed to Forey that a junta composed of thirty five citizens, 'chosen from among the most honourable citizens' of Mexico City, should be charged with a list of powers which he proceeded to elaborate. Three Mexican citizens should be chosen to have executive power while a further 215 should be elected to form an assembly of notables to decide on the 'definitive form of the government'.

This letter from Saligny was very obviously influenced by an undated lengthy note written by Almonte, which seems to have been written after the taking of Puebla. In it he described in detail the system of limited suffrage that he claimed had been used by successive governments and which had been accepted by both the Mexican people and other governments.[23] The similarities between this document and Saligny's letter to Forey are striking, and demonstrate Almonte's influence. Whether or not Forey saw Almonte's note, he accepted Saligny's advice and nominated the committee of 35 notables.

At the end of June he forwarded to Napoleon the list of notables who had been chosen to represent, as far as possible, the universal suffrage which, Forey said, had been impractical for a long time. It was especially so now when the defeated government still instilled fear in the honest sector of the population. Although the Assembly had not yet met to vote on the form of government, Forey remarked to Napoleon that he was certain they would vote for a monarchy, and he was ready to pronounce the name of the Archduke Maximilian.[24] Napoleon was greatly disturbed by this letter, especially as Almonte also pre-empted the work of the Assembly by writing to Napoleon, five or six days before the Assembly was to meet, to say that he would receive by the next steam boat its declaration for the monarchy and the Archduke. Having announced this *fait accompli* Almonte then told Napoleon how the venture should be directed from then on:

> Pour achever l'œuvre, nous désirions que Votre Majesté nous laissa ici comme Commandant en Chef le Général Bazaine et comme directeur exclusive [*sic*] de la politique M. de Saligny; alors tout marchera à merveille.
>
> Je vous prie, Sire, de ne pas oublier que Votre Majesté a offert indirectement à Saligny de le faire Senateur. Il est temps, je crois, Sire, de le recompenser.[25]
>
> [In order to complete the work, we would like Your Majesty to leave General Bazaine as Commander-in-Chief and Mr de Saligny with exclusive direction of political matters; then everything will proceed exceptionally well.
>
> I beg you, Sire, not to forget that Your Majesty indirectly offered to make Saligny a Senator. It is time, I believe Sire, to reward him.]

A remark in Napoleon's handwriting beside this last comment makes it quite clear that Almonte was being over-presumptuous in his relations with the Emperor, and that Napoleon had no intention of rewarding Saligny for his efforts in Mexico. He wrote: 'erreur, ni directement ni indirectement' [wrong, neither directly nor indirectly].

These letters seem to have been the catalyst for Napoleon recalling Forey as well, as there would have been no reason for him to recall both his commander and his minister if they were, in fact, carrying out his instructions satisfactorily. Also, if Forey believed he was doing what the Emperor wanted there would be little reason for him to justify his actions as he did in his letter of 30 June 1863, or to complain of the problems he foresaw in carrying out a vote, as he did in that of 11 January 1863.[26] Previous analyses have lacked this evidence of apparent cause and effect, which is possibly the reason so many have been convinced Napoleon was determined to impose a monarchy on Mexico.

The news of Saligny's recall was greeted in Mexico with both delight and relief by the French army and the Mexicans, none of whom had any respect or liking for him. General du Barail described the arrival of this news as follows:

de toutes les nouvelles apportées par le courrier de France, ce ne fut point la moins agréable à l'armée, qui considérait en M. de Saligny l'auteur de toutes les fautes commises, le bourreau de l'amiral Jurien de la Gravière et du général de Lorencez, le fauteur de la politique réactionnaire et cléricale, opposée au goût des Mexicains et même aux institutions politiques des Français, et enfin le principal obstacle à la pacification désirée.[27]

[of all the news brought by the mail from France, this was by no means the least pleasing to the army, who considered Mr de Saligny the source of all the mistakes committed, the tormentor of Admiral Jurien de la Gravière and General de Lorencez, the supporter of reactionary and clerical politics, which are opposed to the ideals of the Mexicans and even to the political institutions of the French, and most of all, the principal obstacle to the desired pacification.]

This is in stark contrast to Saligny's view of the role he played, for he is reported to have been convinced that the Emperor and his government were looking for a pretext for a military occupation of the country, and that he had done all he could to help realise that aim. To Ernest Louet he said some time later: 'Mon seul mérite est d'avoir deviné l'intention de l'Empereur d'intervenir au Mexique, et d'avoir rendu l'intervention nécessaire.'[28] [My only merit is to have correctly guessed the Emperor's intention to intervene in Mexico, and to have made the intervention necessary.] If Saligny was correct in his assumption, then Napoleon would have had no reason to order his recall. Napoleon's decision to do this, and to continue to press for the opinion of all the people regarding the form of government after Saligny's recall seems to deny any validity to this claim. Saligny also had to be ordered three times by the Foreign Minister to leave Mexico where he was determined to stay.

Was Saligny deliberately treacherous then, and if so, why? It is difficult to accept that Saligny was doing what the Emperor wanted, because he had arrived in Mexico in December 1860 with instructions to conciliate with the two governments claiming authority, to achieve a single, stable government. It is highly unlikely that at that time Napoleon would have advised him personally that he intended to intervene to impose a monarchy. There is also no record of any correspondence between Napoleon and Saligny, and all his instructions were conveyed by Thouvenel and were far more circumspect than Saligny claimed. But, most importantly, in his conversation with Louet, he said that he had 'correctly guessed (*deviné*) the Emperor's intention to intervene in Mexico', which indicates he had no direct communication that this was so. It is only possible to speculate on the reason Saligny thought he was doing something to please the Emperor, but Barker has shown, fairly conclusively, that his personal, financial interests necessitated a continued French involvement in Mexico. Perhaps, also, it was to gain recognition from the Emperor in a bid to enhance his previously nondescript diplomatic career. Unfortunately he was destined to live in oblivion. After Maximilian's death he wrote to the Emperor saying that he believed the intervention had been justified, and he requested an audience with him. This was denied.[29]

Whatever Saligny's motivation, his and Almonte's influence was bringing to fruition the plans they attributed to Napoleon. The predictions made by Almonte and Forey proved correct, and all but two of the Assembly of Notables voted in favour of a monarchy and to offer the crown to Maximilian. They also decided to nominate a Regency of three to rule Mexico until Maximilian's arrival, the three being Almonte, a General Salas, and the Archbishop Labastida, who was to be represented by the Bishop of Mexico City until his return from Rome.[30] Forey supported the election of Maximilian, believing that it was for the best, as the only way to end the era of revolutions was to have a foreign prince to rule the country, which, if he was not mistaken, was the thinking of the Emperor.[31]

Forey had good reason to support the idea of a foreign prince as ruler because the difficulties that continued with the opposing factions, even after the election of the Regency, were far too testing for him. He declared to Drouyn de Lhuys, now Minister of Foreign Affairs, that the role of diplomat in such a country as Mexico was beyond him.[32] Within a month he was writing to Randon expressing his earnest hope that Maximilian would soon arrive to take over the pacification of the country. There were, he said, only two parties, the Liberals and the Conservatives, neither one better than the other, and to speak to them of moderation, justice or conciliation was to waste one's time. He continued:

Ils ne comprennent pas ce langage parce qu'il n'existe pas le parti modéré, de parti vraiment national. Chacun ne veut le retour au pouvoir de ses partisans que pour pouvoir opprimer la faction opposée. Ainsi, cédant à de regrettables influences, la régence se laisse entrainer dans une voie réactionnaire que je ne puis tolérer, et décrète les mesures auxquelles je dois m'opposer.[33]

[They do not understand this talk because the moderate party, a truly national party, does not exist. Each party only wants its partisans to return to power so it can oppress the opposing faction. So, yielding to regrettable influences, the Regency is allowing itself to be carried along a reactionary path that I cannot tolerate, and enacting measures I must oppose.]

The combination of all these difficulties convinced Forey that a monarchy was the best solution for Mexico, with a foreigner unaligned with any of the factions to lead it. He told Napoleon that only those who were opposed to the Regency favoured a republic, and they were by far in the minority.[34]

Napoleon, in the meantime, was determined to consult the people as a whole, and looked on the vote of the Regency as purely an indication of the will of the people. He had been following events with a cautious optimism, which was reflected in his correspondence with Maximilian. After the fall of Puebla he advised Maximilian that there were 'still many obstacles to be overcome', while at the news of Maximilian's proclamation as Emperor by the provisional government he wrote: 'I am glad of this first result, I hope that the whole of Mexico will soon follow the example of the capital and summon Your Imperial Highness to regenerate her.'[35] In Maximilian's reply he expressed his admiration for the fact that Napoleon had not 'abandoned [his] original design of calling, not only upon the notables of the capital, but upon the whole country, to declare themselves with regard to its destiny'.[36] In Napoleon's next letter to Maximilian, accompanying a copy of the resolution of the Assembly of Notables at Mexico City and Vera Cruz, he said: 'I am happy to see that Your Imperial Highness's name is rallying to it a great number of adherents; however, in order that the will of the Mexicans should be more manifest, I should like an appeal made to the people to ratify the choice of the notables by their votes.'[37] To which Maximilian replied:

Your intention, Sir, of appealing to the whole nation to ratify the act of these two great cities is an unequivocal proof that Your Majesty intends, in your exalted wisdom, to establish a firm and lasting structure in Mexico. The expression of the will of the nation will give the Government the conviction that the intention is to establish a strong moral force both at home and in foreign relations.[38]

In a later letter Maximilian revealed that he disagreed entirely with Almonte's suggestion that the vote of the notables of Mexico City was an 'expression of the desires of the nation: Your Majesty, like myself, has from the outset seen in it no more than a *first result*, in itself very happy, but which must be completed by the adhesion of the whole country, or, at least, of the large majority of provinces composing it.'[39]

Although Napoleon would have preferred that the choice of the desired form of government had been put directly to the people, he was now faced with a train of events he could do little to stop. What he could do was ensure that the wishes of the Assembly were at least submitted to the people for ratification or rejection. Instructions in this vein were sent to the new commander, General Bazaine, by Drouyn de Lhuys well before the arrival of the above letter from Maximilian. They stated that the Assembly's role now, as a result of their own vote, was to recommend to the people the adoption of a monarchical institution and offer the name of a prince for their vote. He continued:

Il appartient maintenant au Gouvernement provisoire de recueillir ces suffrages de manière qu'il ne puisse planer aucun doute sur l'expression de la volonté du pays. Je n'ai pas à vous indiquer le mode à adopter pour que ce résultat indispensable soit complètement atteint: c'est dans les institutions et les habitudes locales qu'il faut le chercher. Soit que les municipalités doivent être appelées à se prononcer dans les diverses provinces à mesure qu'elles auront reconquis la disposition d'elles-mêmes, ou que les listes soient ouvertes par leurs soins pour recueillir les votes, le mode le meilleur sera celui qui assurera la plus large manifestation des vœux des populations dans les meilleurs conditions d'indépendance et de sincérité. L'Empereur, Général, recommande particulièrement ce point essentiel à toute votre attention.[40]

[It is now up to the provisional government to gather these votes in a manner which casts no doubt over the expression of the will of the country. I cannot tell you the method to adopt to ensure this indispensable result is achieved: you must determine that from the local institutions and customs. Whether the municipalities should be called upon to pronounce a decision in the diverse provinces in so far as they have the same disposition as themselves, or whether the lists should be opened through their good offices to gather the votes, the best method will be that which will ensure the manifestation of the wishes of the majority of the people, in circumstances of independence and sincerity. This is the principal point that the Emperor particularly wants brought to your attention, General.]

From this there seems little doubt of Napoleon's sincerity in wanting as wide a consultation as possible, but he recognised that the means of achieving that was now out of his hands.

Was Napoleon naïve in his determination to obtain the will of the people as he had done in France to inaugurate his own empire? Perhaps he can be justly accused of not understanding the country, its traditions and culture well enough, but he nevertheless refused to dismiss out of hand a section of the population, notably the Indians, from being involved in the vote. Regardless of his commanders' opinions, he seemed to adhere to his belief that all people were equal, regardless of race. Although Saligny and Almonte may have been correct in their descriptions of the traditional methods of choosing a government in Mexico, it was precisely these traditions that Napoleon hoped to change in order to bring to an end the decades of revolution and *pronunciamentos* that had brought Mexico to its present state of anarchy and poverty. This was why he was so disturbed by the action taken by the Assembly of Notables and its appointment of a Regency, which began to make more decisions in opposition to his clearly expressed aims and ideals.

The reality of determining the voice of the people, however, was to be far more difficult than Napoleon had expected. The problems associated with conducting such a suffrage in this country of far-flung provinces with appalling means of communication, were recorded in the memoirs of General du Barail. The French army was charged with the task of determining the wishes of the people and du Barail wrote cynically of the attempt to do this:

> Nous allions faire une campagne électorale, dont le succès ne pouvait pas être douteux, car ces populations, habituées à voter aujourd'hui pour Pierre, demain pour Paul, auraient acclamé le diable ou le Grand Turc, si nous avions présenté leur candidature au bout de nos sabres et de nos baïonnettes. Nous allions donc transporter à la fois des urnes et des canons, et faire le double office de soldats et de courtiers électoraux.[41]

[We were going to conduct an electoral campaign, the success of which could not be doubtful. For these populations, accustomed to voting today for Peter, tomorrow for Paul, would have acclaimed the devil or the Grand Turk, if we had presented their candidature at the end of our swords and bayonettes. Thus we were going to carry urns and cannons at the same time, and play the double role of soldiers and electoral agents.]

Whatever du Barail's views of their orders, Napoleon was unlikely to commit the army to such a task if he were not genuine in his intentions.

This was not the only problem confronting the Emperor, as the relationship of the Regency with the clergy was becoming particularly alarming. In August 1863, Forey wrote to both Napoleon and Randon that he was hoping for the early arrival of Maximilian to pacify the country and to end the disastrous management by the Regency. Not only did they want to compel all dissidents to proclaim in writing their adherence to the provisional government under pain of arrest and imprisonment, but, most importantly, Forey said, they refused to reassure the new owners of national and church properties, and this was leading those legitimate owners to mistrust Napoleon's intentions. Forey concluded: 'If it places itself under clerical domination, as it seems to intend, it will be following a reactionary policy, and it will not rally round it moderate men who are truly but simply religious.'[42] Some of their early actions included refusing the Last Sacraments and Christian burial to those who would not return property they had bought; issuing an ordinance forbidding work on Sundays; and decreeing that everyone had to go down on their knees when they encountered the Holy Sacrament, and to remain there until it had disappeared and the bells could no longer be heard. Forey likened it to the Inquisition.[43] Napoleon's concern at this news was evident when he wrote to Maximilian telling him of these latest developments and remarking that he thought that the establishment of a monarchy would be impossible unless the sale of national property was ratified.[44] The position of the clergy was to cause Maximilian difficulties also, partly because of the long history of the clergy's financial power and corruption, but also because Maximilian failed to settle the issue with the Pope before his departure for Mexico.

Although the process of obtaining the vote of the people and the establishment of a more reliable government was not yet complete, it was obvious that Napoleon was already envisaging that the French involvement in Mexico would change when this had occurred. This is partly evident from the fact that he decided to replace Forey with a general who was subordinate to him, General Bazaine, instead of sending another commander from France. Having realised that he had undertaken the intervention on the basis of erroneous and misleading information provided by Saligny, Napoleon was determined that his commitment would not be increased. This was why Bazaine was appointed, not because Almonte had suggested it.[45]

Napoleon's instructions then became directed more towards the development of the self-sufficiency of Mexico as soon as possible, and in this regard he instructed Bazaine to improve the strength and organisation of the Mexican army. He also advised that in Paris the government was discussing the financial measures necessary to develop the resources of the country, and suggested that once the new government demonstrated some stability it would be easy to organise a loan. He then told Bazaine that he had read an engineer's reports on the mines of Sonora and that a company was being formed which would develop them at their own expense. They promised to give a portion of the produce to the French government, which the Mexican government could tax, thus providing a ready source of income. To this end Bazaine was asked to obtain from the provisional government mining concessions for all the mines in Sonora. In compensation, France would later negotiate a reduction in the reimbursements, for the costs of the war, owed to France by the Mexican government.[46]

In the meantime, the prolonged campaign was losing popularity in France, and was to be debated in the *Corps législatif* in January 1864. According to Fleury the basis of this unpopularity was that many in the Emperor's government doubted the likely success of the government that had been created, because it was far too reactionary and out of sympathy with French politics and with the more liberal sentiments of the Mexican people.[47] What had begun as a seemingly powerful moral demonstration against a reprehensible government had turned into a war, which to the public and the Opposition had confusing aims and no foreseeable outcome. Charles de Mazade commented that the misdirection given to the campaign by Almonte, along with his inaccurate information, had done nothing to increase its popularity or to help the French cause, and what had been envisaged as a short campaign had already lasted two years.[48] But by the end of 1863 Napoleon thought that a stable government would soon be established in Mexico, and when he was given the results of the consultation of the people, dubious though they proved to be, he prepared for the eventual withdrawal of the French army.

7
The Empire Does Mean Peace

Many historians have claimed that it was the turn of events in Europe during 1863, most notably the uprisings in Poland and later the conflict over the Danish Duchies, that forced Napoleon to begin reducing France's involvement in Mexico, but many indications have been seen already that Napoleon never intended that France should have a lengthy involvement in Mexico. Napoleon was not considering abandoning Mexico to Maximilian because of the problems in Europe. It had always been his intention to see a new regime set up there that would be favourable to France and the rest of Europe, and when looked at in the light of his overall policy, which is revealed in his proposal for a European Congress in November 1863, it can be seen that, in fact, Napoleon had no need to remain actively involved in Mexico once such a regime was established.

In his address at the opening of the legislative session in November 1863, he said that 'France's distant expeditions, such as those in Cochin-China and Mexico...were not the result of a premeditated plan: force of circumstances had brought them about.' But he asked how France could develop her external commerce if she gave up the idea of any influence in the Americas. While they had encountered an unexpected resistance in Mexico, their efforts would not have been wasted and they would be compensated for their sacrifices 'when the destiny of the country, which will owe its regeneration to France, was handed over to a Prince whose ideas and policies make him worthy of such a noble mission'.[1]

With the belief that this Prince might soon be taking responsibility for Mexico, Napoleon continued to exercise his concern for events in Europe. He was intensely interested in helping resolve the issue of Russian dominance of Poland, but for him the problem was an international one, which was why he proposed that England, France and Austria conclude an entente to influence Russia and Prussia in the resolution of the problem. When both England and Austria rejected his proposal, he believed it was not appropriate for France to try and resolve the issue alone. The reasons he gave are entirely consistent with those behind his insistence that the expedition to Mexico had to be undertaken as a joint venture with England and Spain. He said of the Polish situation:

Nous ne prétendons pas, toutefois, imposer nos solutions aux Puissances qui sont intéressées, autant ou même plus directement que nous, au règlement des difficultés pendantes. Dans une question essentiellement européennes, il n'est conforme ni à nos obligations ni à nos droits d'aller seuls au-devant d'une responsabilité qu'il appartient à tous de partager.[2]

[We have no intention of imposing our own solutions on the powers who are as much, or more directly concerned, with the settlement of the pending difficulties. In an essentially European question we have neither the obligation nor the right to face alone a responsibility which everyone should share.]

The same principle was evident in Napoleon's instructions to Forey in July 1862, when he recognised that Mexico's location between the Atlantic and the Pacific was commercially significant to both Europe and the Americas, and therefore could not remain the province of a single nation. In relation to the Emperor's proposal of a joint venture to Mexico, Marshal Randon commented:

Cette action à plusieurs était devenue dans l'esprit de l'Empereur un système. Ainsi avait-on fait en Crimée avec les Turcs, en Italie avec les Piémontais, en Chine avec les Anglais, en Cochinchine avec les Espagnols; et cette politique était bonne. Le malheur fut qu'au Mexique on ne put la suivre jusqu'au bout.[3]

[The concept of joint action had become for the Emperor a system. It was used in the Crimea with the Turks, in Italy with the Piedmontese, in China with the English, in Cochin-China with the Spanish; and this policy was good. It was unfortunate that in Mexico it could not be followed to completion.]

The idea of a community of nations gathering to discuss and try to resolve issues that affected them was not new for Napoleon. He had proposed on previous occasions the idea of a congress to resolve the Italian and Roman problems, in 1848 and 1860, but each time the idea was rejected. The failure of his attempts to resolve the Polish situation in 1863 prompted him to issue another proposal for a congress. In presenting his idea to the legislative assembly in November 1863, he asked rhetorically if the only avenues now open were either to go to war or to remain silent. Not wanting to accept either of these alternatives, he thought the Polish cause should be submitted to a European tribunal along with all other questions disturbing Europe. He had already written a letter to the sovereigns of Europe, which said:

> Toutes les fois que de profondes secousses ont ébranlé les bases et déplacé les limites des Etats, il est survenu des transactions solennelles, pour coordonner les éléments nouveaux et consacrer en les revisant, les transformations accomplies. Tel a été l'objet du traité de West-phalie, au dix-septième siècle, et des négociations de Vienne en 1815. C'est sur ce dernier fondement que repose aujourd'hui l'édifice politique de l'Europe; et cependant ... il s'écroule de toutes parts.
>
> Si l'on considère attentivement la situation des divers pays, il est impossible de ne pas reconnaître que, presque sur tous les points, les Traités de Vienne sont détruits, modifiés, méconnus ou menacés. De là, des devoirs sans règle, des droits sans titre et des prétentions sans frein. Péril d'autant plus redoutable que les perfectionnements amenés par la civilisation, qui a lié les peuples entre eux par la solidarité des intérêts matériels, rendraient la guerre plus destructives encore.
>
> C'est là un sujet de graves méditations. N'attendons pas pour prendre un parti que des événements soudains, irréstibles, troublent notre jugement et nous entraînent, malgré nous, dans des directions contraires. Je viens donc proposer à Votre Majesté de régler le présent et s'assurer l'avenir dans un Congrès.[4]

> [Each time profound upheavals have shaken the foundations and altered State boundaries, they have been followed by solemn agreements to arrange the new situations and to revise and sanction the changes that had been achieved. This was the object of the Treaty of Westphalia in the seventeenth century, and the negotiations at Vienna in 1815. It is on this latter foundation that the political structure of Europe rests today; however ... everywhere that structure is crumbling.
>
> If the situation of various countries is considered closely, it is impossible not to notice in almost every direction that the Treaties of

Vienna have been destroyed, modified, misunderstood or threatened. Hence there are obligations without constraints, unofficial laws, and unrestrained claims. This danger is much more alarming because the advances brought by civilisation, which have united peoples by the strength of material interests, makes war even more destructive.

This is a subject for serious consideration. Let us not wait until sudden, irresistable events cloud our judgement and drag us, in spite of ourselves, in contrary directions, before we decide on a course of action. I am therefore proposing to Your Majesty that we normalise the present situation, and make sure of the future in a Congress].

Napoleon's proposal was greeted with either minor reservations or none at all by Portugal, Hanover, Italy, Prussia, Bavaria and the German Confederation. Tsar Alexander of Russia requested only that Napoleon outline the questions he thought should be discussed at the congress. The Emperor Franz-Josef of Austria expanded on this idea, saying that specifying the questions in advance and having agreement on the direction intended would help avoid any unforeseen obstacles. His decision about involvement would be made after his Ambassador, Metternich, had discussions with Napoleon. Franz-Josef's Foreign Minister, Rechberg, conveyed his ideas to Metternich:

> Pour apporter à un Congrès notre loyal concours, nous devons connaître quel sera le programme exact de ses délibérations, et être assurés que ce programme remplit toutes les conditions requises pour préparer l'élaboration d'une œuvre de paix et de conciliation.[5]

> [In order to bring our frank assistance to a Congress, we must know what the precise programme of its deliberations will be, and be assured that this programme will fulfil all the conditions necessary to prepare for the implementation of an agreement on peace and conciliation.]

Austria's reply was very similar to England's, and they both focused on the point that Napoleon had made about the Treaties of Vienna being menaced or modified, and showed that they were both afraid that Napoleon intended some rearrangement of Europe. I believe this could not be further from the truth, but Cowley's immediate reaction, and the later replies of both England and Austria, show that this fear was very real on their parts. Cowley's initial comment to Russell was that he considered the proposal 'mischievous' and 'dangerous . . . for the Continental Powers. The position of Austria is terrible. Acquiescence implies the loss of Gallicia and perhaps Venetia. Refusal may induce the Emperor, aided by the Italians, to try if he cannot reach Poland thru [*sic*] Austria.'⁶ There is no evidence that this observation is anything other than supposition on Cowley's part. Russell responded, though, that he thought a congress was 'practicable but that they must soon arrive at the question of war or no war. Is it easier to solve that question in a Congress, or by common diplomatic means? That question requires much and long deliberation.'⁷ It is interesting to speculate, however, on the influence of Cowley's remark on the forthcoming responses of England and Austria.

Rechberg asked Metternich to determine in what respects Napoleon thought the Treaties of Vienna were no longer effective because Franz-Josef believed they still formed 'the basis of public law in Europe'. Russell wrote to Cowley that his government believed 'the main provisions of the Treaty of 1815 are still in full force' and that the balance of power in Europe still rested on its foundations. He added:

> If instead of saying that the Treaty of Vienna has ceased to exist or that it is destroyed, we inquire whether certain portions of it have been modified, disregarded or menaced, other questions occur. Some of the modifications which have taken place have received the sanction of all the Great Powers, and now form part of the public law of Europe.
>
> Is it proposed to give those changes a more general and solemn sanction? Is such a work necessary? Will it contribute to the peace of Europe?⁸

It is no coincidence that these replies are similar because Bloomfield, British Ambassador to Vienna, reported on 12 November that Austria was concerned that it be in agreement with England about the congress and wanted to make sure that their written replies agreed, but were not word for word.⁹

As far as those parts of the Treaty of Vienna that were currently being 'menaced' were concerned, Russell wanted to know what Napoleon's proposals were, and, if they were agreed by a majority of the powers, would they be enforced by arms? England's main concern was that specific issues should be addressed by the congress, for

> they would feel more apprehension than confidence from the meeting of a Congress of Sovereigns and Ministers without fixed objects ranging over the map of Europe and exciting hopes and aspirations

which they might find themselves unable either to ratify or to quiet.

Drouyn de Lhuys replied that Napoleon had deliberately addressed all the courts simultaneously without any preconceived ideas about ententes with any of them, in order to show his sincere impartiality and be able to approach the discussions free from any obligations. As the newest Sovereign, Drouyn de Lhuys said, Napoleon did not believe he had the right to assume the role of arbitrator or determine in advance the programme for the congress. He proceeded, however, to outline some of the areas for concern in Europe such as: the Polish uprising; the pending dispute over the Danish Duchies; the unresolved conflict between Italy and Austria; the continued occupation of Rome; and most importantly, the excessive armaments maintained by all countries because of the mistrust harboured between them. Suggesting that these were probably the main issues for discussion, he added:

> Lord Russell n'attend pas, assurément, que nous indiquons ici le mode de solution applicable à chacun de ces problèmes, ni le genre de sanction que pourraient comporter les décisions du Congrès. C'est aux Puissances qui y seraient représentées qu'appartiendrait le droit de prononcer sur ces divers points. Nous ajouterons seulement que ce serait, à nos yeux, une illusion que de poursuivre ces solutions à travers le dédale de correspondances diplomatiques et de négociations séparées, et que, loin d'aboutir à la guerre, la voie proposée est la seule qui puisse conduire à une pacification durable.[10]

> [Lord Russell surely does not expect that we indicate here the kind of solution applicable to each of these problems, nor the kind of sanctions the decisions of the Congress could call for. The right to make decisions relating to such diverse issues would belong to the powers who are represented there. We will only add that, in our opinion, we would be deluding ourselves if we thought solutions can be found through a maze of diplomatic correspondence and separate negotiations, and that far from leading to war, the avenue proposed is the only one that can lead to a durable peace.]

At no time had Napoleon made any suggestion that any nation should be asked to cede territory, but England was convinced that this might be his fundamental aim, and pointed out all the difficulties that would prevent a congress from resolving such demands. Russell also doubted that any benefit would be gained from convening a large number of representatives, which included those from nations totally unaffected by many of the current issues, who would express 'opinions and wishes' that could not be enforced. Not being able to see any 'beneficial consequences' likely to arise from the proposed congress, the British government declined the invitation, thereby dealing Napoleon a severe blow.

Despite this rejection, Napoleon received great support for his idea from other countries, notably Denmark, and from within his own country. The Senate voted unanimously in favour of the proposal, and, speaking on behalf of the entire country, the President of the Senate said:

Elle a donc applaudi avec transport à votre proposition d'un Congrès: prévoyante idée qui offre à notre patrie des satisfactions exemptes d'ambitions; à l'Europe, des garanties de paix et le désarmement; à la civilisation une libre et vaste carrière pour ses développements. Puissent les souverains, guidés par leur haute raison et par les lumières du siècle, s'unir à Notre Majesté pour une tâche qui, allant au-devant les luttes au lieu d'en attendre l'explosion, réglera les prétentions et mettra le droit des gouvernements en harmonie avec les vœux légitimes des peuples.[11]

[France has loudly acclaimed your proposal of a Congress: it is a far-sighted idea which offers our nation satisfactions free of ambitions; to Europe it offers guarantees of peace and disarmament; to civilisation it offers a vast scope for its developments. May the sovereigns, guided by their high ideals and by this age of enlightenment, join with Your Majesty in an undertaking which, as it is put in place before conflicts erupt instead of afterwards, will settle claims and ensure that the law of governments is in harmony with the legitimate wishes of the people.]

Napoleon was delighted with this address and the support his idea received, and despite his disappointment at England's rejection, he later said that 'I could not at heart find fault with her course, for I knew that she always prefers to settle her own affairs alone, in the best way for her own interests.'[12]

Political writer, Thornton Hunt, who was connected with a major English newspaper, had discussions with Napoleon when he was in exile in England after the fall of the Empire, and was impressed with the benefits that could have resulted if the Congress had gone ahead. Napoleon had suggested an International Council might meet every few years and its deliberations could clear up differences, because 'it would impose on the contesting parties the weight of international opinion, and thus settle the dispute for years'. If a quarrel arose again before the Council was due to meet, other nations would advise those involved to have patience and wait for the question to be brought before it. This latter point may have been idealistic, but the final comments made by Napoleon illustrate how broad was his view of the world, and how much his interests were outward looking:

> the minutes of this International Council would serve as bases for a code of international laws. This would be an important innovation, for, properly speaking, international laws do not exist, and we have at present no other guide than the works of learned jurisconsults, the statutes of various nations, and theory.
> . . . to these anticipated results of the International Council there will also have to be added this important fact: it would not be long before the Congress would found an international parliament, which would serve, not only for sanctioning fresh laws, but also for amending those old laws which have been rendered obsolete by the ever-increasing progress of our times.[13]

His optimism may have been tested by the decades it took for some of his ideas to come to fruition.

Count de la Chapelle, a friend in exile, said that Napoleon had intended to develop his thoughts further and had commissioned him to prepare them, but unfortunately he died before this could be done. He described Napoleon's idea as 'that admirable system which will be no doubt adopted when governments are wiser, and when they give to the interests of the peoples under them a higher place than to their own personalities'.[14] Hunt commented that when an International Council did eventuate, he hoped that mankind would remember that Napoleon 'was the founder of this court of legislation and of judicial appeal for nations'.[15] And these ideas do not seem so Utopian when the establishment of the League of Nations, and later United Nations, are considered, as well as the relatively recent European Parliament. The name of Napoleon III, however, is remembered by very few when the origin of these organisations is discussed.

Can a parallel really be drawn between Napoleon's grand proposal and his involvement in Mexico? My research shows that it can.

Napoleon's concern for better relations among all nations, as expressed
in his proposal of a congress, is difficult to dispute. Why then should
his intentions have been any different in Mexico, when they were based
on the same principle – a community of nations working together
to resolve a situation for the benefit of all nations, with the aim of
ensuring prosperity and stability? This comparison has not been considered previously, but there are some obvious parallels which help explain
Napoleon's involvement in Mexico. William Echard is one of very few
historians to have studied seriously Napoleon's proposals for congresses
and he concluded that he was a true Europeanist.[16] This conclusion can
be expanded to show that Napoleon's wider foreign policy was consistent with his European policy, which was exposed so fully in November
1863. Napoleon's correspondence shows clearly that he had no intention of claiming territory for France, or exclusive control of commerce
in the Americas, and that his troops were to be withdrawn immediately
a stable government was established. While some might argue that his
correspondence might not reveal his *true* intentions, nobody has been
able to offer substantive evidence to support such claims. The most
important similarity with his congress proposal is his stated belief that
he was acting to ensure benefits for all nations, including Mexico.

Many historians have been as suspicious as England was of Napoleon's intentions, and remain convinced that he was determined to
ensure France regained her supremacy in Europe and as a world power.
It was British ministers who doubted Napoleon's motives and thwarted
his hopes for a united Europe, and also for a combined approach to one
of the world's problems, Mexico. Nor was Napoleon's cause helped by
British journalists such as Charles Mackay, who wrote in October 1863:

> No impartial man who studies the history of the expedition can
> entertain the slightest doubt that the Emperor Napoleon designed
> from the very beginning the dispute between the Allies, and the with-
> drawal of England and Spain ... He got rid of [England's] cooperation
> just at the point when it ceased to be a convenience and would have
> become an embarrassment. The period had come when France must
> either retreat or openly assume the policy of invasion and conquest.
> The dispute between the Allies, deliberately provoked and rendered
> necessary by France, afforded a decent opportunity for the French
> intervention to emerge into the light, and assume its true character.[17]

Just why Napoleon should resort to such an elaborate exercise if he
intended all along to act alone, is not explained. This assessment can

have been based only on limited access to official documents, and, quite probably on conjecture, but it would no doubt have influenced some sections of the British public, and added to the suspicion with which France was already regarded by many.

At the same time the unpopularity of the campaign was becoming more evident in France. The *Corps législatif* showed that it opposed a prolonged involvement in Mexico, although its members were prepared to support the government if protection of France's honour necessitated an extension of time. These sentiments were expressed in the report of the Commissions of the Budget on the supplementary credits of 1863:

> Dans les prévisions actuelles, le Gouvernement espère que la fin de 1864 marquera le terme de l'expédition. Nous sommes unanimes à conseiller de mettre un terme à l'expédition du Mexique, non pas à tout prix, Dieu nous en garde! mais aussi promptement que l'honneur et l'intérêt de la France le permettront. L'expression de ce vœu répond au sentiment général du pays.[18]

> [In the light of current expectations, the government hopes that the end of 1864 will signal the end of the expedition. We are unanimous in recommending a term be put on the Mexican expedition – not at any price, God forbid! – but as quickly as the honour and interests of France will allow. This desire corresponds with the general feeling in the country.]

Napoleon's instructions to Bazaine in August 1863, had stressed that the government was anxious to limit the duration of their involvement, and that Bazaine had to undertake the immediate development of the Mexican army with that view in mind, so this report was congruent with Napoleon's own thoughts.

Unfortunately, events out of Napoleon's control were to continue to undermine his intentions, the first of these being the actions of Archbishop Labastida on his arrival in Mexico to take his position in the Regency. The Archbishop informed Bazaine that the Emperor approved his proposal to restore the power of the clergy, and at a meeting of the Regency on 24 October he claimed that the French had only been accepted in the capital because of the influence of the clergy, and if Bazaine refused to work with him he could no longer count on their support. Despite Labastida's opposition, and in accordance with his instructions, Bazaine managed to get the Regency to insert in the official journal a notice that all legitimate sales of national property would be confirmed.[19] Although Almonte had supported Bazaine's move, he thought that Bazaine should take a more conciliatory approach to the clergy, because they could still use the influence that they exercised in the country.[20]

It was the apparent association of the French with the clergy that created many difficulties for Bazaine and his army, but Saligny's and Almonte's support for the nomination of Labastida to the Regency was mostly responsible. General du Barail wrote that when they were trying to clear some bandits out of the north of Mexico they encountered two French miners who gave them an account of how the Liberals felt about the French:

Ne croyez pas ... un seul instant, que les libéraux soient hostiles aux Français et qu'ils aient envie de se battre avec eux. Ils n'ont qu'un plan: vous fatiguer par des marches continuelles et inutiles, et vous forcer à rentrer à Mexico. Leurs chefs considèrent la France comme la source du progrès et le flambeau de la civilisation; mais jamais ils n'accepteront le gouvernement réactionnaire et clérical que vous voulez leur imposer.[21]

[Do not believe ... for an instant, that the Liberals are hostile to the French and want to fight them. They have only one plan: to tire you out with continual and useless marches, and force you to return to Mexico City. Their leaders consider France the source of progress and the light of civilisation; but they will never accept the reactionary and clerical government that you want to impose on them.]

They commented that the Liberals already hated Maximilian because they imagined that the priests would play a large role in his government. The French cause was seriously damaged, then, by the refusal of the Supreme Court to hear any of the cases referred to it for confirmation of sales of legitimately-bought church property. Public outcry demanded that the judges be dismissed for 'upholding the pretensions of the archbishop and his clergy, which were as unjust as they were impolitic'.[22] The provisional government reminded the judges that they had to uphold the decrees of the previous Liberal government, but Labastida encouraged the judges to oppose this directive and then went even further. On 30 December 1863 he and his bishops served a document on the Regency which threatened excommunication of anyone who supported the nationalisation of church property. The judges then declared they would not execute the decrees and as a result were dismissed by the government. Labastida would not submit to the pressure of the two other Regents, Almonte and Salas, to leave this question to be resolved by the future Emperor, so they in turn rejected his proposal that the decrees of 1861 be overturned. In anger Labastida refused to attend any further meetings of the Regency.

Regardless of the steps taken by the Regency and Bazaine, the issue of the influence that the clergy might exercise in the forthcoming government was to remain a concern. Michel Chevalier commented that the seriousness of this 'embarrassment' could not be underrated:

> We have here to deal not merely with the clergy lands, nor with the opening of a chapel at Mexico, in which the Protestants may worship God in the form agreeable to their conscience: the question is a far wider one. In reality, the point to be settled is whether the new Government of Mexico shall adopt the mass of those liberal and progressive ideas to which all civilized States have successively rallied, or whether it shall run in the fated track of those antiquated maxims, according to which all Liberty, religious, political, or economic, is a curse.[23]

The only chance he saw for Maximilian to institute a progressive government was for him to appeal to the Holy See to order cooperation from the Mexican clergy. Maximilian, however, left Europe without negotiating such support from Rome. Corti remarked that when Labastida had demanded of Maximilian, during discussions in Europe, a commitment to the restitution of Church property, 'they had parted without any definitive pronouncement upon this highly important subject, for the Archduke was afraid it might be prejudicial to his candidature'.[24] The result was a problem that Maximilian never successfully resolved.

Unaware of the difficulties with the clergy, Napoleon gave his address, *Exposé de la situation de l'Empire*, to the *Corps législatif* and the Senate. In discussing foreign affairs, he only briefly mentioned the Mexican campaign, but he did emphasise that the majority of the people had to accept the decision of the notables before Maximilian could be expected to go to Mexico. Napoleon advised that the expedition had been undertaken to protect France's interests, but it was hoped that the salvation of Mexico would be a possible consequence of the campaign. While they were expecting in the near future to obtain guarantees from the new government, there were still many questions to be settled, and 'the resolution of the military situation could only prepare the way for later negotiations'.[25]

Although pressing matters in Europe were said to have made Napoleon impatient to see Maximilian take over responsibility for Mexico, he had commented to Metternich, in December 1863, that were he in Maximilian's place he would defer his departure until the situation was a little more advanced. This remark was probably influenced by confusing reports from Almonte in October 1863 which claimed that soon two-thirds of the country would have voted for the monarchy. But, in the same letter, he had added that if Maximilian did not arrive soon it might be necessary to send a further two brigades to reassure the 'timid people' who might begin to doubt Maximilian was coming, or that France would persevere in its enterprise. He thought the arrival of Maximilian would be equal to that of an army.[26] Napoleon's reserve apparently impressed Metternich, who remarked to Rechberg:

> Cette assertion me paraît importante, au milieu des bruits qui commencent à courir sur les impatiences et la mauvaise humeur de l'Empereur au sujet de l'Archeduc...
>
> L'Archeduc devrait peut-être s'assurer personnellement des intentions réelles de l'Empereur.[27]

> [This assertion seems important to me, coming amidst the rumours that are beginning to beheard about the Emperor's impatience and ill humour on the subject of the Archduke...
>
> The Archduke should perhaps be reassured of the true intentions of the Emperor.]

He added, however, that the campaign was becoming more unpopular in France, but that in the Senate the Emperor's address relative to affairs in Mexico was passed after the government assured the Senate that France had not declared war against Mexico just for the benefit of the Archduke.

Yet contradictions in opinion as to the state of pacification of the country continued to make it difficult to know the real situation. *The Times* correspondent wrote of the 'cordial reception' accorded to the French, and the ease with which they had occupied all of the largest cities, proving that the claims in Europe that Mexico was essentially republican and supported Juarez were wrong. The rumours that had abounded that the Mexicans would 'shed the last drop of their blood in defence of their *much loved* President and Constitution' were, he said, propagated by those who wished to keep the country in a state of anarchy to support their own contraband trade. He then intimated Santiago Vidauri, ruler of two of the Mexican states, was about to declare in favour of the intervention, and that by the end of December 'the election of the Archduke will have been ratified by all the principal States and at least seven-eighths of the population of the country'.[28]

This report, referred to in the *Moniteur* two days later, was used to support the government's policy. The *Moniteur* claimed the report also helped to refute the extracts from a brochure on Mexico, printed in Opposition journals, which exaggerated 'the difficulties of the expedition', denied 'the advantageous results which may arise from it', and declared that 'only a small portion of that country has declared in favour of France'. The article in the *Moniteur* concluded by saying: 'It is melancholy to think that in order to render justice to French foreign policy, there should be a necessity of seeking the truth in foreign journals, and not in those of France.'[29] The dispatches of *The Times* correspondent in the following month gave even more glowing reports of the peaceful state of the country and the lack of resistance to the French occupation. He concluded in January that: 'The military part of the expedition is now at an end, and an active police force is all that will be required for the future.'[30]

Diverse opinions continued to be expressed, and Napoleon was accused not only of concealing the true situation in Mexico, but also of having self-interested and imperialistic motives for being there. Public opinion was influenced by varying reports on Mexico, by assertions contained in letters printed in newspapers, and articles in both French and foreign journals and newspapers. Napoleon's habit of not revealing all his ideas to the parliament or the public did not encourage support for the enterprise either. Charles de Mazade remarked at the end of 1863 that it was the unsupported assertions of individuals that provoked profound opposition to the politics of the government. As an example, he quoted the public correspondence in *Le Temps*, of Hidalgo, one of the Mexicans intimately involved in promoting the intervention with European governments, with a Spanish friend. Hidalgo had said in one letter that if, as he expected, the Mexicans were in favour of a monarchy, there was no doubt that similar movements would follow in the other Spanish-American republics. As a result of such remarks France, Mazade said, was suddenly transformed into the promoter of such a movement, and he concluded:

C'est ainsi que le commentaire obscurcit notre œuvre réelle en donnant à notre politique une portée qui devient à notre insu une provocation à la méfiance contre nous, et qui dépasserait la limite de tous les intérêts de la France.[31]

[It is in this way that commentary obscures our real achievement by giving our politics an interpretation which, behind our backs, provokes mistrust of us, and which would be beyond the limits of France's interests.]

Declarations on the Emperor's supposed motives by British journalist, Charles Mackay, have already been seen, and Mackay also claimed that the venture was unpopular in France because it was 'the work of Imperial ambition'. However, he added that there were those who said 'that Imperial ambition itself was but an instrument, and that the two proverbial agencies of immemorial mischief – the priest and the petticoat – are the true founders of the Empire of Mexico'.[32] It is evident that Napoleon was not influenced by the clergy and had no intention of restoring their power, but without access to contrary information many accepted such claims. Similarly, there has been much support for the idea that the Empress Eugenie encouraged Napoleon to intervene in Mexico, but the evidence for this is also far from conclusive.

Was Napoleon himself, however, responsible for the proliferation of motives that were ascribed to him by others? As seen in Chapter 5, perhaps it was the secrecy over his 'elevated motives' that led to conjecture and determined assertions about his motives. Yet some understanding of this method of handling foreign affairs can be gained from a letter to Prince Napoleon in response to some suggestions relating to the Polish situation earlier in 1863. Historians of the Mexican campaign appear to have ignored this, but it provides a significant insight into Napoleon's thinking, and a plausible explanation of his habit of secrecy:

the very greatest prudence and the greatest skilfulness is required to reach a good result . . . I have to deal with powers who are very touchy, and the moment they have any reason to see ambitious views on my part they will reject any kind of alliance. On the other hand, if the Press determines to make me go faster than I think is wise, I shall be compelled to make declarations which will interfere with my policy. I want neither manifestations nor provocations, which always force one to make compromising declarations.[33]

As seen above, Mazade offered similar comment on the impact of statements in the press on public opinion of government policy, and on the policy itself. When the suspicion with which Napoleon's intentions were regarded, particularly by England, is considered, it is possible to see that his silence about his motives in Mexico was based on the same principles as those quoted above. It is not difficult to see some factors that forced Napoleon to move faster, or in a different direction, than he wanted in Mexico. One was the precipitate action of the Mexican emigrants who approached Maximilian well before Napoleon was ready to proceed that far, and another was the action taken by Forey, and directed by Saligny and Almonte, of appointing a Regency and using the vote of the notables to declare Mexico was in favour of a monarchy.

Because of the continually conflicting reports of the situation in Mexico, and concerns in the parliamentary chambers about a lengthy campaign, it was inevitable that the expedition would be debated again. Surprisingly, in January 1864, an amendment to the Emperor's address to the *Corps législatif*, 'that France should withdraw from Mexico', was defeated soundly by 201 votes to 47. The results of the vote, however, do not indicate the intensity of the discussion. The debate was opened by the Vice President of the Council of State, M. Chaix d'Est-Ange, who admitted that while France may only occupy one-tenth of the country of Mexico, 5.5 million of the 7.7 million Mexicans had supported the intervention. He recognised that the Assembly was not favourable to distant expeditions which were said to cause uneasiness in the country, but asked if that was a good enough reason not to undertake them. France's industries had setbacks recently, which meant they had to be more active against foreign competition and increase their markets, and this could only be achieved through such expeditions.

He also referred to the expedition against Mexico in 1838 by the July Monarchy, which only resulted in the seizure of the port of St Jean d'Ulloa because they did not have enough landing troops. The Mexicans easily defeated them, expelled all the French from the country, and closed their markets to France. This, and other ill-prepared expeditions to Montevideo and Morocco in 1844, severely damaged the honour of France, so the Emperor was not prepared to leave Mexico this time until France's honour was avenged. This argument is supported by an article which Napoleon had written in an Opposition journal, *Le Progrès du Pas de Calais*, in the early 1840s, in which he criticised these ineffective undertakings of the government. When quoting this article in January 1864, the Paris correspondent of *The Times* commented that 'the Prince who wrote it will not imitate the Government he denounced, or return from Mexico until he has established order and good government on a solid basis. By doing so he will be entitled to the gratitude of France'.[34]

The Opposition arguments put forward by Favre, Thiers and Berryer were based on criticisms of the management of the campaign, and the likelihood of a prolonged period in Mexico. Favre declared that the claims France had on the Mexican government were only a pretext for enthroning Maximilian, and that they only really controlled that part of the country their soldiers occupied, a view supported by correspondents in Mexico. He also questioned the influence of the Mexican emigrants on France's involvement, and demanded to know whether France had fulfilled the conditions demanded by Maximilian. Favre stated that it was not true that all of the great cities of Mexico were in their favour, and that, therefore, much more fighting and money would be required. Thiers declared that having reached Mexico City, France's honour was satisfied, and they should have treated with Juarez, retained the customs ports for revenue, and saved France 14 or 15 million francs per month. He believed it would be impossible for Mexico to support a monarchy, and France would have to continue to do so for many years. So far France had not pledged its honour to Maximilian, but the moment he left for Mexico under France's guarantee, they would be bound to him. Berryer added that the United States would not accept a monarchy in Mexico, and perhaps in time Spain and England would be jealous of France's influence there and problems among the three nations would arise.

Berryer's opinion was consistent with the sentiments expressed in the brochure written in 1864 by A. Malespine, entitled 'Solution de la question mexicaine', a copy of which was found amongst Berryer's papers. Malespine suggested that in order to find out the people's wishes, there should be an armistice of three months during which time a vote should be held, under the supervision of delegates for both the provisional government and Juarez. This would determine whether they wanted a monarchy or to maintain the Republic and the Constitution of 1857. If the French and Juarez each agreed to accept the decision of the people, then whichever government was chosen would have the support of the people, and the Clerical party would lose its influence. He concluded by asking if it would not be more sensible to treat with Juarez and avoid further bloodshed by putting the choice to the people, which would also prevent conflict with the United States.[35]

Eugène Rouher, who was appointed Minister of State after the death of Billault, concluded the argument for the government, strongly influencing the vote that followed.[36] He dismissed the idea of treating with Juarez because it had been agreed by the allied governments before their departure that his government had been discredited. He added that one of the government's strongest arguments for remaining in Mexico was for the protection of its maritime and commercial interests in that part of the world, particularly the West Indies. Although their commerce with Mexico only amounted to about 20 million francs at present, that with other states of South America had almost doubled in ten years, from 268 million in 1852 to 572 million francs in 1862. The government could not say how long they would need to stay to protect their interests but they wished to leave as soon as possible. Rouher concluded his address with an emotional statement, speaking of the Emperor:

> si quelqu'un prend la plume de l'historien, il dira: Celui-là fut un homme de génie qui, à travers les résistances, les obstacles et les défaillances, eut le courage d'ouvrir des sources de prospérités nouvelles à la nation dont il était le chef. (*Applaudissements.*) Celui-là fut l'apôtre d'une politique hardie, mais prévoyante et sage, qui reconnut que l'équilibre européen n'est plus comme aujourd'hui sur les Alpes, les Pyrénées, ou le Pont-Euxin, mais qu'il embrasse le monde entier, et que de si grands intérêts doivent être l'objet de la sollicitude de la France, si loin qu'il faille aller les protéger par le drapeau français. Oui, cette page sera glorieuse! (*Applaudissements prolongés.*)[37]

> [if someone takes the pen of the historian, he will say: This was a man of genius who, in the face of resistance, obstacles and failures, had the courage to open up sources of new prosperity for the nation of which he was the leader. (*Applause*) He was the apostle of a daring, but far-sighted and wise politics, who recognised that the balance of power in Europe is no longer, like today, on the Alps, the Pyrenees, or the Black Sea, but embraces the whole world, and that such great interests must be the object of France's concern, however far it is necessary to go to protect them with the French flag. Yes, this page will be glorious! (*Prolonged applause*)]

While it is obvious that Rouher was a staunch supporter of Napoleon, this is still a further illustration of how the Mexican campaign can be seen to be consistent with Napoleon's proposal for a congress, and with his overall policy.

Émile Ollivier commented that after this rousing reception, the Assembly did not want to hear Favre's response, even though it was always the custom to allow someone to respond to a minister. Despite the overwhelming defeat of the motion, Ollivier claimed that, in fact, 'at the bottom of their hearts' three-quarters of the Assembly disapproved the government's politics in relation to Mexico. The correspondent for *The Times* remarked that some had obviously been persuaded by the eloquence of Rouher, because there were many who voted against the amendment who had expressed rather different opinions previously. His own opinion was that, regardless of the truth of the Opposition's arguments, the fact was 'that the French Army cannot be withdrawn before it shall have founded order in a country whose normal condition has long been the most frightful disorder'.[38]

Sensitive to the opposition to involvement in Mexico, Napoleon continued in the direction that Rouher had outlined in his address, which was to reduce France's commitment as quickly as possible. He had done what he had set out to do and prepared the way for the establishment of a stable government. He had laid the groundwork for the development of the country and its resources, and ensured that Europe maintained access to American markets by preventing the southward encroachment of the United States. His negotiations with Maximilian during the ensuing weeks illustrate his commitment to reducing France's involvement at an early date, but to achieve this it was important that the new government be established as soon as possible. Napoleon's endeavours to get commitment from Maximilian, however, have led many to insist he was determined to impose a monarchy on Mexico, and Maximilian's vacillations after accepting the throne did not help Napoleon's case.

8
'A Noble and Chimerical Utopia'

When the initial results of the plebiscite reached Europe, Maximilian gave his commitment to accept the throne of Mexico, subject to certain conditions that were negotiated with Napoleon. Napoleon then was anxious that he take up his position as quickly as possible, so France's commitment could be reduced. But the Emperor had been criticised for pressuring Maximilian, and accused of wanting him to take responsibility for a situation which he knew was out of hand, and in which he no longer wanted to be involved. Much of the criticism was based on the validity of the plebiscite in Mexico, which Émile Ollivier challenged. He had information claiming that if the army found notables in a town or village who were prepared to accept municipal functions, they would install them and make them declare their agreement with the vote for a monarchy. If no Mexican notables were found, the local administration was given to the French military, who then threatened any important persons they could find with expulsion from Mexico if they did not vote for the empire. Another method was to count the total population of an area as the number of adherents to the monarchy.[1] Although Ollivier does not cite his source for this information, in view of General du Barail's comments it is quite possible that individuals in the army may have conducted the vote in such a manner. But this was not at the bidding of Napoleon.

Bazaine did, however, write to Napoleon admitting that the votes 'were not the result of universal suffrage', adding:

> Mais ce n'est pas moins l'expression de la grande majorité des États délivrés, car l'élément indien qui habite les campagnes suit toujours l'élément mexicain qui habite les centres principaux. La masse indienne n'a jamais été sincèrement consulté par aucun parti, et le prétexte en

est simple: on les regarde comme des gens sans raison. Pour les amener *gente de razón* [*sic*], il faudrait changer par un coup de baguette l'organisation sociale du pays. Comment établir des listes électorales quand ici l'état civil n'existe pas? Tout en étant convaincu que les actes d'adhésion représentent l'opinion des *gens de raison* du Mexique, et que l'Archeduc peut sans remords s'appuyer sur cette manifestation, je n'en ai pas moins fait préparer un plébiscite et n'ai point le moindre doute sur le vote.[2]

[But it is nevertheless the manifestation of the great majority of the freed states, for the Indians who inhabit the countryside always follow the Mexicans who inhabit the major centres. The Indian population has never really been consulted by any party, and the reason is simple: they are regarded as men who cannot reason. To help them become reasoning men would need the wave of a wand to change the social organisation of the country. How can electoral lists be established when a civil state does not exist here? While I am convinced that the votes collected represent the opinion of the men of reason in Mexico, and that the Archduke can rely on this manifestation without any compunction, I will nonetheless organise a plebiscite and I have not the least doubt of the vote.]

Napoleon was not happy, as the vote reflected the wishes of only the majority of the States that had been liberated, and he instructed that a proper plebiscite be held. There have been many examples cited to show Napoleon was adamant that the people had to make this choice, and Pierre de la Gorce showed that the sovereignty of the people was the first article in Napoleon's political creed:

Le peuple peut déléguer l'autorité, mais il garde un droit supérieur, celui de ressaisir et de reprendre ce qu'il a donné. Telle est la doctrine développé dès 1832 dans les *Rêveries*. Ce que Bonaparte proclame à vingt-quatre ans, il le redira en ses jours de prospérité; et cette reconnaissance du droit populaire sera comme l'hommage du souverain qui gouverne à un souverain plus auguste encore.[3]

[The people can delegate authority, but they maintain a higher right, that of seizing again and taking back that which they have given. This is the doctrine developed in 1832 in the *Rêveries*. What Bonaparte proclaimed at the age of twenty four, he will repeat in his days of prosperity; and that recognition of the rights of the people will be like the homage of the governing sovereign to an even more noble sovereign.]

Again there is no reason to believe Napoleon would suggest for Mexico a system opposed to that in France. In a recent analysis, Alain Minc commented on Napoleon III's commitment to consultation of the people: 'la société, malgré son corset, a pu s'exprimer et le pouvoir a été obligé, certes avec lenteur et en multipliant les demi-mesures, de s'y soumettre'.[4] ['Society, despite the constraints on it, could express its wishes, and the power was obliged to submit to it, even though it certainly did so slowly and with many half-measures'.] But, whatever its limitations, Napoleon showed that he was prepared to submit himself to the demands of his country, and Minc concluded that Louis Napoleon's attachment to universal suffrage was not purely rhetoric. Yet he was accused of only ever intending 'a sort of universal suffrage' be consulted in Mexico. Britain had been quick to accuse Napoleon of this, but Minc made an interesting comparison of the French and British systems at this time:

> Le second Empire est mille fois moins libéral que l'Angleterre victorienne, mais il pratique le suffrage universel, alors que la Chambre des communes est encore élue sur une base censitaire.[5]

> [The Second Empire is a thousand times less liberal than Victorian England, but it practises universal suffrage, while the Chamber of Commons is still elected through a franchise based on property ownership.]

This did not prevent criticism and condemnation of the Emperor.

Despite Napoleon's wishes, Bazaine decided, in view of a recent resurgence of opposition by Juarez's army, that he would leave it to Maximilian when he arrived to decide if he wanted to accept the situation, or have it confirmed in a vote by universal suffrage.[6] By this time Maximilian was committed to go to Mexico, and Napoleon agreed that this process should be followed. Although the result of the vote was questionable, Maximilian had accepted it and negotiated guarantees from France which were satisfactory to him. Napoleon had guaranteed material support for the new Empire in the form of French troops who would be withdrawn gradually as the Mexican army and the foreign forces were developed. After their withdrawal he would leave the Foreign Legion of 6,000 men for six to eight years. His plans in this respect were made quite clearly to Maximilian, as were his reasons for not being able to help indefinitely. Corti summarised the Emperor's intentions as follows:

> the Archduke might rest assured that he had every interest in not leaving his work unfinished, and that the French troops would not

be withdrawn so long as any danger to the stability of the Government remained; but Ferdinand Maximilian must realize that, in view of the opposition of public opinion in France and of the Corps législatif, the Emperor could not promise in advance to leave the troops in Mexico for a definite period.[7]

Maximilian had responded that he was prepared to accept the throne if Napoleon increased the Foreign Legion to 8,000 men and accepted his proposals for repayment of Mexico's debt to France. In March 1864, final negotiations were carried out in Paris and a loan floated for the new empire, after which Maximilian returned to Austria to prepare to leave for Mexico.

However, when he arrived in Vienna he suddenly began to hesitate over his decision to go to Mexico. Franz-Josef had asked him to sign an agreement not to make any claim on the Austrian throne for himself or the sons he might have. Maximilian was mortified, and declared that he would no longer go to Mexico. Napoleon and the Emperor Franz-Josef were then forced to remind him of his duty and of upholding both his own and their honour. They, in turn, were to be accused of putting undue pressure on the Archduke. But having assured his own country that France would not be committed in Mexico indefinitely, Napoleon was unexpectedly confronted with the possibility that Maximilian would not go and that new negotiations might have to be undertaken. He wrote to Maximilian:

> By the treaty concluded between us, and mutually binding upon us, by the assurances given to Mexico, by the pledges exchanged with the subscribers of the loan, Your Imperial Highness has entered into engagements which you are no longer free to break. What, indeed would you think of me if, once Your Imperial Highness had arrived in Mexico, I were to say that I can no longer fulfil the conditions to which I have set my signature?
> ... It is absolutely necessary in your own interests and those of your family that matters should be settled, for the honour of the house of Habsburg is at stake.[8]

General Frossard, Napoleon's close aide-de-camp, delivered the letter so he could impress on Maximilian the gravity of the situation.

Maximilian's dilemma is interesting, because Frossard learned from Franz-Josef on his arrival in Vienna, that Maximilian had known before he went to Paris that he would have to renounce any claim to the

Austrian throne. However, Franz-Josef blamed himself for Maximilian's hesitations because he should have discussed having the renunciation in writing before the Archduke left for Paris, as it was this that concerned Maximilian. Frossard reported this conversation to Napoleon, saying that he had remarked to Franz-Josef that he could see that this issue was a pressing question of honour for the Archduke, but the Austrian Emperor had responded:

> Oui, une question d'honneur pour nous tous; il faut que cela s'accomplisse; j'y fais tous mes efforts; mais aussi il faut que mon frère se soumette aux conséquences de la nouvelle situation, en ce qui regarde notre propre pays.[9]

> [Yes, a question of honour for us all; it must be concluded; I have put all my effort into it; but also my brother has to accept the consequences of the new situation, insofar as our own country is concerned.]

When approached by Frossard, Maximilian claimed he had not been given all the details before he went to Paris, and his honour as an Archduke, a husband and son made him act as he did. Frossard reminded him that beyond his own private honour there was his political honour owed to Napoleon, France and the world. Maximilian said he recognised this, as did his wife, but he could not help being anxious about the future for his wife, and the children he hoped to have. As far as the Archduchess was concerned, Frossard commented to Napoleon that she seemed as upset as the Archduke, but still she was very decided about becoming the Empress of Mexico and unconcerned about her eventual rights to the crown of Austria.

Corti, among others, showed that, until this point, Maximilian had been naïvely excited at the idea of being Emperor, particularly for the sake of his young wife. He is reported as saying, however, that he would have jumped for joy if someone had come to tell him that everything had fallen through, but that Charlotte was the one who would have been disappointed. Paul Gaulot, who recounted this, added:

> Ce prince, épris d'art, de littérature, de poésie, poète même à ses heures, avait été séduit un instant par l'éclat d'un trône, par ce rêve d'empire qui le mettait, dans sa pensée, l'égal de son frère aîné et de Napoléon III, sinon comme puissance, du moins comme prestige extérieure, mais son âme n'avait point la sécheresse des politiques ni l'énergie des ambitieux. Son rêve l'éblouissait; la réalité l'effrayait.[10]

[This prince, enamoured of art, literature, poetry – a poet himself in his time – had been seduced for a moment by the glamour of a throne, by the dream of an empire which would make him, in his mind, the equal of his older brother and Napoleon III, if not in power at least in outward prestige. But his spirit did not have the hardness of real politicians nor the energy of the ambitious. His dream dazzled him; reality frightened him.]

Napoleon was becoming more anxious, and before he received the above account from Frossard he sent him a telegram:

Une décision prompte est indispensable. La nouvelle de l'indécision fera naître des complications au Mexique. Déjà, en Angleterre, la Bourse fait des difficultés pour le nouvel emprunt. Toutes ces questions de famille auraient dû être réglées d'avance. On ne peut, sans grand inconvénient, laisser un peuple en suspens, vis-à-vis de grandes difficultés et l'escorte dans les Terres-Chaudes en proie aux atteintes de la fièvre jaune.[11]

[A prompt decision is indispensible. The news of the indecision will create complications in Mexico. Already, in England, the Stock Exchange is making difficulties for the new loan. All these family questions should have been settled in advance. One cannot, without severe inconvenience, leave a people in a state of uncertainty faced with great difficulties, and the escort in the hot regions prey to attacks of yellow fever.]

Meanwhile Frossard learned that all the difficulties emanated from the repeated and firm advice of King Leopold of Belgium, the father of Princess Charlotte. He had earlier impressed on Maximilian the need to have in writing Napoleon's commitment to the gradual withdrawal of French troops so that if things went badly Napoleon could not suddenly withdraw them.[12] Maximilian showed Frossard a letter in which Leopold had told him not to give in over his claim to the Austrian throne, but to treat tactfully the Mexican deputies, who were waiting to receive his official acceptance, while the issue was being resolved. The obstinacy of this influence offended both Napoleon and Franz-Josef, Frossard told Maximilian, and he added to Napoleon that he felt the Prince was entirely dominated by his father-in-law. Frossard then expressed his personal opinion of Maximilian which perhaps should have sounded a warning to Napoleon, but previous impressions had been so different and it was really too late to consider alternatives:

Avec une intelligence distinguée et un esprit cultivé, il n'a pas assez de caractère, et si j'osais le dire, de fermeté d'âme. Sa pensée est tout à des éventualités chimériques; il tourne trop vers l'Europe ses regards d'avenir, et ne me semble pas avoir assez de confiance dans la grande entreprise qu'il va faire.[13]

[While he has a distinguished intelligence and a cultured mind, he does not have enough character, and, dare I say, strength of spirit. He is totally occupied with chimerical possibilities; his thoughts of the future are focused too much on Europe, and he does not seem to me to have enough confidence in the great venture he is about to undertake.]

Count Fleury also was concerned about Maximilian and told Napoleon he had heard that Maximilian was 'very fickle in character', and that he focused more on trivialities than important issues. For example, even though he was not yet emperor he had spent a year deciding on the uniforms for his court and the livery for his household.[14]

Try as he might, Frossard had been unable to get the Archduke to fix a day for his official acceptance, and he wrote to him at Miramar, his home, to announce the arrival of a M. Herbet who was bringing the treaties which needed to have his signature. Frossard told Maximilian that he knew that he had decided to accept, and it was not possible to defer any longer the written assurance that was awaited by both Napoleon and Mexico. Maximilian replied with a friendly note, but indicated only vaguely that he would receive the Mexican deputation either the following Saturday or Sunday. When he received the above telegram from Napoleon, Frossard showed it to Maximilian and emphasised the problem of the troops waiting longer in the unhealthy zone to escort him to Mexico City. Maximilian was waiting for Charlotte to return from Vienna, but he agreed to accept the deputation on the Saturday and leave for Rome and Mexico on the Sunday. Maximilian finally gave his formal commitment to the Mexican deputies and signed a Convention with France[15] on the appointed day, but his departure was delayed several days because of a mysterious illness brought on, it was surmised, by his anxiety. This did not augur well for the future. While many had expressed their doubts about his capabilities, nobody was to know at this point just how inept Maximilian would prove to be.

Despite accusations of pressuring Maximilian and wanting only to serve his own interests, Napoleon has been shown to have been the most cautious of all the interested parties about imposing a monarchy, and the most anxious to ensure that it was the will of the people. He did not exert any pressure on Maximilian until after he had concluded lengthy negotiations with him in Paris, during which Maximilian had obtained from the Emperor all that he wanted, especially in relation to payment of the indemnity of Mexico to France, the number of French troops to remain in Mexico, and other concessions that Metternich had thought would be impossible.[16] Thus, there is another question to be considered: whether Maximilian should be completely exonerated while Napoleon is condemned. Once the Archduke left Paris Napoleon accepted that he was committed to go, and certainly his negotiations had never revealed the possibility of his reneging. Napoleon's anxiety was therefore understandable. Ollivier, however, sympathised with the unfortunate Prince, whom he believed to be subjected to undue pressure by the two Emperors, the Mexican envoys and 'a wife consumed with ambition, who was not going to let an imperial crown fall from her head'.[17]

Arguments that Napoleon wanted to finish with Mexico because of the crises that were looming in Europe can only be partially substantiated. His interest in Mexico continued, but his efforts after Maximilian's departure were directed towards encouraging the development of Mexico's resources and army so that he could reduce France's involvement, as he always intended. Alfred and Kathryn Hanna assert that the rejection of Napoleon's congress had caused him to try to 'get the Mexican Empire on its feet as quickly as possible so that the onus would be shifted to the shoulders of the new ruler'. If the new Emperor was successful in gaining control over most of Mexico and having his Empire accepted by the United States, they said, Napoleon could withdraw his troops and turn his attention to Europe.[18] Yet the rejection of his congress could equally be claimed as a reason for maintaining his interest elsewhere, not freeing himself of it. There were indeed more issues, such as the Danish–German question, that were claiming the Emperor's attention, but having committed his resources to resolving an international problem in Mexico, he did not intend to withdraw until a satisfactory result was in sight.

With Maximilian's departure for Mexico, and Bazaine's reports of continued French military successes, Napoleon might reasonably have expected that Mexico would soon be less demanding of French resources. He wrote to Bazaine in August 1864, two months after Maximilian's arrival, emphasising the need to develop the indigenous army so the French could leave as soon as possible. The early news from Mexico also indicated that the prosperity of the country, at least in those areas controlled by the French, was improving, with the Paris correspondent of *The Times* reporting that the receipts at the Vera Cruz customs house had increased every month but one since the beginning of the year.[19] In November 1864, Napoleon wrote to Maximilian impressing the need for his government to establish its credit in the light of bonds issued in Paris for a new loan, which would provide a considerable sum for him by early 1865. He added that it was necessary for Maximilian to establish a sound bank in Mexico, as leading bankers in Paris and London had agreed to 'place themselves at the head of this establishment'.[20] His advice about developing the resources of Sonora and other areas of Mexico, however, was incomprehensibly rejected by Maximilian, prompting Alfred and Kathryn Hanna to comment:

> The importance of this rejection lies in the insight it affords into the Austrian's own thinking on Mexico. He had just underwritten a staggering debt for his unknown realm whose chief difficulty had been financial confusion and bankruptcy. At the same time he denied what at the moment seemed the quickest means of discovering new wealth.[21]

A few days after Napoleon wrote to Maximilian, a report in *The Times* indicated that the Mexican people had already begun to be disillusioned by Maximilian's apparent inactivity. They were concerned that he had left the capital to explore the country even before he had established a ministry, and without having issued any decrees. *The Times* correspondent, however, felt the people would soon appreciate Maximilian's decision to get to know the country, the people and their resources before making decisions, and when Maximilian realised the Mexican commissioners he had left in charge had achieved nothing, then he would take action.[22] This was perhaps a rather optimistic view of the situation.

Whether Napoleon was concerned at such reports is difficult to say, but the reports that arrived in Paris in 1865 certainly presented a very confusing picture. By mid-1865, both Napoleon and Randon greatly concerned at the lack of progress in the development of Mexico's resources, and, particularly, that Maximilian's government seemed to think that the French government would continue to support the country indefinitely. Also, while Bazaine's military reports indicated that the pacification of the country was proceeding well, he still requested that more troops be sent, in anticipation of the losses that would occur in the next few months due to both sickness and battle. Randon pencilled a succinct '*non*' on Bazaine's request of 22 April 1865, and a more lengthy comment that there was no intention of sending reinforcements, on his request of 27 May. Bazaine was in the habit of writing political reports, military reports and personal letters, sent separately, and Randon queried the contradictory impressions that they conveyed. The political reports seemed to say that there was no chance of regenerating the country under the empire, while his other reports and letters showed great progress being made, at least as far as control of the country was concerned. Both Randon and the Emperor were moved to ask if they were written or influenced by the same person.[23] Having read a huge number of them myself, I can appreciate why they should ask such a question.

Napoleon and Randon also became aware of negative views of the situation from officers returned from Mexico, and expressed in personal letters from Mexico. When these were raised with Bazaine, he wrote to Randon that he had told his men to be very reserved in what they had to say or write, but that Randon should know how much the spirit of criticism was inherent in the French nature and how little the French liked to have their natural vivacity suppressed. He concluded that their negative opinions could not be considered valid because they were only formed on their own limited contact with Mexicans and foreigners and they could not have an overall picture of the real situation. His current view was that Paris needed to be patient and realise that the empire could not be expected to be self sufficient in such a short time, even if much of the blame was due to Maximilian's weakness and impracticality. He assured Randon that things would progress quickly after a rail link was forged between Vera Cruz and Mexico City, although he had never expressed such conditions before.[24]

What course was now open to Napoleon when both he and his government had anticipated commencing withdrawal from Mexico? Certainly the Chambers would not sanction an increase in the budget for Mexico after their reserved passing of the supplementary budget in November 1863. Napoleon was reminded, in August 1865, of the feelings of the Chambers and of the people, by one of his ministers without portfolio, and long-time friend, Magne, who remarked that while it was accepted that France's intentions in Mexico had been noble, it was now up to the new government to free the country from anarchy. Neither the people nor the majority of the *Corps législatif* would sanction sending more troops, nor vote more money for the expedition. Magne believed that if there was a universal feeling about the situation it was that their first setbacks had been gloriously avenged, their honour was safe and their interests satisfied, so there was no need to prolong their occupation. Two other issues added to the desirability of leaving as soon as possible, and they were the possibility of conflict with the United States, and the situation in Europe, particularly in Spain and Germany.[25]

These observations, however, only added to Napoleon's already firm desire to withdraw from Mexico, but he must have been frustrated at reports that Maximilian had apparently applied himself industriously to a study of the urgent reforms needed, had signed numerous decrees and submitted countless projects to close study, but that he had in fact achieved very little.[26] He wrote in determined fashion to Maximilian in August 1865 that it was imperative that he develop a strong government that would be accepted by America, and 'should cause no embarrassment to France, who is making so many sacrifices for Mexico'.[27] Bazaine's frustrating reports then led Randon to suggest Napoleon hasten the departure of the French troops because of the difficulty of stabilising far-flung regions in the country. The confusion that was arising in responsibilities between the French, Austrian and Belgian troops, also suggested it might be best to leave only foreign troops there to tame the country.[28] The Emperor's patience finally was overstretched by a report from Bazaine, at the end of October, which showed that things were not going well. Napoleon told Bazaine that France could no longer remain in such a situation of uncertainty with its prolonged demands on their finances, and he had to make an 'energetic resolution'. His impatience was obvious:

Il faut que l'Empereur Maximilien comprenne que nous ne pouvons rester indéfiniment au Mexique, et qu'au lieu de bâtir des théâtres et les palais, il est essentiel de mettre de l'ordre dans les finances et sur les grandes routes. Qu'il sache bien qu'il sera beaucoup plus facile d'abandonner un gouvernement qui n'a rien fait pour pouvoir vivre que de le soutenir malgré lui.[29]

[The Emperor Maximilian must understand that we cannot remain indefinitely in Mexico, and that instead of building theatres and palaces, it is essential that he brings some order to the finances and to the main transport routes. He should know that it will be much easier to abandon a government which has done nothing to support itself than to support it in spite of itself.]

Napoleon then optimistically advised his two Chambers in January 1866, that as Mexico was now governed by 'a regular power which was ready to fulfil its commitments, and respect foreigners and their property in Mexico', he would soon be able to advise the date by which the expeditionary forces would be withdrawn – after necessary arrangements were concluded with Maximilian.[30]

It was with the realisation that there was nothing more that he could do for Mexico, except pour money in with absolutely no prospect of a return, or of new revenue from Mexico's resources, that Napoleon turned his attention to Europe. This period, as he was preparing to withdraw his troops, provides another opportunity to witness an *exposé* of his policy. In May 1866 he again proposed a congress, this time involving France, England and Russia, to discuss the issues of Venetia, the Danish Duchies and the reform of Federal Germany. Once again England, in the person of Lord Clarendon, assumed that the idea would be to force the offending countries to take certain action. In this case, Clarendon believed, Prussia would either be prevented from annexing the Duchies, or, alternatively, allowed to do so, and Austria made to cede Venetia to Italy, and 'the British Government could not be a party to such transactions'.[31] When this congress was rejected, Napoleon expressed to Drouyn de Lhuys what he had hoped to achieve in the congress:

Nous aurions, en ce qui nous concerne, désiré, pour les Etats Secondaires de la Confédération une union plus intime, une organisation plus puissante, un rôle plus important; pour la Prusse plus d'homogenéité et de force dans le nord; pour l'Autriche le maintien de sa grande position en Allemagne. Nous aurions voulu en outre, que, moyennant une compensation équitable, l'Autriche put ceder la Vénétie à l'Italie; car si, de concert avec la Prusse et sans se préoccuper du traité de 1852, elle a fait au Danemark une guerre au nom de la nationalité allemande, il me paraissait juste qu'elle reconnut en Italy le même principe, en complêtant l'indépendance de la peninsule.
    Telles sont les idées qui, dans l'intérêt du repos de l'Europe, nous aurions essayé de faire prévaloir. Aujourd'hui, il est à craindre que le sort des armes seul en décide.[32]

[As far as we are concerned, we would have wanted, for the secondary states of the Confederation a closer union, a more powerful organisation, a more important role; for Prussia, more homogeneity and strength in the north; for Austria, the maintenance of her leading position in Germany. In return for a reasonable compensation we would also have wanted Austria to cede Venetia to Italy; for if, in concert with Prussia and without worrying about the treaty of 1852, she went to war with Denmark in the name of German nationality, it seemed just to me that she should recognise the same principle in Italy by effecting the independence of the peninsula. Such are the ideas which, in the interest of peace in Europe, we would have tried to have prevail. Today, it is to be feared that it will be decided only by a resort to arms.]

British statesmen, however, could never see that his ideas were aimed at the peaceful solution of long-term problems.

In August, Lavalette, Minister of the Interior and temporarily responsible for Foreign Affairs, suggested to Napoleon that his policy was not really understood by the majority of his countrymen. In an open letter to the Emperor he suggested that public opinion fluctuated between hopes of territorial aggrandisement, fears of the expansion of Prussia, regrets at the powerlessness of Austria, and doubts about the future of Italy. To end this state of uncertainty Lavalette suggested that if the Emperor explained his policy the country would be behind him. He then continued with a lengthy *exposé* of how he saw that policy. Apparently in response to Lavalette's prompting, Napoleon drafted a letter to his Ministers in the European capitals expressing his view of the future of Europe in the light of the recent Austro-Prussian conflict, and the advantages of the movement towards larger national states. This letter, attributed to Lavalette, appeared in the *Moniteur* on 17 September 1866.

Europe knew, the Emperor wrote, that the greatness of a nation no longer depended on the weakness of its neighbours, and that true equilibrium could only exist when the wishes of all the European nations were satisfied. He added:

le Gouvernement impérial a depuis longtemps appliqué ses principes en matière d'extension de territoire. Il comprend, il a compris, les annexions commandées par une nécessité absolue, réunissant à la patrie des populations ayant les mêmes mœurs, le même esprit national que nous et il a demandé au libre consentement de la Savoie et du comté de Nice le rétablissement de nos frontières naturelles. La France ne peut désirer que les agrandissements territoriaux qui n'altéreraient pas sa puissante cohésion; mais elle doit toujours travailler à son agrandissement moral ou politique, en faisant servir son influence aux grands intérêts de la civilisation.

Son rôle est de cimenter l'accord entre toutes les puissances qui veulent à la fois maintenir le principe d'autorité et favoriser le progrès. Cette alliance enlèvera à la révolution le prestige du patronage dont elle prétend couvrir la cause de la liberté des peuples et conservera aux grands États éclairés la sage direction du mouvement démocratique qui se manifeste partout en Europe.[33]

[the imperial government has for a long time applied these principles relating to extension of territory. It understands, has understood, annexations which were dictated by absolute necessity, reuniting to the country populations having the same customs, the same national spirit as we, and it asked the free consent of Savoy and the county of Nice to the reestablishment of our natural frontiers. France can only desire extensions of territory which do not affect her powerful cohesion; but she must always work for her moral or political growth, using her influence in the service of the great interests of civilisation.

Her role is to consolidate the alliance among all the powers who want at the same time to maintain the principle of authority and to encourage progress. This alliance will remove from revolution the prestige of patronage by which means it claims to protect the cause of freedom, and will allow the great enlightened states to continue the sound management of the democratic movement which is evident everywhere in Europe.]

Napoleon advised his agents to present these ideas to the governments to which they were accredited. Those governments, however, neither understood nor supported them, and only saw Napoleon as seeking to increase his power in Europe. But, as Albert Guérard said, while to Napoleon 'the doctrine of nationalities...was the very condition of permanent peace...it was bound to disturb the *status quo*'. He commented, though, that Napoleon's ideals should not be regarded as too Utopian because they were 'essentially the same as Woodrow Wilson's principle of self-determination'.[34]

William Echard has shown that historians have failed to understand Napoleon's foreign policy because they, too, assumed that his conference policy was really intended to achieve territorial growth for France. In addition, some, such as Albert Pingaud, decided that Napoleon's efforts to conclude alliances with Britain, Russia, Austria and Prussia at varying times during his reign indicated he could not decide with whom to have an alliance.[35] Others concluded that, because he approached so many different courts, he did not in fact ever have a policy. Echard's study, however, reveals that Napoleon believed the only way his congress idea could be successful was if there were general understandings between some of the major powers before such a congress took place, and this was why he was prepared to approach different courts, regardless of the relationships between individual powers.[36]

Napoleon III's foreign policy was neither indeterminate nor vacillating, and his *exposé* of his policy in his addresses, and, more particularly, in his letters and notes in 1866, confirm that he remained faithful to the ideas expressed in his youth. Unfortunately, if his views regarding Europe were to be doubted by other nations, the idea of extending his policy beyond Europe could only be considered as self-seeking. Yet Mazade, whose incisive articles show his merit as a keen and unbiased observer, said his 15 years of watching the progress made in France convinced him of Napoleon's selfless motivation.[37] His desire to bring stability and development to nations consumed by anarchy was often expressed in his addresses to the chambers and supported by the observations of ministers such as Rouher and Lavalette. Pierre de la Gorce commented that Napoleon's first concern was always for civilisation and humanity:

Bien que très zélé pour servir ses sujets, il ne dit pas: France d'abord, mais d'abord la civilisation et l'humanité. Cette tendance, à la fois magnifique et dangereuse, inspira toutes ses entreprises: en lui, une conception tout internationale de ce qui était, de ce qu'il croyait le bien.[38]

[Although very zealous in serving his subjects, he does not say: France first, but rather civilisation and humanity first. That tendency, at once magnificent and dangerous, inspired all his undertakings: in him, a completely international conception of what was, and of what he believed to be, good.]

He supported Lavalette's views by showing that, after all the conflicts Napoleon was involved in he never sought any compensation, in terms of territory, for France, but was concerned only for the freedom or betterment of other peoples.

This was one of his hopes for Mexico, but while he was clarifying his policy to his neighbours, he was being bombarded with more confusing reports from Bazaine. They were boringly repetitive, occasionally adding how much better all would be when the railway was completed, or pressing the need to augment the number of troops in case of increased threat from American filibusters in the north, or from the United States themselves.[39] Then there were reports from Maximilian contradicting those from Bazaine, with each blaming the other for the lack of progress in Mexico. While Bazaine complained of Maximilian's inactivity, he, in turn, was accused of using funds and materials to support the French army instead of organising a Mexican army. Because of Maximilian's inability to establish a strong financial base for the Empire, the situation was becoming desperate. In a determined bid to get continued support from Napoleon, the Empress Charlotte came to Paris in August 1866. Napoleon, however, could only tell her that they could do no more for Maximilian, except to help him to leave.[40] Tragically, this rejection seemed to be the catalyst which led to the emotional breakdown of the Empress Charlotte, from which she reportedly never recovered.[41]

Napoleon then decided to send one of his most trusted generals, General Castelnau, to Mexico to make a thorough assessment of the situation. Castelnau was instructed to encourage Maximilian to abdicate if he determined that the imperial government could not sustain itself after the departure of the French. At the same time Napoleon did not wish to see Mexico abandoned once more to anarchy, and if this seemed likely, Castelnau was to propose that Bazaine should remain for a short time as dictator while the people decided the leader and kind of government they wanted. He added:

> Mon seul but, mon seul vœu est de ne pas voir se perdre les germes de civilisation qu'a pu semer dans ce pays, auquel tant d'intérêts nous rattachent et que j'ai voulu, à un jour donné, sauver de son propre désordre, la présence pendant cinq années du drapeau et de l'esprit français.[42]

> [My sole aim, my only wish is not to lose the germs of civilisation which the presence of the flag and the French spirit during five years has been able to spread throughout this country, to which we are attached by so many interests, and which I wanted, at one time, to save from her disorder.]

While Napoleon's instructions to Castelnau show his disappointment at what had transpired in Mexico, they also remind us that his aims had been, and were still, humanitarian. If they had been purely self-seeking there would have been no need for him to reiterate this to Castelnau, or even to send Castelnau to Mexico.

Shortly after his arrival Castelnau noted, from information gathered from Mexicans, that the financial measures Maximilian had undertaken were only expedients, more often than not ill-advised, and the most fundamental issue of the nationalised property of the clergy had been the subject of a series of regulations, each more impractical than the others. He added:

> Pour avoir gaspillé un temps précieux, accumulé des fautes sans nombre, passé à côté du programme que lui traçaient les conditions mêmes de son avènement, l'empire, dès les premiers jours de l'année 1865, se trouva irréparablement condamné. Maximilian, si bien accueilli à son entrée dans Mexico, le 12 juin précédent, était arrivé, dans un délai paradoxalement bref, à la plus complète impopularité. Le sentiment public à cet égard se traduisait tout haut par un jeu de mots cruellement expressif. 'Ce n'est pas un *empereur* que nous a envoyé la France', disait-on parmi le peuple, 'c'est un *empireur*'.[43]

[For having squandered precious time, amassed numerous mistakes, failed to carry out the programme which was laid down in the conditions of his accession, the empire, from the earliest days of 1865, was irreparably condemned. Maximilian, so warmly welcomed on his entry into Mexico City on the 12 June prior to this, attained the most complete unpopularity in a paradoxically brief period. Public feeling in this regard was expressed aloud by a cruelly expressive play on words. 'It is not an emperor that France sent us', was said amongst the people, 'it is someone who made things worse'.]

While Castelnau concluded that the only solution was for Maximilian to abdicate, the Emperor proved to be just as indecisive about abdicating as he had been about all his actions in Mexico. In November Castelnau reported that Maximilian was ready to leave Mexico, but, in the ensuing weeks, many of his associates – including Bazaine, who had a Mexican wife and personal interests he wished to maintain in the country – tried to convince him that the Empire still had some chance of surviving. After receiving Castelnau's letter of 9 December detailing Maximilian's vacillations and all the intrigues to persuade him to remain in Mexico, Napoleon sent a cable to Castelnau:

Reçu dépêche du 9 décembre. Ne forcez pas l'Empereur d'abdiquer mais ne retardez pas le départ des troupes. Repatriez tous ceux qui ne voudront pas rester. La plupart des navires sont partis.[44]

[Received dispatch of 9 December. Do not force the Emperor to abdicate but do not delay the departure of the troops. Repatriate all those who do not wish to remain. Most of the ships have departed.]

Bazaine had reportedly told Maximilian that if he decided to remain in power Napoleon would continue to support him with troops.[45] However, he later wrote to Randon that he had only told Maximilian that the Foreign Legion and those French soldiers put at the disposition of the Mexican government would remain, and that he was authorised to say this until a telegraphic dispatch from Napoleon, dated 13 December, ordered him to repatriate the Foreign Legion and all French soldiers.[46] Despite his denials Bazaine did continue to press Maximilian to stay.

In the meantime Maximilian advised Castelnau that he was ready to set his crown aside, but he wanted to do it honourably for himself and usefully for the country. Because he had been called by the country to be its Emperor, it was up to the people to decide whether he should leave. He had decided to convoke a national congress and propose an armistice, which would allow all parties to come together to decide the destiny of the country. He would abide by their decision, whatever it might be. Castelnau advised him that this might have been a reasonable suggestion a year ago, but now when his own ministry considered the empire 'a noble and chimerical Utopia', and the republicans were in control of most of the country, the only thing to do was to abdicate, and spare himself and the country from the disaster that would follow such a proposition. Maximilian was unmoved, even when shown a declaration signed by Castelnau, Dano, the French minister, and Bazaine, suggesting this was the only step to take. Instead, he showed them a dispatch from Bazaine, dated the previous day, urging him to keep the crown, for the empire was the only solution for Mexico, and he, Bazaine, would do all he could to support it. While Castelnau was astounded at Bazaine's duplicity, Maximilian said he had been subjected to it for a long time and believed Bazaine was influenced by his Mexican wife and her family. Regardless, he was committed to his decision to convene a congress, and asked Castelnau if he might ask the United States to mediate by urging Juarez to be involved in the congress.[47]

But Castelnau realised there was nothing more that could be done, so the French troops began leaving Mexico City on 5 February 1867, while

Maximilian remained to negotiate with Juarez to bring about peace under a government that might be arranged between the two of them. Yet already Maximilian had conceded to Castelnau that if a congress was convened it would decide in favour of Juarez. This, he thought, would be the best solution for Mexico, which could only be constituted successfully as a federal republic.[48] Juarez, however, refused to negotiate, and Maximilian and his army continued to fight Juarez's troops until May. Maximilian then decided perhaps he should leave the country, but his plans, in the end, were thwarted when one of his most trusted generals betrayed his plans to the Liberals, who demanded his unconditional surrender. A request to Juarez that he be allowed to leave the country was refused, and he and two of his generals were court-martialled. At no time would Juarez meet Maximilian, his determination to destroy this foreign Empire being far greater than anyone in Europe realised. The astonishing decision of the court-martial was to sentence Maximilian and his generals to death, and on 19 June 1867, the three were executed by firing squad.[49] Thus was brought to an end what many had called the dream of the Emperor Napoleon III, who was then to be accused of being responsible for the fate of Maximilian and his Empire.

9
La Plus Grande Pensée du Règne?

After Maximilian's execution, the French Minister in Mexico, Alphonse Dano, wrote to the Foreign Ministry that opposition from the United States had probably had the most impact on the future of the Mexican Empire. But the most serious obstacle to the success of the Empire was Maximilian himself, who 'reasoned well and acted entirely to the contrary', not having the common sense to realise he could not live by traditional Habsburg protocol in Mexico.[1] This view was supported by Castelnau, whose first dispatch from Mexico summarised the feelings of everyone associated with Maximilian, including those who had been close to him:

> Ce malheureux prince est condamné sans appel, sa cause est perdue sans rémission et n'est pas discutable. C'est qu'en effet son incapacité absolu qui, dès les premiers jours de son règne, avait alarmé les hommes clairvoyants, est devenue aujourd'hui évidente pour tous. C'est que ses irrésolutions, ses maladresses, ses contradictions, ses dissipations, son inertie surtout lui ont enlevé successivement jusqu'au dernier de ses adhérents. Et pourtant chacun s'accorde à reconnaître que, si difficiles que fussent les circonstances dans lesquelles il a pris le pouvoir, il avait en mains plus de moyens qu'il n'en fallait pour les maîtriser.[2]

> [This unfortunate prince is condemned without appeal, his cause is lost beyond redemption and is not debatable. The fact is that from the very first days his absolute incapacity alarmed the perceptive people, but now it has become evident to everyone. His indecisiveness, his blunders, his inconsistencies, his dissipation, his inertia, above all, have successively driven away the last of his supporters. Everyone

is in agreement in acknowledging that while the circumstances in which he took power were difficult, he had more resources available to him than he needed to overcome them.]

General du Barail, on the other hand, saw the initial cause in the unlimited powers assumed by the Regency, which tried to introduce laws that had already been rejected in France, thus severely damaging the credibility of Napoleon's intentions in Mexico. He believed that if it were not for their actions, particularly those of Labastida, the various factions may have been reconciled happily under Maximilian, and the United States 'would probably have resigned themselves to the *fait accompli*'.[3]

While the Regency and Maximilian played in the final acts of what was ultimately a disastrous venture, events prior to this also determined the outcome. One contributing factor, 'the tyranny of distance', was a substantial cause of many of the problems. Delays in communication resulted in many decisions being made without the counsel of the government or Napoleon, and there was little that could be done when an action had already been taken. As the Emperor's cousin, Prince Napoleon, observed in relation to the conduct of the Crimean War:

When a war is carried on at such a distance it is not only at an enormous cost in men and money, but, further, the Government is not in a position to direct it owing to the time required for the interchange of communications. From this fact arises the necessity of entrusting the Commander-in-chief with extraordinary powers, which is always dangerous, and of leaving to him the absolute direction of events.[4]

Prince Napoleon went on to comment how difficult it was to find someone worthy and capable of effectively exercising such a responsibility, and the problems caused by the representatives in Mexico have been well illustrated.

Yet the role of others in this campaign, although recognised, has been played down by both contemporary critics and historians, except for Nancy Barker's work on Saligny. There was far more correspondence between Napoleon and his commanders, and between the Ministers for Foreign Affairs and War and their representatives, now held in the three major French archives, than has been used in any other study of this campaign. The mining of this correspondence has revealed a number of facts: that Jurien admitted taking decisions opposed to his instructions, and accepted responsibility for doing so; that Lorencez misinterpreted

Napoleon's intentions regarding a change in the form of government in Mexico; and that Saligny and Almonte used their own initiative in directing the actions of Forey to achieve the end they themselves desired. When the Regency was appointed as a result of all their intrigues, the situation in Mexico was beyond Napoleon's control, and events were put in train that led to the tragic conclusion of the venture.

Should Napoleon perhaps be blamed for having made the wrong choice of personnel? This is difficult to sustain, because nobody anticipated that the campaign would be long or difficult when, in late 1861, the three governments decided to intervene. Saligny's appointment has been examined, and given his record, it is obvious that he would not have been chosen as the permanent minister to Mexico, or to any other country. The experience and abilities of Lorencez and Forey have also been considered, and it would seem neither was really up to the task demanded of them. The problem was that the task did not seem so demanding, particularly politically speaking, when each of them was appointed to take command. Perhaps Napoleon should have listened to Marshal Randon, in June 1863, when he suggested that he send a trusted *aide-de-camp* to Mexico to make a thorough analysis of the situation, and to assess more accurately the needs of the expeditionary forces.[5] But as news of the fall of Puebla arrived shortly after Randon made his suggestion, again Napoleon could be forgiven for not thinking the situation was desperate enough to take such measures.

He could not have anticipated the contrary actions of his envoys, but Charles de Mazade, who had observed the government for more than 15 years, believed many of the Emperor's projects were compromised because of the people who were meant to direct their operation. He wrote to this effect to the Empress in 1865, when she was acting Regent during the Emperor's absence in Algeria, suggesting that many of his delegates imposed their own ideas in the implementation of Napoleon's plans and he was not always aware that they were not carried out as he intended:

> Forcément, involontairement peut-être, insensiblement, ceux qui exé-
> cutent substituent leurs idées, leurs intérêts, leurs préoccupations à la
> pensée de celui qui croit avoir pourvu à tout par une direction
> générale ou par un ordre. L'Empereur se fait-il par hasard l'illusion que
> tout ce qu'il dit se fait, que ce qui est de son intérêt, c'est à dire de
> l'intérêt public, prédomine? Ce serait une singulière méprise. Il faut
> bien qu'il sache qu'il trouve quelquefois ses ennemis les plus dan-
> gereux, d'autant plus dangereux qu'ils sont involontaires, dans les

agents eux-mêmes, qui le plus naivement, le plus consciencieusement du monde cherchent avant tout à faire prévaloir leurs vues propres, à se faire une influence, à soigner leur position.[6]

[Inevitably, unintentionally perhaps, imperceptibly, those who carry out instructions substitute their own ideas, their interests, their concerns for the idea of the one who thought he had provided for all eventualities with a general direction or an order. Has the Emperor by chance the illusion that what he says is what is done, that what is in his interest, that is to say the public interest, prevails? That would be a singular mistake. He has to understand that sometimes his most dangerous enemies – much more dangerous because they are unintentionally so – are to be found in the agents themselves, who quite innocently, most conscientiously, try above all to win agreement for their own views, to gain influence, and to look after their own positions.]

This tendency to put their own mark, either involuntarily or deliberately, on the interpretation of their instructions has been well illustrated in the Mexican campaign. But what has perhaps been overlooked is the fact that once Napoleon realised that his plans had gone astray, he took firm control to ensure that his representatives were very clear about his intentions and their instructions. He was not successful in achieving this, but the volume of correspondence between himself and Forey, Almonte and Maximilian shows conclusively that his ideas relating to Mexico were unchanged from his first clear *exposé* in his letter to Flahault in October 1861. They also reveal his anger when he learned his ideas and instructions were misconstrued. Those who have not studied this correspondence, or who have dismissed it, have criticised Napoleon for being deceived for so long by Saligny, or asserted that Saligny and his colleagues were carrying out the 'secret' instructions of their Emperor.

Many believed another reason for the failure of the campaign was that the Emperor lost interest in Mexico after the rejection of his congress proposal in 1863, and because his deteriorating health reduced his interest in, and mental ability to cope with, affairs of state. The fact that he spent much of his time writing his *History of Julius Cæsar* has been used to support these claims, and his preoccupation with it did give rise to much speculation, both within and outside France, about his health and political intentions. Émile Ollivier observed, however:

Comme on ne pouvait se résigner à interpréter aucune de ses actions naturellement et sans y supposer une trame, on vit dans ce témoignage pacifique une habilité inquiétante qui dissimulait des projets belliquex.[7]

[As they could not bring themselves to interpret any of his actions naturally and without imagining an intrigue, they saw in this peaceful testimony a disquieting activity which was covering up some warlike projects.]

Ollivier then added that it was not 'political indolence', as some believed, that led Napoleon to write this history, but that he needed something else to focus on after more than ten years of total responsibility for leading the people of France. He was indeed affected by the rejection of his congress proposal, but after some weeks of appearing angry and morose he recovered and again became actively concerned about the Schleswig-Holstein question.[8] He even spent several weeks in Algeria, in mid-1865, assessing the situation there and determining what could be done to improve the lot of the Arabs. His political correspondence, his speeches, his personal letters in these later years, and his writings in exile, after the fall of his own empire, also show his mind was just as keen as ever, despite continued reports of his deteriorating health and loss of ability to manage affairs of state.

In the immediate aftermath of the collapse of the Mexican Empire there were many claims that the greatest contributing factor to the withdrawal of the French from Mexico was the conclusion of the American Civil War, and Napoleon's fear of a war with the United States. The American press, particularly, claimed that Napoleon had decided to withdraw from Mexico after their Foreign Secretary, Seward had put pressure on France by writing to Napoleon's Minister, Montholon, in Washington, in December 1865. General J. Watson Webb, American Ambassador in Brazil, however, had had discussions in Paris with Napoleon in November that year, and knew that he had decided to withdraw from Mexico well before Seward had written to Montholon on 5 December. In April 1866 Webb wrote a letter to Napoleon in which he accused Seward of unjustly giving the impression that he had influenced the French with his letter to Montholon, when he had known the day before he wrote it that Webb had already told the President of Napoleon's decision.[9]

In fact, in August 1865, Drouyn de Lhuys had written to Dano, the French minister in Mexico, after considerable correspondence relating to the settlement of both Mexico's debts to France and the claims of French nationals, saying that it was time to conclude a definitive agreement with the Mexican government. The Emperor and his government realised by this time that Maximilian was incapable of organising his country's finances and continued to expect France to provide loans. Between September 1865 and January 1866 a convention was negotiated and agreed between the two governments, and in that time the decision was taken to begin preparations for a withdrawal of French troops. On 14 January, the Foreign Minister advised Dano that, as the Mexican government had not fulfilled its part of the Convention of Miramar, the agreement concluded between Maximilian and France in April 1864, France was no longer bound by it, and could no longer afford to meet the expenses of the expedition, which were to have been taken over by the Mexican government. Public opposition was also growing in France and the Emperor did not want to provoke that opposition any longer. Napoleon wished to begin repatriation of his troops in the following autumn, now that reclamation of their claims had been regulated in a convention, and the withdrawal would be completed by the autumn of 1867.[10]

The argument that it was pressure from the United States and fear of war that forced Napoleon to withdraw, is difficult to sustain. Correspondence from Bigelow, the American Ambassador in Paris, after a discussion with Drouyn de Lhuys in October 1865 shows that the United States knew France had decided to withdraw, but was hoping that the United States would be prepared to recognise Maximilian's government. Alfred and Kathryn Hanna used this discussion to support their argument that Napoleon was looking for an excuse to get out of Mexico. They suggest that Bigelow's comment to Drouyn de Lhuys, that if the French troops did withdraw, the United States might have to recognise the Empire, gave France the opening to withdraw while saving her prestige.[11]

It is true that Napoleon wished to avoid antagonising the United States, but it was the realisation that Maximilian was expecting the financial and military support of France to continue indefinitely, as well as the unpopularity this was engendering in France, that had most influence on Napoleon. He could not, and did not want to have to, justify continued expenditure in Mexico when he had not intended a prolonged occupation in the first place. It was another twelve months before the troops were to begin leaving Mexico, so pressure from the United States could not have been too intense, and nor does it appear so in the diplomatic correspondence. The Secretary of State, Seward, was mainly concerned that France maintained her timetable of withdrawal and would have left Mexico by the end of 1867 as indicated.

When Castelnau was sent to Mexico, Montholon wrote that there were once again claims that France was yielding to pressure from the

United States. On 19 October 1866 Napoleon advised Drouyn de Lhuys to send an official dispatch to Montholon 'qui prouve que nous avons pris nos résolutions à l'égard du Mexique sans y être amené par une pression des états unis, et par conséquent avant l'arrivée du Général de Castelnau' [which proves that we made our decision regarding Mexico without being forced by pressure from the United States, and therefore before the arrival of General de Castelnau]. Drouyn de Lhuys also told Montholon that while the Emperor had intended to withdraw the French troops in three convoys, the last leaving in November 1867, the news from Mexico was so bad that he did not want to leave a small number of troops exposed and isolated at such a great distance from France, so they were now all to be withdrawn in the spring. This was why he had sent Castelnau, to advise Maximilian that, if he wished to remain in Mexico, he could no longer count on French support.[12] When Maximilian decided to stay in Mexico at the beginning of 1867 Napoleon had no choice but to withdraw his troops and leave him to do the best he could, alone.

This leads to a consideration of how important intervention in Mexico was to Napoleon. Can it be regarded as *la plus grande pensée du règne* when, compared to other foreign matters, particularly those relating to Europe, it occupied relatively little of his time? References to Mexico in Napoleon's annual addresses to the parliamentary chambers are comparatively short, while the reports on the situations in Italy and Poland, for example, are quite lengthy. The idea of seeing a stable government established in Mexico was indeed part of a 'grand idea', but not in the sense seen by many historians and even some of Napoleon's contemporaries. Some believed he was obsessed with the idea of a canal, but if that were so, why is there no mention of it in correspondence relating to the development of Mexican resources? The importance of European access to Central America is evident, and it has been shown that this concerned not only Napoleon. His intention to leave Mexico as soon as a government was established also belies an obsession with constructing and controlling a canal in the region. Another view of *la grande pensée*, the creating of a Latin Catholic bloc, is too simplistic and not supported by the facts. Why would Napoleon insist on the involvement of Britain in the enterprise if his idea was to strengthen the Latin culture and suppress the influence of the Anglo-Saxons to the north? He also demonstrated he was not prepared to support the clergy in Mexico, and his commanders had instructions to provide places of worship for the Protestant faithful. Neither is there evidence to sustain claims that he intended to substitute monarchies for the republics in South America, other than in the publication of Hidalgo's letters referred to by Mazade.[13] Others who have analysed the Mexican venture in terms of *la grande pensée* have said that its failure was inevitable because of Napoleon's ineptitude. Principal among such critics was Christian Schefer, who blames him for not having enough information about either the natural resources of Mexico or its political traditions. According to Schefer, the enterprise was based solely on distant hopes and unverified assertions, which became for Napoleon 'articles of faith'. He supported this claim with a scathing analysis of Napoleon's intellectual abilities:

Napoléon III a été souvent qualifié de visionnaire; il l'est réellement, dans toute la force du terme, et au point de ne plus savoir lui-même s'il constate ou s'il imagine. Il est radicalement incapable de séparer le rêve de la réalité. Les hypothèses qu'il a forgées deviennent pour lui des vérités démontrées et les fictions qu'il évoque lui masquent les obstacles. Des doutes ne l'effleurent donc que rarement. Le succès final lui paraît toujours certain. Et il ne songe pas un instant que ses soldats s'aventurent peut-être au Mexique, à la poursuite d'un mirage.[14]

[Napoleon III has often been described as a visionary; he truly was one, in the full meaning of the term, and to the point of no longer knowing himself if he was stating fact or fancy. He was completely incapable of separating daydream from reality. The hypotheses that he concocted became for him proven truths, and the illusions that he evoked obscured the obstacles from him. Doubts rarely crossed his mind. Ultimate success always seemed certain to him. And he did not imagine for an instant that his soldiers were perhaps venturing to Mexico, in pursuit of a mirage.]

Schefer admitted that much of the information Napoleon received was wrong or deliberately misleading, but he was culpable for not verifying it. Yet the information given him by Saligny was confirmed initially by opinions from Wyke, and, later, by those of the Belgian and Prussian envoys and *The Times* correspondent in Mexico. Schefer went even further in his criticism of Napoleon, adding that if he seemed to be hesitating about a decision it was not because he was considering and reflecting on what he was told, as he hardly knew how to reflect. He continued in similar vein:

Critiquer ou approfondir, pour prendre ensuite une décision raisonnée, exige un travail qui lui répugnait, car son intelligence nébuleuse et désordonnée était, par surcroît, d'une indolence extrême. S'informer méthodiquement des affaires mexicaines, prescrire des enquêtes et confronter leur résultats eût été besogne dépassant ses forces.[15]

[To study critically or deeply in order to make a well-reasoned decision demanded an effort which was distasteful to him, for his nebulous and disorderly intelligence was, moreover, the result of extreme indolence. To inform himself methodically of Mexican affairs, to arrange investigations and examine their results would have been a task beyond him.]

These conclusions are extremely harsh and Schefer provided nothing to support them, although he probably drew on the writings of contemporary critics and opponents of Napoleon.

There are others, however, who give a far different view of the personality and abilities of this enigmatic man. Ernest d'Hauterive, who published the correspondence of Napoleon III with Prince Napoleon, said he

wore the appearance of irresolution, because he concealed his will. Extremely good hearted, of a kindness of disposition exaggerated in the head of a State, and of a patience which nothing could wear down, he knew how to wait; and, because he was master of himself, concealed his impressions, reflected at great length, and did not yield to first impulses, he was accused of indecision.[16]

In his memoirs Count Fleury said that Napoleon was always willing to listen to the advice of others and even change his mind on the basis of that advice, but that, unfortunately, many of his Ministers and *aides-de-camp* were too timid to give advice when it may have prevented him committing an error.[17] Émile Ollivier also confirmed Napoleon's habit of carefully considering all sides of the situation before acting:

Avant de s'engager il pesait lentement, mûrement le pour et le contre, embrassait les divers aspects de la situation, parfois passait, pour un instant, avant de se fixer, d'un parti à l'autre: c'est ce que les historiens 'qui n'ont jamais mis le nez aux conseils' ont appelé ses hésitations.[18]

[Before committing himself he slowly and carefully considered the for and against, taking in the diverse aspects of the situation, sometimes changing for an instant from one decision to another before finally settling on one: it is this that historians, 'who have never shown their faces in decision-making bodies' have called his wavering.]

The inability of many of his acquaintances and foreign diplomats to come to terms with Napoleon's reflective nature, demonstrated by his silences and lack of positive response to their ideas, and partly a result of his years as a conspirator, led to conjecture about his ideas and intentions. In particular, his foreign policy has been seen as inconsistent and often decided on a whim.

It was inevitable, then, that Napoleon's intervention in Mexico would be considered in a similar light. But, as Rouher said, he was a man who had the courage to take a risk to open up new avenues for prosperity for his country and to recognise that European equilibrium now embraced the entire world. There were few who believed, as he did, that free trade was the basis of peace between nations, and that protectionism was the sacrifice of the many to the few, but this was why Rouher called the Mexican venture *la grande pensée du règne*. Napoleon's aim in Mexico therefore, was just as he had stated it to Forey: to maintain for Europe, not just for France, access to the markets of the Americas which Europe had every reason to suspect the United States wished to monopolise. He could also help to bring peace and prosperity to a country ruined by anarchy and in danger of being absorbed by the United States.

These intentions were far beyond the narrow idea of creating a Latin–Catholic bloc or of extending monarchies throughout republican America. As William Smith said, to accept these as his motives is to misunderstand the mission that Napoleon believed France had:

> To him the vision was one of a world which would be based upon national groupings, so balanced as not to be competitive, held together by a common desire to promote trade, prosperity and international peace. His war would be one of words, his battlefields the green baize of the tables, where met the congresses of the Powers. Whole armies of words would march at his command and his opponents could not but be overcome by logic and common sense. They would, he always felt, understand his dream. It was a reasonable assumption in that most of his contemporaries had in their youth waded, as he had, through the flood waters of romanticism and had not emerged bone dry.[19]

But if they had been consumed by the same ideas in their youth, many of his contemporaries, especially the British, had relinquished their youthful ideals, perhaps because they had become more concerned with remaining in power. Richard Cobden thought this of Lord Russell, and he told the House of Commons that foreign governments felt that the Foreign Office had no power, because the power rested in the House, 'and foreign Governments more than suspect that your Foreign Minister is often playing a game with them from time to time merely to suit his policy and his prospects in this House'.[20] This has been shown to have been so in 1861, when the confusing messages being given to Napoleon by the British ministers had considerable impact on the course of the intervention.

Napoleon III pursued a foreign policy that was too idealistic and threatening to his fellow sovereigns, yet, despite their rejections of his ideas of congress diplomacy, he was not easily disillusioned, as can be seen in his repeated attempts to convene a congress. But neither was he single-minded in pursuit of his policy, or prepared to pursue it at any cost. One of his criticisms of his uncle, Napoleon I, was that he fell because he tried to accomplish in ten years the work of several centuries. Napoleon III had much more patience and was prepared to wait and take advantage of opportunities as they arose. The question is, should he be condemned for the failure of the expedition to Mexico, or should he be given due credit for a grand vision of the world?

Had the venture succeeded, it would, no doubt, have been hailed by all as *la plus grande pensée du règne*. But it did not succeed, and Napoleon III has been criticised, not only for its failure, but for his motives, real or supposed, for becoming involved in Mexico. Many have conveniently ignored the fact that the decision to go to Mexico, to demand the repayment of debts and retribution for continuing offences against their nationals, was taken jointly by the governments of France, Britain and Spain. They all agreed that the Mexican government could no longer be negotiated with, and a show of force was needed to pursue their claims. It was also agreed that Mexico needed a more stable government to ensure any agreements would be honoured in the future. The fact that Spain and Britain agreed with Napoleon that a monarchy was the most suitable form of government has been overlooked by Napoleon's critics. Instead, the focus has been on the activities of Napoleon's representatives in Mexico, and the blame for the breakdown of the Tripartite Convention placed on their shoulders. The activities of the British and Spanish representatives have been played down or ignored, even though it was their decision to negotiate with Juarez instead of demanding retribution for their claims.

Napoleon was determined that an expedition would only be undertaken in conjunction with the two nations he hoped to make firm allies, but what he did not appreciate was the influence of internal politics on the Spanish players, Collantes, O'Donnell and Prim, and the constraints imposed on the British ministers, Palmerston and Russell, who agreed verbally with his ideas, but would not discuss them with the parliament. Could Napoleon have anticipated the consequences for the joint venture of these different political situations? After the breakdown of the Convention Palmerston and Russell condemned Napoleon, but at the same time they commented that success in Mexico could benefit Britain but at no cost to her government. This would seem to confirm their agreement with Napoleon's ideas, and that the messages they gave him in the period of negotiations were misleading, to say the least.

Perhaps, as with many other aspects of Napoleon's reign, perception of the Mexican campaign has been clouded by 'the appearance of things'. William Smith recognised that one of the tragedies of the Empire was that the brilliant court life that was developed to help improve the prestige of France with other older European monarchies gave a false impression of both Napoleon and Eugenie.[21] It gave those who saw only this aspect of Napoleon the impression that he was frivolous and inept. Similarly, consideration of the Mexican venture has been clouded, first by too much attention to anecdotal evidence, which said there were secret instructions and that Napoleon was determined to impose a monarchy on Mexico, and, second, by the unquestioned following of early historians of the venture, such as Corti. Corti's conclusions about Napoleon's intentions were based on limited evidence, and he misinterpreted some of that evidence. Napoleon's correspondence with Maximilian, Forey and Bazaine has revealed that he was not blindly obsessed with achieving a goal, but was sensitive to the difficulties, and was prepared to abandon or modify his plans if necessary. There would have been no need to recall Jurien, Lorencez, Forey and Saligny if they had been carrying out his instructions. One of the telling pieces of evidence to support this is Saligny's comment that he believed he had correctly *guessed* the Emperor's intentions.[22]

Napoleon has been blamed for having inadequate knowledge of the country, the people and its political traditions, when he decided to intervene. According to Jack Dabbs, 'The French policy seems to lie in the feeling, common among military intruders, that they faced a plastic, wieldy, unformed society that could easily substitute new social patterns for old.'[23] But what colonial power, missionary group or military invader in the nineteenth century approached other cultures any differently? There were consequences, though, to the limited understanding of the firmly entrenched stratification in Mexican society. For example, when it came to organising support for either the republican or monarchical causes, the Indians could be easily organised by 'aggressive creoles or mestizos' to support one or other cause. But, as Dabbs observed, the Indians 'had no real interest in the avowed principles of either group, and they deserted easily...Often they passed without resistance from one army to the other.'[24] It was difficult, then, for the French to know just how much physical support they had. At the same time there is evidence of strong support of the Empire by the Indian population, and it is this that was accepted in Paris to validate the intervention. Many French agents had convinced the Indians that the French had come to alleviate the oppression they had suffered under the Spanish, and the Juarists had alienated Indian support by banning religious parades and pageants. They therefore turned to Maximilian and their support was generally maintained, at least in the central part of Mexico, until the last days of the Empire.[25] When the French finally left Mexico the Juarists executed many Indian leaders, and under the new regime of Porfirio Diaz the Indians 'slipped back into the same status as before the Intervention'.[26] So, while popular support for the intervention was evident, republican opposition was much stronger than Napoleon had anticipated, and the campaign demanded more resources than he was prepared to commit.

The failure of the intervention has, however, prevented due recognition of the value of the Emperor's ideas in going to Mexico and, as a result, serious consideration of his world view. Napoleon was reminded, some time after Mexico, of a saying of La Rochefoucauld:

> As most people consider only the appearance of things, their judgements are based solely on results, so that a design of a plan seems to them well formed or well carried through only when the result is good.[27]

Judgement on results is clearly evident in most accounts of the Mexican campaign, but given the number of players involved, and their contributions to its failure, there is merit in considering whether Napoleon's ideas have value. While most saw his world view as self-seeking, there was a vast difference between his intentions to develop Mexico and save it from the devastating effects of anarchy, and those of various

United States diplomats who sought to annex regions of Mexico, particularly those richest in natural resources, as payment for their debts. In such a comparison Napoleon III must be recognised as having selfless and humanitarian motives. Had the government of Maximilian been able to sustain itself and quell Juarez, Napoleon would have been praised for bringing stability and prosperity to the nation. If European influence had been maintained in Central America, the United States almost certainly would have been unable to introduce a policy of protectionism, which began to affect Europe in the decades before the First World War. Of the influence of the United States, Paul Gaulot asked in 1906:

> Que deviendrait l'Europe – et l'on peut dire aujourd'hui: que deviendra l'Europe? – que deviendrait l'Europe si cette population de marchands, riche parce qu'elle travaille, forte parce qu'elle est riche, se servait de ses navires de guerre et de ses navires de commerce pour dominer le vieux continent et lui imposer les produits de son agriculture et de son industrie?[28]

> [What would become of Europe – and one can say today: what will become of Europe? – what would become of Europe if this population of merchants, rich because they work, strong because they are rich, make use of their warships and merchant vessels to dominate the old continent and impose on it the produce of their agriculture and industry?]

Was Napoleon III in fact more perceptive than his more conservative contemporaries? There can be no doubt, when in the late twentieth century we see some of Napoleon's ideas have come to fruition, that he was a visionary, but unfortunately out of step with his contemporary statesmen. The main difference between them and Napoleon III was that he was not a traditionalist. As Albert Guérard said:

> his distinction among rulers is that he anticipated and tried to shape the future; his genuine greatness is that, in many important fields, he proved a true prophet, and that the solutions for which he worked are still our hope today ... But if failure must be admitted as an indictment, it need not be accepted as an all-embracing and conclusive condemnation. A man may fail, as Saint-Louis, Napoleon I, Lafayette, and Woodrow Wilson did fail, without being branded as a knave or a fool.[29]

Because his contemporaries could not accept Napoleon's aims, and could not rid themselves of their conviction that he was looking for compensation for France in Europe and the New World, many branded him as at least a 'knave', if not also a 'fool'.

Perhaps his intentions were not understood or accepted because he expected that they would be, without his having to justify or explain himself. When he wrote *Des Idées napoléoniennes*, he concluded his description of the system Napoleon I had intended to introduce by saying: 'Il n'est plus besoin maintenant de refaire le systême de l'Empereur, il se refera de lui-même; souverains et peuples, tous aideront à le rétablir, parce que chacun y verra une garantie d'ordre, de paix et de pros-périté.'[30] [There is no longer a need to rebuild the Emperor's system for it will rebuild itself; sovereigns and peoples will all help to reestablish it, because everyone can see in it a guarantee of order, peace and prosper-ity.] He expected the companions of his youth would retain the ideals they had all shared, but instead, lack of understanding fostered rumour, conjecture and suspicion of his intentions.

After the defeat at Sedan in 1870, and the subsequent collapse of the Empire, recriminations in France against Napoleon were strong. Immedi-ately after his death in 1873, the French republican press savagely criti-cised the man who had led them for over twenty years, many conveniently remembering only the later failures and ignoring the achievements of the early years of the reign. *Le Temps* was almost vitriolic, claiming Napoleon alone was responsible for the ruin of the later years and the troubles that had continued after the defeat of 1870. He had led France into the abyss, thereby demonstrating that Bonapartism had only ever led to the invasion and dismemberment of France. The author added:

Insensible à sa chute et aux malheurs de la France, affligé peut-être de la voir se relever sans lui, Napoléon III est mort sans doute plein de chimères et d'espérances. Il ne faut pas douter que ces chimères ne tâchent de lui survivre. Mais cela n'importe pas. Ce qui importe, c'est que la France soit à jamais guérie de la folie bonapartiste, et elle a, certes, payé sa guérison assez cher pour se garder de toute rechute.[31]

[Indifferent to his fall and to the misfortunes of France, grieved to see her recover without him, Napoleon III has died, no doubt full of wild dreams and hopes. There is no doubt that these dreams will try to survive him. That is not important. What is important is that France be forever cured of the Bonapartist folly, and she has, certainly, paid dearly for the recovery in order to guard against further setbacks.]

These negative views tainted the majority of early histories of the Second Empire, which attached little but failure to the entire period. Alain Corbin highlighted the fact that the proponents of the *'légende noire'* [black legend] relating to the Second Empire were led by two *'artisans de génie'*, [artisans of genius] Victor Hugo and Leon Gambetta, who cast the mould for many of the republican histories of the Empire.[32] While Corbin and others have criticised the basis of these early analyses of Napoleon III and the Empire, their influence is evident, even in works as late as the 1970s.

However, other opinions in the wake of the Emperor's death, in newspapers such as *La Presse, Moniteur Universel, La France*, and *Paris-Journal*, reminded the French people that the Empire had not experienced only disasters. *La France* commented:

> ni les fautes extérieures et intérieures de l'Empire . . . ni les faiblesses des derniers jours contre lesquelles l'opinion publique s'est déchaînée ne doivent nous faire oublier que le règne de Napoléon III a été marqué par un développement de prospérité matérielle dont nous ressentons encore les effets; que la France, après les guerres de Crimée et d'Italie, avait recouvré sa prépondérance en Europe.[33]

> [neither the mistakes in foreign and internal affairs of the Empire . . . nor the failures of the final days, against which public opinion was unleashed, should allow us to forget that the reign of Napoleon III was significant for the development of economic prosperity whose effects we are still experiencing; nor that France, after the Crimean and Italian wars, regained her ascendancy in Europe.]

In similar vein *Paris-Journal* wrote:

> Pour nous, le règne de l'empereur Napoléon III est un des plus féconds en grands résultats que l'histoire de notre pays aura à enregister; il comptera, malgré les malheurs de la fin, parmi les plus prospères.
>
> L'ordre maintenu à l'intérieur, le progrès dans les institutions constitutionnelles, le développement de la richesse nationale sous l'influence d'une législation économique libérale, constituent un ensemble qui a sa grandeur.[34]

> [For us, the reign of the Emperor Napoleon III is one of the most prolific in great achievements that the history of our country will ever record; it will count among the most prosperous, in spite of the misfortunes of the end.

The order maintained in the interior, the progress in constitutional institutions, the development of national prosperity under the influence of liberal economic legislation, together constitute an achievement which has its greatness.]

The *Moniteur Universel* criticised the radicals and their press, who focused their condemnation of Napoleon on the *coup d'État*, forgetting their own actions in 1848 and 1870 which were much more revolutionary, and in some cases more violent. It then added:

L'empereur n'eut pas toutes les qualités d'un souverain, mais il en eut plusieurs et il serait absurde de supposer qu'il dut uniquement au hasard les succès qui marquèrent la première partie de son règne. Peut-être voulait-il faire trop de choses, mais il en fit inconstestablement beaucoup d'utiles. À l'intérieur, il favorisa avec suite et intelligence les progrès de l'agriculture, de l'industrie et du commerce; à l'extérieur, si sa politique ne fut pas toujours conforme à nos traditions, elle ne manqua pas d'éclat.[35]

[The Emperor may not have possessed all the qualities of a sovereign, but he had several, and it would be absurd to imagine that the success that marked the first part of his reign was due purely to chance. Perhaps he wanted to do too many things, but it is indisputable that he did do many useful things. Domestically, he encouraged agricultural, industrial and commercial progress in a coherent and intelligent manner; externally, if his policy did not always conform to our traditons, it did not lack panache.]

Paradoxically, the British press, particularly *The Times*, devoted pages to a resumé of his reign, and accounts of his illness. Although critical of some aspects of his reign and his seemingly erratic foreign policy, *The Times* said, in part: 'All his schemes for her domestic improvement, for the emancipation of her trade and industry, and the extension of commerce by new and unheard of channels were magnificent.'[36] It also commented on the reaction of the French press, which, it said, wanted to put the blame for all France's problems on the shoulders of one man, and to condemn him for his failures while conveniently forgetting his successes. They seemed to forget that France was at the present time in a state of political turmoil, which was perhaps more worrying than some of the years under Napoleon:

Not one of the many factions into which France has divided herself is at all in a condition to boast either of what it has done since the

downfall of the Emperor, of its present position, or of its prospects.
A third year has come upon this sea of troubles, and finds them all
engaged in a vain attempt to agree upon the mere outlines of the
Constitution that is to be.[37]

Despite his defeat and failures, it is impossible to deny his personal
qualities of kindness and gentleness and a refusal to blame others who
were equally or more responsible for the final disaster. As a person the
English admired him greatly, and more than twenty thousand people
visited Chislehurst, the place of his death, in the days before his funeral.
A journalist with *The Times* commented that Napoleon was justified in
feeling bitter after his defeat. Also, his illness, the bladder stones that
had plagued him for so many years, was so bad he had every reason to
be deeply depressed, but

> he not only preserved his apparent serenity, but displayed invariably
> that dignified courtesy which denotes a man too stable to be easily
> shaken . . . Beset by a mortal malady which would have made most
> men irritable and captious, the Emperor has shown himself invariably
> calm and strong. Nothing perhaps, is so admirable in the life of this
> remarkable man as the silence he has consistently preserved with
> regard to those whose ill-advised counsels, incapacity and self-inter-
> ested falsehoods contributed so largely to his ruin.[38]

Émile de Girardin, a journalist with *Liberté*, also wrote of Napoleon's
qualities, concluding with a well-known epithet:

> L'empereur possède au plus haut degré deux qualités souveraines: la
> bonté et la douceur. S'il n'en eût pas été essentiellement doué, nous
> eussions eu, le lendemain du 2 décembre 1851, le despotisme et le
> despote, tandis que nous avons eu la tyrannie sans avoir le tyran . . .
> Nul n'a des intentions meilleures. Nul n'a des tendances plus
> justes. Nul n'a plus profondément le sentiment qui correspond aux
> inspirations des masses, aussi existe-t-il entre elles et lui un courant
> sympathique qui a résisté à des épreuves sous lesquelles eût suc-
> combé tout autre prince régnant.
> Au temps où l'on décernent aux souverains des surnoms, on l'eût
> surnommé Napoléon *le Bien-intentionné*.[39]

> [The Emperor possessed two sovereign qualities to the highest
> degree: kindness and gentleness. If he had not been blessed with

these qualities we would have had, in the aftermath of the 2 December 1851, despotism and the despot, but instead we have had tyranny without the tyrant... None had better intentions. None had sounder sympathies. None had a deeper understanding of the people's wishes, and between them and him was a sympathetic accord which withstood the hardships under which any other reigning prince would have given way. In a time when one confers epithets on sovereigns, he would be known as 'Napoleon the well-intentioned'.]

Foremost among those good intentions was his desire for a united Europe with a respect for nationalities. However, it was his attachment to the principle of nationalities that, in the end, caused his downfall. It encouraged him to accept the eventuality of German unification, his hatred of the Treaties of Vienna perhaps preventing him from seeing the dangers, envisaged by Talleyrand and others, of the potential aggression of such a large national group. Jean-Michel Gaillard concluded that his passion for nationalities prevented him seeing that the interests of France were better served by a divided Germany:

Ainsi, guidé par des idées généreuses mais contradictoires, Napoléon III a mené une politique extérieure ambitieuse qui aboutit à l'inverse de ce qui était souhaitable pour son pays. Certes, le principe des nationalités a triomphé en Italie et en Allemagne, et l'ordre de Vienne a été détruit. Mais le prix payé en vies humaines dans les conflits qu'il a conduits (lui qui avait promis la paix) et la nouvelle carte de l'Europe qui en est résultée montrent à l'évidence que son règne peut être considéré comme l'une des pages les plus noires de l'histoire diplomatique de la France et de l'Europe.[40]

[Thus, guided by generous but contradictory ideas, Napoleon III conducted an ambitious foreign policy whose result was entirely contrary to what was most desirable for his country. Certainly, the principle of nationalities triumphed in Italy and Germany, and the order determined by the Treaties of Vienna has been destroyed. But the price paid in human lives in the conflicts in which he was involved – he who promised peace – and the new map of Europe which has resulted shows quite clearly that his reign can be considered as one of the blackest pages in the diplomatic history of France and of Europe.]

Italy and Germany were finally united, but Napoleon III's ideas for a new European order, based on nationalities and shared interests, did not come to fruition as he had hoped, and France was to suffer again. The suspicions of his conservative neighbours and their memories of the First Empire prevented such forward-looking ideas being achieved in the nineteenth century. Were they Utopian, and should his reign be condemned, as Gaillard has condemned it? His plans were not achieved, but others, who have seen the necessity of following his pioneering role, have realised some of them. That he was genuine in his intentions is difficult to doubt, for foremost among Napoleon's characteristics were those of sincerity and concern for others. In all his correspondence that I have read, both official and to family, friends and others entirely unknown to him, that quality of sincerity is striking. He may be accused of making errors of judgement relating to the situation in Mexico and to his representatives, for example, but his stated motives were genuine.

It was almost inevitable, however, that a more traditional and ambitious politician ensured that Napoleon's view of the world was unfulfilled for a hundred years. It was 'Bismarck who, carried forward by romantic enthusiasm and the unmatched discipline of a nation at the height of its powers which he was able to galvanise into action, reached his deliberately restricted objectives and so clothed the tattered Europe of Napoleon III in his own kind of tunic'.[41] It took some decades and two devastating world wars before others began the slow process of fulfilling his vision, at least in part. Napoleon III was not so unrealistic after all, but little, if any, recognition has been given to him as the visionary who foresaw the establishment of the United Nations and related organisations, and a European Parliament.

Appendix 1

Convention between Great Britain, Spain and France, relative to Combined Operations against Mexico.
Signed at London, October 31, 1861.
Ratifications exchanged at London, November 15, 1861.

Sa Majesté l'Empereur des Français, Sa Majesté la Reine d'Espagne et Sa Majesté la Reine de la Grande-Bretagne et d'Irlande se trouvant placées, par la conduite arbitraire et vexatoire des autorités de la république du Mexique, dans la nécessité d'exiger de ces autorités une protection plus efficace pour les personnes et les propriétés de leurs sujets, ainsi que l'exécution des obligations contractées envers elles par la république du Mexique, se sont entendues pour conclure entre elles une convention, dans le but de combiner leur action commune, et, à cet effet, ont nommé pour leurs plénipotentiaires, savoir:

Sa Majesté l'Empereur des Français, S. Exc. le comte de Flahault de la Billarderie, sénateur, général de division, grand'croix de l'ordre impérial de la Légion d'honneur, son ambassadeur extraordinaire auprès de Sa Majesté la Reine de la Grande-Bretagne et d'Irlande;

Sa Majesté la reine d'Espagne, S. Exc. don Xavier de Isturiz y Montero, chevalier de l'ordre insigne de la Toison d'or, grand'croix de l'ordre royal de Charles III, grand'croix de l'ordre impérial de la Légion d'honneur, sénateur du royaume, son envoyé extraordinaire et ministre plénipotentiaire à la cour de Sa Majesté la Reine du royaume-uni de la Grande-Bretagne et d'Irlande;

Sa Majesté la Reine de la Grande-Bretagne et d'Irlande, le très-honorable Jean comte Russell, vicomte Amberley de Amberley et Artsalla, pair du royaume-uni, conseiller de Sa Majesté en son conseil privé, principal secrétaire d'État de Sa Majesté pour les affaires étrangères;

Lesquels, après avoir échangé leurs pouvoirs, sont tombés d'accord pour arrêter les articles suivants:

Art. 1er. Sa Majesté l'Empereur des Français, Sa Majesté la Reine d'Espagne et Sa Majesté la Reine de la Grande-Bretagne et d'Irlande s'engagent à arrêter, aussitôt après la signature de la présente convention, les dispositions nécessaires pour envoyer sur les côtes du Mexique des forces de terre et de mer combinées dont l'effectif sera déterminé par un échange ultérieur de communications entre leurs gouvernments, mais dont l'ensemble devra être suffisant pour pouvoir saisir et occuper les différentes forteresses et positions militaires du littoral mexicain.

Les commandants des forces alliées seront, en outre, autorisés à accomplir les autres opérations qui seraient jugées, sur les lieux, les plus propres à réaliser le but spécifié dans le préambule de la présente convention, et notamment à assurer la sécurité des résidents étrangers.

Toutes les mesures dont il s'agit dans cet article seront prises au nom et pour le comte les hautes parties contractantes, sans acception de la nationalité particulière des forces employées à les exécuter.

Art. 2. Les hautes parties contractantes s'engagent à ne rechercher pour elles-mêmes, dans l'emploi des mesures coercitives prévues par la présents convention, aucune acquisition de territoire ni aucun avantage particulier, et à n'exercer, dans les affaires intérieures du Mexique, aucune influence de nature à porter atteinte au droit de la nation mexicaine de choisir et de constituer librement la forme de son gouvernement.

Art. 3. Une commission composée de trois commissaires, un nommé par chacune des puissances contractantes, sera établie avec plein pouvoir de statuer sur toutes les questions que pourraient soulever l'emploi et la distribution des sommes d'argent qui seront recouvrées au Mexique, en ayant égard aux droits respectifs des parties contractantes.

Art. 4. Les hautes parties contractantes désirant, en outre, que les mesures qu'elles ont l'intention d'adopter n'aient pas un caractère exclusif, et sachant que le gouvernement des États-Unis a, de son côté, des réclamations à faire valoir, comme elles, contre la république mexicaine, conviennent qu'aussitôt après la signature de la présente convention il en sera communiqué une copie au gouvernement des États-Unis; que ce gouvernement sera invité à y accéder, et qu'en prévision de cette accession, leurs ministres respectifs à Washington seront immédiatement munis de leurs pleins pouvoirs à l'effet de conclure et de signer collectivement ou séparément, avec le plénipotentiaire désigné par le président des États-Unis, une convention identique, sauf suppression du présent article, à celles qu'elles signent à la date de ce jour. Mais comme les hautes parties contractantes s'exposeraient, en apportant quelque retard à la mise à exécution des articles 1 et 2 de la présente convention, à manquer le but qu'elles désirent atteindre, elles sont tombées d'accord de ne pas différer, en vue d'obtenir l'accession du gouvernement des États-Unis, le commencement des opérations susmentionnées au delà de l'époque à laquelle leurs forces combinées pourront être réunies dans les parages de Vera-Cruz.

Art. 5. La présente convention sera ratifiée, et les ratifications en seront échangées à Londres dans le délai de quinze jours.

En foi de quoi, les plénipotentiaires respectifs l'ont signée et y ont apposé le sceau de leurs armes.

Fait à Londres, en triple original, le trente et unième jour du mois d'octobre de l'an de gráce mil huit cent soixante et un.

(L.S.) Signé FLAHAULT
(L.S.) Signé XAVIER DE ISTURIZ
(L.S.) Signé RUSSELL

[His Majesty the Emperor of the French, Her Majesty the Queen of Spain, and Her Majesty the Queen of Great Britain and Ireland, being compelled by the arbitrary and vexatious conduct of the authorities of the Republic of Mexico to demand from those authorities more effective protection for the persons and properties of their subjects, as well as the fulfilment of the obligations contracted towards them by the Republic of Mexico, have agreed to conclude a Convention with a view to combining their common action, and, for this purpose, have named as their Plenipotentiaries, to wit:–

His Majesty the Emperor of the French, His Excellency the Count de Flahault de la Billarderie, Senator, Lieutenant-General, Grand Cross of the Imperial Order of the Legion of Honour, His Ambassador Extraordinary to Her Majesty the Queen of Great Britain and Ireland;

Her Majesty the Queen of Spain, His Excellency Don Xavier de Isturiz y Montero, Knight of the Illustrious Order of the Golden Fleece, Grand Cross of the Royal Order of Charles III, Grand Cross of the Imperial Order of the Legion of Honour, Senator of the Kingdom, Her Envoy Extraordinary and Plenipotentiary Minister at the court of Her Majesty the Queen of the United Kingdom of Great Britain and Ireland;

Her Majesty the Queen of Great Britain and Ireland, the Right Honourable John Earl Russell, Viscount Amberley of Amberley and Artsalla, a Peer of the United Kingdom, a Member of Her Britannic Majesty's Privy Council, Her Majesty's Principal Secretary of State for Foreign Affairs;

Who, after having exchanged their credentials, have agreed upon the following Articles:–

ARTICLE I: His Majesty the Emperor of the French, Her Majesty the Queen of Spain, and Her Majesty the Queen of Great Britain and Ireland, engage to make, immediately after the signature of the present Convention, the necessary arrangements for dispatching to the coasts of Mexico combined naval and military forces, whose strength shall be determined by a further exchange of communications between their Governments, but of which the total shall be sufficient to seize and occupy the several fortresses and military positions on the Mexican coast.

The Commanders of the allied forces shall be, moreover, authorised to execute other operations which may be considered, at the time, most suitable to effect the aim specified in the preamble of the present Convention, and specifically to ensure the security of foreign residents.

All the measures contemplated in this Article shall be taken in the name and on the account of the High Contracting Parties without reference to the particular nationality of the forces employed to execute them.

ARTICLE II: The High Contracting Parties engage not to seek for themselves, in the employment of the coercive measures contemplated by the present Convention, any acquisition of territory nor any special advantage, and, not to exercise in the internal affairs of Mexico any influence of a nature to prejudice the right of the Mexican nation to choose and to freely constitute the form of its Government.

ARTICLE III: A Commission composed of three Commissioners, one to be named by each of the Contracting Powers, shall be established with full authority to determine all questions that may arise as to the application and distribution of the sums of money which shall be recovered from Mexico, having regard to the respective rights of the Contracting Parties.

ARTICLE IV: The High Contracting Parties desiring, moreover, that the measures which they intend to adopt should not bear an exclusive character, and being aware that the Government of the United States on its part has, like them, claims to enforce upon the Mexican Republic, agree that immediately after the signature of the present Convention a copy thereof shall be communicated to the Government of the United States; that that Government shall be invited to accede to it, and that in anticipation of that accession, their respective Ministers in Washington shall be at once furnished with full powers for the purpose of concluding and signing, collectively or separately, with the plenipotentiary designated by the President of the United States, a Convention identical to that which they sign this day, except for the suppression of the present Article. But as by delaying the execution of Articles I and II of the present Convention, the High Contracting Parties would risk failing in the object which they desire to attain, they have agreed not to defer, with the view of obtaining the accession of the Government of the United States, the commencement of the above-mentioned operations beyond the time at which their combined forces can be assembled in the vicinity of Vera Cruz.

ARTICLE V: The present Convention shall be ratified, and the ratifications thereof shall be exchanged at London within fifteen days.

In witness thereof the respective Plenipotentiaries have signed it, and have fixed thereto the seal of their arms.

Concluded at London, in triplicate, the thirty-first day of the month of October, in the year of grace one thousand eight hundred and sixty-one.]

Appendix 2

Convention concluded at Miramar 10 April 1864 between France and Mexico

Le Gouvernement de S.M. l'Empereur des Français et celui de S.M. l'Empereur du Mexique, animés d'un désir égal d'assurer le rétablissement de l'ordre au Mexique et de consolider le nouvel empire, ont résolu de régler par une convention les conditions du séjour des troupes françaises dans ce pays, et ont nommé pour leurs plénipotentiaires à cet effet, savoir:

S.M. l'Empereur des Français, M. Charles-François-Edourad Herbet, ministre plénipotentiaire de 1er classe, conseiller d'État, directeur au ministère des Affaires étrangères, grand-officier de son Ordre impérial de la Légion-d'honneur, etc.,

Et S.M. l'Empereur du Mexique, M. Joaquin Velasquez de Léon, son ministre d'État sans portefeuille, grand-officier de l'ordre distingué de Notre-Dame de Guadelupe, etc.,

Lesquels, après s'être communiqué leurs pleins pouvoirs, trouvés en bonne et due forme, sont convenus des articles suivants:

Article 1er. Les troupes françaises qui se trouvent actuellement au Mexique seront réduites le plus tôt possible à un corps de 25,000 hommes, y compris la légion étrangère.

Ce corps, pour sauvegarder les intérêts qui ont motivé l'intervention, restera temporairement au Mexique dans les conditions réglées par les articles suivants.

Art. 2. Les troupes françaises évacueront le Mexique au fur et à mesure que S.M. l'Empereur du Mexique pourra organiser les troupes nécessaires pour les remplacer.

Art. 3. La légion étrangère au service de la France, composée de 8,000 hommes, demeurera néanmoins encore pendant six années au Mexique, après que toutes les autres forces françaises auront été rappelées conformément à l'article 2. À dater de ce moment, ladite légion passera au service et à la solde du Gouvernement mexicain. Le Gouvernement mexicain se réserve la faculté d'abréger la durée de l'emploi au Mexique de la légion étrangère.

Art. 4. Les points du territoire à occuper par les troupes françaises, ainsi que les expéditions militaires de ces troupes, s'il y a lieu, seront déterminés de commun accord et directement entre S.M. l'Empereur du Mexique et le commandant en chef du corps français.

Art. 5. Sur les points où la garnison ne sera pas exclusivement composée de troupes mexicaines, le commandement militaire sera dévolu au commandant français.

En cas d'expéditions combinées de troupes françaises et mexicaines, le commandant supérieur de ces troupes appartiendra également au commandant français.

Art. 6. Les commandants français ne pourront intervenir dans aucune branche de l'administration mexicaine.

Art. 7. Tant que les besoins du corps d'armée français nécessiteront tous les deux mois un service de transports entre la France et le port de Vera-Cruz, les frais de ce service, fixés à la somme de 400,000 francs par voyage (aller et retour), seront supportés par le Gouvernement mexicain et payés à Mexico.

Art. 8. Les stations navales que la France entretient dans les Antilles et dans l'océan Pacifique enverront souvent des navires montrer le drapeau français dans les ports du Mexique.

Art. 9. Les frais de l'expédition française au Mexique à rembourser par le Gouvernement mexicain sont fixés à la somme de 270 millions pour tout le temps de la durée de cette expédition jusqu'au 1er juillet 1864. Cette somme sera productive d'intérêts à raison de 3 pour 100 par an.

A partir du 1er juillet, toutes les dépenses de l'armée mexicaine restent à la charge du Mexique.

Art. 10. L'indemnité à payer à la France par le Gouvernement mexicain, pour dépense de solde, nourriture et entretien des troupes du corps d'armée à partir du 1er juillet 1864, demeure fixée à la somme de 1,000 francs par homme et par an.

Art. 11. Le Gouvernement mexicain remettra immédiatement au Gouvernement français la somme de 66 millions en titres de l'emprunt au taux d'émission, savoir: 54 millions en déduction de la dette mentionnée dans l'article 9, et 12 millions comme à compte sur les indemnités dues à des Français en vertu de l'article 14 de la présente convention.

Art. 12. Pour le payement du surplus des frais de la guerre et pour l'acquittement des charges mentionnées dans articles 7, 10 et 14, le Gouvernement mexicain s'engage à payer annuellement à la France la somme de 25 millions en numéraire. Cette somme sera imputée: 1° sur les sommes dues en vertu desdits articles 7 et 10; 2° sur le montant, en intérêts et principal, de la somme fixée dans l'article 9; 3° sur les indemnités qui resteront dues à des sujets français en vertu des articles 14 et suivants.

Art. 13. Le Gouvernement mexicain versera, le dernier jour de chaque mois, à Mexico, entre les mains du payeur général de l'armée, ce qu'il devra pour couvrir les dépenses des troupes françaises au Mexique, conformément à l'article 10.

Art. 14. Le Gouvernement mexicain s'engage à indemniser les sujets français des préjudices qu'ils ont indûment soufferts et qui ont motivé l'expédition.

Art. 15. Une commission mixte, composée de trois Français et de trois Mexicains, nommés par leurs Gouvernements respectifs, se réunira à Mexico dans un délai de trois mois pour examiner et régler ces réclamations.

Art. 16. Une commission de révision, composée de deux Français et de deux Mexicains, désignés de la même manière, siégeant à Paris, procédera à la liquidation définitive des réclamations déjà admises par la commission désignée dans l'article précédent, et statuera sur celles dont la révision lui aura été réservée.

Art. 17. Le gouvernement français remettra en liberté tous les prisonniers de guerre mexicains dès que l'Empereur du Mexique sera entré dans ses États.

Art. 18. La présente convention sera ratifiée et les ratifications en seront échangées le plus tôt que faire se pourra.

Fait au château de Miramar, le 10 avril 1864.

Signé: HERBET, JOAQUIN VELASQUEZ DE LEON

[The Government of His Majesty the Emperor of the French and that of His Majesty the Emperor of Mexico, prompted by the same desire, to ensure the reestablishment of order in Mexico and to consolidate the new empire, have resolved to regulate by means of a convention the terms relating to the sojourn of French troops in that country, and have named as their plenipotentiaries for this purpose, to wit:

His Majesty Emperor of the French, M. Charles-François-Edouard Herbet, plenipotentiary minister first class, Senior member of the Council of State, under-secretary to the Ministry of Foreign Affairs, grand officer of the Imperial Order of the Legion of Honour, etc.

And His Majesty the Emperor of Mexico, M. Joaquin Velasquez de Léon, his Minister of State without portfolio, grand officer of the Distinguished Order of Our Lady of Guadelupe, etc.

Who, after having exchanged their credentials which have been found in good and due order, have agreed upon the following Articles:-

ARTICLE 1: The French troops who are at present in Mexico will be reduced as soon as possible to a corps of 25,000 men, including the Foreign Legion.

This corps, in order to safeguard the interests which have prompted the intervention, will remain in Mexico temporarily, under conditions regulated by the following articles.

ARTICLE 2: The French troops will leave Mexico progressively, as the Emperor of Mexico is able to organise the necessary troops to replace them.

ARTICLE 3: The Foreign Legion in France's service, comprising 8,000 men, nevertheless will remain in Mexico for six years, after all the the other French forces have been withdrawn in compliance with Article 2. From that time, the said Legion will pass into the service and pay of the Mexican Government. The Mexican Government reserves the right to determine the duration of the employment of the Foreign Legion in Mexico.

ARTICLE 4: The areas of the territory to be occupied by the French troops, as well as the military expeditions of these troops, if they occur, will be determined by joint agreement directly between His Majesty the Emperor of Mexico and the Commander-in-Chief of the French corps.

ARTICLE 5: In those areas where the garrison is not composed exclusively of Mexican troops, the military command will be devolved to the French commander.

In the case of expeditions combining French and Mexican troops, the senior command of these troops will also belong to the French commander.

ARTICLE 6: The French commanders may not intervene in any branch of the Mexican administration.

ARTICLE 7: As long as the requirements of the French army corps necessitate a transport service between France and the port of Vera Cruz every two months, the cost of this service, fixed at 400,000 francs per return voyage, will be borne by the Mexican Government and be paid in Mexico.

ARTICLE 8: The naval stations that France maintains in the Antilles and in the Pacific Ocean will regularly send ships to show the French flag in Mexican ports.

ARTICLE 9: The costs of the French expedition to Mexico which are to be reimbursed by the Mexican Government are fixed at the sum of 270 million for the entire period of the expedition up to 1 July 1864. This sum will incur interest at the rate of 3 per cent per annum.

Commencing from 1 July, all the expenses of the Mexican army remain the responsibility of Mexico.

ARTICLE 10: The compensation to be paid to France by the Mexican Government for expenditure, involving pay, provisions and maintenance of the troops of the army corps, will remain fixed at the rate of 1,000 francs per man per year, commencing from 1 July 1864.

ARTICLE 11: The Mexican Government will immediately pay the French Government the sum of 66 million as security for the loan at the rate of issue, that is: 54 million deductable from the debt specified in Article 9, and 12 million as payment of compensation due to French nationals as laid out in Article 14 of the present convention.

ARTICLE 12: In payment of the surplus costs of the war and in settlement of the expenses mentioned in Articles 7, 10 and 14, the Mexican Government agrees to pay France annually the sum of 25 million in legal tender. This sum will be defrayed to: (1) the amount owing in virtue of the said Articles 7 and 10; (2) to the total, in interest and principal, of the amount fixed in Article 9; (3) to the compensation which will still be owed to French subjects as laid out in Articles 14 and following.

ARTICLE 13: On the last day of each month the Mexican Government will pay to the army paymaster in Mexico City the amount necessary to cover the expenses of the French troops in Mexico, in accordance with Article 10.

ARTICLE 14: The Mexican Government agrees to compensate the French subjects for the losses they have unduly suffered and which motivated the expedition.

ARTICLE 15: A joint commission, composed of three French and three Mexicans, nominated by their respective governments, will meet in Mexico City in three months to examine and settle these claims.

ARTICLE 16: A commission of review, located in Paris, composed of two French and two Mexicans, designated in the same way, will carry out the final settlement of the claims already admitted by the commission designated in the preceding Article, and give a ruling on those for which it is the final authority.

ARTICLE 17: The French Government will release all Mexican prisoners of war when the Emperor of Mexico is fully instated.

ARTICLE 18: The present convention will be ratified and the ratifications will be exchanged as soon as possible.

Concluded at the château of Miramar, 10 April 1864.

Signé: HERBET, JOAQUIN VELASQUEZ DE LEON

Notes and References

Introduction

1. Paul Gaulot, *L'Expédition du Mexique 1861–1867 d'après les documents et souvenirs de Ernest Louet Payeur en chef du Corps Expéditionnaire*, 2 vols (Paris, 1906).
2. Egon Cæsar Count Corti, *Maximilian and Charlotte of Mexico*. Translated from the German by Catherine Alison Phillips (Archon Books, 1968 © 1928).
3. Michel Chevalier, *Mexico Ancient and Modern*, 2 vols. Translated under the author's superintendence by Thomas Alpass (London, 1864).
4. Daniel Dawson, *The Mexican Adventure* (London, 1935).
5. Christian Schefer, *La Grande Pensée de Napoléon III: Les Origines de l'Expédition du Mexique (1858–1862)* (Paris, 1939).
6. Carl H. Bock, *Prelude to Tragedy: The Negotiation and Breakdown of the Tripartite Convention of London, October 31 1861* (Philadelphia, 1966).
7. Ralph Roeder, *Juarez and his Mexico*, 2 vols (New York, 1947). Roeder's work was termed a biographical history, and was praised as one of the best books written in English on the history of Mexico. He has an enormous bibliography but has provided no citations whatsoever, which makes it difficult to confirm the validity of his sources. However, his opinions on Saligny, for example, are generally supported by other sources I have quoted. His archival sources included the private archives of Benito Juarez and the ten-volume Bazaine archives kept in Texas, which contain valuable material relating to the intervention. His secondary sources include Mexican, French and English published works.
8. See Joan Haslip, *Imperial Adventurer: Emperor Maximilian of Mexico and his Empress* (London, 1974 © 1971); Shirley Black, *Napoleon III and the French Intervention in Mexico: A Quest for Silver* (PhD dissertation, University of Oklahoma, 1974); Gary M. Poulton, *Great Britain and the Intervention in Mexico 1861–1865* (PhD dissertation, Miami University, 1976).
9. Shirley Black, *op. cit.*, pp. 109–10.
10. Jean-François Lecaillon, *Napoléon III et le Mexique: Les illusions d'un grand dessein* (Paris, 1994).
11. James F. McMillan, *Napoleon III* (London, 1991), p. 65.
12. Lynn M. Case (ed.), *French Opinion on the United States and Mexico 1860–1867* (Archon Books, 1969 © 1936), pp. 331ff.
13. William E. Echard, *Napoleon III and the Concert of Europe* (Baton Rouge, 1983).
14. James F. McMillan, *op. cit.*, p. 81.
15. Stuart L. Campbell, *The Second Empire Revisited: A Study in French Historiography* (New Jersey, 1978), p. 2.
16. Napoleon III, 'Des Idées napoléoniennes', *Œuvres de Napoléon III*, Vol. I (Paris, 1869), p. 158.
17. Émile Ollivier, 'Napoléon III: Son dessein international', *La Revue des Deux Mondes (RDM)*, 146 (1 March 1898), p. 50.

18. A. J. Hanna and K. A. Hanna, *Napoleon III and Mexico: American Triumph Over Monarchy* (Chapel Hill, 1971), pp. 66–7.
19. Napoleon III, 'Le Canal de Nicaragua', *Œuvres de Napoléon III*, (Paris, 1869), Vol. 2, pp. 542–3.
20. Discours de l'Empereur à l'ouverture de la Session Legislatif de 1854, le 1 février 1854. Archives Nationales (AN): 400AP 54, Archives napoléon.
21. Lord Augustus Loftus to Russell, 19 April 1860. Public Record Office (PRO): FO519/198, Cowley Papers.
22. Persigny to Conseil général de la Loire, 27 August 1860. Recounted by Émile Ollivier, *L'Empire libéral*, Vol. 5 (Paris, 1900), pp. 66–7.
23. Émile Ollivier, 'Napoléon III: Son dessin international', p. 53.
24. Napoleon III, 'Des Idées napoléoniennes', p. 162.
25. William E. Echard, *op. cit.*, pp. 2–3.
26. *Ibid.*, pp. 182–3.
27. Alain Plessis, *The Rise and Fall of the Second Empire 1852–1871*. Translated by Jonathon Mandelbaum (Cambridge, 1987), pp. 8–9. In 1840, after a failed attempt to enter France at Boulogne and overthrow the Orleanist regime, Louis Napoleon was arrested, tried and sentenced to life imprisonment at the fortress of Ham in Picardy. He remained there for six years before escaping to England where he waited for a further opportunity to pursue his destiny in France.
28. Discours de l'Empereur à l'ouverture de la Session Legislatif de 1859, le 7 février 1859. AN: 400AP 54, Archives napoléon.
29. F. J. C. Hearnshaw, 'The European Revolution and After, 1848–1854', *The Cambridge History of British Foreign Policy 1783–1919*, edited by Sir A. W. Ward and G. P. Gooch (Cambridge, 1923), pp. 335–6.
30. Kenneth Bourne, *The Foreign Policy of Victorian England 1830–1902* (London, 1970).

1 Prelude to Intervention

1. G. M. Poulton, *Great Britain and the Intervention in Mexico* (PhD, Miami University, 1976) pp. 12–13.
2. William H. Goetzmann, *When the Eagle Screamed: The Romantic Horizon in American Diplomacy 1800–1860* (New York, 1966), pp. 19–20.
3. *Ibid.*
4. *Ibid.*, pp. 74–5.
5. *Ibid.*, p. 82.
6. *The Times* (London), 3 June 1856. Quoted by Kenneth Bourne, *Britain and the Balance of Power in North America 1815–1908* (London, 1967), pp. 200–1.
7. *The Economist*, 14 June 1856.
8. William H. Goetzmann, *op. cit.*, p. 82.
9. See note 27 in the Introduction.
10. Wilfred Hardy Callcott, *Church and State in Mexico, 1822–1857* (New York, 1965, © 1926), pp. 88ff. and 132ff.
11. *Ibid.*, p. 249.
12. *Ibid.*, p. 315.
13. *Ibid.*

14. Ralph Roeder, *Juarez and his Mexico* (New York, 1947), Vol. 1, p. 193.
15. Walewski to Pelissier, French Minister in London, 18 September 1858. Archives du Ministère des Affaires Étrangères (AMAE): Correspondance Politique (CP) Angleterre, Vol. 711.
16. In a dispatch from Pelissier to Walewski, 27 September 1858. AMAE: CP Angleterre, Vol. 711.
17. Fournier, the French minister in Madrid, to Walewski, 7 November 1858. AMAE: CP Espagne, Vol. 852.
18. Buchanan to Russell, 7 November 1858. PRO: FO 72/940.
19. Buchanan to Russell, 8 November 1858. PRO: FO 72/940.
20. Fournier to Walewski, (n.d.) AMAE: CP Espagne, Vol. 852.
21. Raymond Carr, *Spain 1808–1939* (Oxford, 1975, © 1966), p. 260.
22. Collantes to Mon, 9 December 1858. *Archives Diplomatiques (AD)*, Vol. 3, 1862, pp. 207–8.
23. *Ibid.*
24. Buchanan to Russell, 20 July 1859 and 24 August 1859. Quoted by Daniel Dawson, *The Mexican Adventure* (London, 1935) p. 39.
25. Letter from Mexico, printed in *The Times*, 3 January 1859.
26. Ralph Roeder, *op. cit.*, Vol. 1, p. 205.
27. Collantes to Mon and Isturiz, 18 April 1860. *AD*, Vol. 3, 1862, pp. 211–13.
28. Isturiz to Collantes, 27 April 1860. *Ibid.*, p. 213.
29. Mon to Collantes, 4 May 1860. *Ibid.*, p. 214.
30. Collantes to Isturiz, 11 May 1860. *Ibid.*, p. 215.
31. Russell to Mathew, 24 August 1860. *British and Foreign State Papers (State Papers)*, Vol. 51, pp. 548–9.
32. Dated Mexico City, 15 October 1860, published in *The Times*, 13 November, 1860.
33. Saligny to Serrano, 1 December 1860. *AD*, Vol. 3, 1862, pp. 243–5.
34. Report of the retiring American Minister in Mexico in 1859. Quoted by Ralph Roeder, *op. cit.*, Vol. 1, p. 190.
35. *Ibid.*, p. 191. Although Roeder does not elaborate on this observation it is possible to conjecture that ministers at such a distance from their governments with extreme delays in communication, were either hesitant in their actions from insecurity, or alternatively acted with supreme confidence, as Roeder implies, and were prepared to make momentous decisions without reference to their governments first.
36. Christian Schefer, *op. cit.*, p. 64. Nancy N. Barker, 'The French Legation in Mexico: Nexus of Interventionists', *French Historical Studies*, VIII (1974), p. 411.
37. *Ibid.*
38. *Ibid.*, pp. 412–17.
39. Oseguera to Persigny, 8 April 1861. AMAE: CP Mexique, Vol. 54.
40. Ralph Roeder, *op. cit.*, Vol. 1, p. 278.
41. *Ibid.*, p. 279.
42. Saligny to Thouvenel, 15 March 1861. *AD*, Vol. 1, 1862, pp. 119–20.
43. Saligny to Thouvenel, 28 April 1861. *Ibid.*, p. 121.
44. Saligny to Thouvenel, 7 May 1861 (r. 30 June). AMAE: CP Mexique, Vol. 54.
45. Wilfred Hardy Callcott, *op. cit.*, p. 282.
46. Alain Plessis, *The Rise and Fall of the Second Empire 1852–1871*, translated by Jonathon Mandelbaum (Cambridge, 1987), p. 12.

47. Saligny to Thouvenel, 12 June 1861. *AD*, Vol 1, 1862, pp. 121–2.
48. Saligny to Thouvenel, 5 July 1861. *Ibid.*, p. 123.
49. Ralph Roeder, *op. cit.*, Vol. 1, p. 346.
50. Mathew to Russell, 12 May 1861 (r. 27 June). *State Papers*, Vol. 52, pp. 251–2.
51. Russell to Wyke, 30 March 1861. *Ibid.*, pp. 237–8.
52. *Ibid.*, p. 238.
53. *Ibid.*, p. 241.
54. *Ibid.*, p. 242.
55. Wyke to Russell, 27 May 1861. *Ibid.*, p. 255.
56. Wyke to Russell, 25 June 1861 (r. 29 July). *Parliamentary Papers: Correspondence relating to affairs in Mexico (Parliamentary Papers)* (London, 1862), Part 1, p. 21.
57. *Ibid.*
58. Ralph Roeder, *op. cit.*, Vol. 1, pp. 322–3.
59. Wyke to Zamacona, 19 July 1861. *State Papers*, Vol. 52, p. 297.
60. Zamacona to Wyke, 21 July 1861. *Ibid.*, pp. 298–9.
61. Wyke to Zamacona, 22 July 1861. *Ibid.*, p. 305.
62. Wyke to Zamacona, 23 July 1861. *Ibid.*, p. 307.
63. Zamacona to Wyke, 25 July 1861. *Ibid.*, p. 309.
64. Wyke to Russell, 26 July 1861 (r. 29 August). *Ibid.*, p. 294.
65. Wyke to Russell, 28 July 1861 (r. 29 August). *Parliamentary Papers*, Part 1, p. 51.
66. Wyke to Zamacona, 30 July 1861 (Enclosure Wyke to Russell, 8 August (r. 29 September). *State Papers*, Vol. 52, pp. 333–4.
67. Zamacona to Saligny, 21 July 1861. AMAE: CP Mexique, Vol. 55.
68. Saligny to Thouvenel, 27 July 1861 (r. 30 August). AMAE: CP Mexique, Vol. 55.
69. *AD*, Vol. 4, 1862, p. 146.
70. Thouvenel to Saligny, 5 September 1861. *AD*, Vol. 1, 1862, p. 125.
71. Ralph Roeder, *op. cit.*, Vol. 1, pp. 346–7.
72. Schlœsing to Bazaine, 14 October 1863. Quoted by Paul Gaulot, *op. cit.*, Vol. 1, pp. 425–6.
73. Russell to Wyke, 21 August 1861. *Parliamentary Papers*, Part 1, p. 30.
74. Russell to Wyke, 10 September 1861. *Ibid.*, p. 53.
75. Ministre des Relations Extérieure de la République Mexicaine to Collantes, 21 February 1861. *AD*, Vol. 3, 1862, pp. 284–6.
76. Collantes to Serrano, 9 July 1861. *Ibid.*, pp. 289–90.
77. Mon to the Spanish Chamber of Deputies, 7 January 1863. *AD*, Vol. 2, 1863, p. 39.
78. Wyke to Russell, 27 August 1861 (r. 29 September). PRO: FO 50/354.
79. Saligny to Thouvenel, 28 August 1861 (r. 30 September). AMAE: CP Mexique, Vol. 55.

2   The Tripartite Convention

1. Mon to Collantes, 6 September 1861. *AD*, Vol. 2, 1863, p. 41.
2. Collantes to Mon, 6 September 1861. *AD*, Vol. 3, 1862, p. 290.
3. Mon to Cortes, 7 January 1863. *AD*, Vol. 2, 1863, p. 42.

4. Mon to Collantes, 9 September 1861. *Ibid.*
5. *Ibid.*
6. Collantes to Serrano, 11 September 1861. *AD*, Vol. 3, 1862, pp. 293–7.
7. Crampton to Russell, 16 September 1861. *Parliamentary Papers*, Part 1, p. 55.
8. Mon to the Cortes, 7 January 1863. *AD*, Vol. 2, 1863, p. 45.
9. Barrot to Thouvenel, 18 September 1861. AMAE: CP Espagne, Vol. 859.
10. Cowley to Russell (private), 5 September 1861. PRO: PRO 30/22/56, Russell Papers.
11. Thouvenel to Flahault, 9 September 1861. AMAE: CP Angleterre, Vol. 720.
12. Russell to Flahault (translation) in Flahault to Thouvenel (private), 16 September 1861. AMAE: CP Angleterre, Vol. 720.
13. Cowley to Russell, 17 September 1861. *State Papers*, Vol. 52, pp. 322–3.
14. Russell to Cowley, 23 September 1861. *Parliamentary Papers*, Part 1, p. 57.
15. Crampton to Russell (telegram), 24 September 1861. PRO: FO 72/1010.
16. Russell to Cowley, 23 September 1861. *Parliamentary Papers*, Part 1, p. 57.
17. Thouvenel to Flahault, 26 September 1861. Quoted by L. Thouvenel, *Le Secret de l'Empereur: Correspondance confidentielle et inédite echangée entre M. Thouvenel, le Duc de Gramont et le Général Comte de Flahault 1860–1863*, 2 Vols (Paris, 1889), Vol. 2, pp. 175–6.
18. Lyons to Russell, 10 September 1861 (r. 23 September). *Parliamentary Papers*, Part 1, p. 56.
19. Cowley to Russell, 24 September 1861. *Ibid.*, p. 59.
20. Russell to Cowley, 27 September 1861. PRO: FO 27/1380.
21. *Ibid.*
22. *Ibid.*
23. Russell to Crampton, 27 September 1861. *State Papers*, Vol. 52, p. 332.
24. Russell to Cowley, 30 September 1861. PRO: FO 27/1380.
25. Note by Almonte (dated September 1861 in Thouvenel's hand). AMAE: CP Mexique, Vol. 55.
26. Cowley to Russell, 2 October 1861. PRO: FO 27/1397.
27. Cowley to Russell (private), 2 October 1861. PRO: PRO 30/22/56, Russell Papers.
28. W. H. C. Smith, *Napoleon III* (London, 1972), p. 177.
29. Napoleon to Flahault, 9 October 1861. AMAE: CP Angleterre, Vol. 720.
30. Henry Salomon, 'Le Prince Richard de Metternich et sa correspondance pendant son ambassade à Paris (1859–1871)', *La Revue de Paris*, 31 (1), 1924, pp. 520–1.
31. Napoleon to Flahault, 9 October 1861. AMAE: CP Angleterre, Vol. 720.
32. Russell to Cowley, 12 October 1861. PRO: FO 27/1380.
33. Note, Palmerston to Russell, 15 October 1861. PRO: PRO 30/22/56, Russell Papers.
34. Francis W. Cavendish, *Society, Politics and Diplomacy 1820–1864: Passages from the Journal of Francis W.H. Cavendish* (London, 1913), pp. 218–19.
35. Paul Hayes, *Modern British Foreign Policy: the Nineteenth Century 1814–1880* (London, 1975), pp. 106–7.
36. Granville to Argyll, 31 August 1859. Quoted by Paul Hayes, *op. cit.*, pp. 116-17.
37. Flahault to Thouvenel (personal), 16 October 1861. AMAE: Papiers d'agents – archives privées (PA–AP) 233 Thouvenel.

226 *Notes and References*

38. Flahault to Thouvenel. Report of conversation with Russell, 19 October 1861. AMAE: CP Angleterre, Vol. 720.
39. Flahault to Thouvenel (private), 19 October 1861. AMAE: PA-AP 233 Thouvenel, Vol. 3.
40. Thouvenel to Flahault, 21 October 1861. AMAE: CP Angleterre, Vol. 720.
41. Cowley to Russell, 16 October 1861. PRO: FO 27/1397.
42. Barrot to Thouvenel, 21 October 1861. AMAE: CP Espagne, Vol. 859.
43. Crampton to Russell, 20 October 1861. PRO: FO 72/1010.
44. Thouvenel to Flahault, 25 October 1861. AMAE: CP Angleterre, Vol. 720.
45. Thouvenel to Flahault, 28 October 1861. AMAE: CP Angleterre, Vol. 720.
46. Flahault to Thouvenel (private), 1 November 1861. AMAE: PA–AP 233 Thouvenel, Vol. 8.
47. Wyke to Russell, 29 September 1861 (r. 30 October), *Parliamentary Papers*, Part 1, p. 101.
48. See Appendix 1 for the final content of the Tripartite Convention signed in London on 31 October 1861.

3 The Venture under Way

1. Charles de Mazade, 'L'Expédition du Mexique', *RDM*, Vol. 37, 1 February 1862, p. 768. De Mazade was a political observer who wrote numerous articles in journals such as *La Presse* and *La Revue des Deux Mondes* on aspects of French foreign policy and international politics, as well as the 'Chronique de la quinzaine' in *Revue des Deux Mondes*. He wrote on Mexico, the political events in Spain, the Italian question and on the Polish situation and its importance to the balance of power in Europe.
2. J. H. Tremenheere, 'The Empire of Mexico', *Quarterly Review*, Vol. 115, April 1864, pp. 348–81.
3. Thouvenel to Barrot, telegram (confidential), 5 November 1861. AMAE: CP Espagne, Vol. 859.
4. Barrot to Thouvenel, 6 November 1861. *Ibid.*
5. Thouvenel to Flahault, 11 November 1861. L. Thouvenel, *Le Secret de l'Empereur* ... (Paris, 1889), Vol. 2, pp. 185–6.
6. Thouvenel to Jurien (confidential), 11 November 1861. Quoted by C. H. Bock, *Prelude to Tragedy: The Negotiation and Breakdown of the Tripartite Convertion of London, October 31 1861* (Philadelphia, 1966), pp. 522–3.
7. Flahault to Thouvenel (private), 13 November 1861. AMAE: PA–AP 233 Thouvenel, Vol. 8.
8. Russell to Wyke (copy), 15 November 1861. AN: BB⁴ 1817bis.
9. Wyke to Russell, 29 September 1861 (r. 30 October). *Parliamentary Papers*, Part 1, p. 101.
10. Russell to Wyke (copy), 15 November 1861. AN: BB⁴ 1817bis.
11. *Ibid.*
12. Collantes to Prim, 17 November 1861. *AD*, Vol. 3, 1862, p. 322.
13. Charles de Mazade, 'L'Expédition du Mexique et la Politique Française', *RDM*, Vol. 48, 1 December 1863, pp. 682–3.
14. Wyke to Russell, 28 October 1861. *State Papers*, Vol. 52, p. 384.

15. Russell to Crampton and Cowley, 28 November 1861. *State Papers*, Vol. 52, pp. 388–9.
16. Saligny to Serrano, 24 November 1861. *AD*, Vol. 3, 1862, pp. 342–3.
17. Saligny to Serrano, 24 November 1861. *Ibid*. Also see comments on these events in Ralph Roeder, *Juarez and His Mexico* (New York, 1947), Vol. 1, pp. 386–9.
18. Serrano to Collantes, 26 November 1861. *AD*, Vol. 3, 1862, p. 323.
19. Francis W. H. Cavendish, *Society, Politics and Diplomacy* (London, 1913), pp. 122 and 134.
20. Collantes to Mon, 10 November 1861. *AD*, Vol. 3, 1862, p. 316.
21. Challié to Minister of Marine and Colonies, 30 November 1861. AN: BB[4] 799.
22. Challié to Minister of Marine and Colonies, 12–20 December 1861. AN. BB[4] 799.
23. *Ibid*.
24. Wyke to Russell, 29 December 1861 (r. 29 January). PRO: FO 50/354.
25. *Ibid*.
26. Commodore Dunlop became the British representative with Sir Charles Wyke in place of Admiral Milne who was directed to Bermuda to help resolve the *Trent* affair.
27. Jurien to Minister of Marine, 28 December 1861. AN: BB[4] 799.
28. Thouvenel to Mercier, 3 December 1861. Quoted by Émile Ollivier, *L'Empire libéral*, Vol. 5, p. 268.
29. Lynn M. Case, *Edouard Thouvenel et la Diplomatie du Second Empire*. Traduction française par Guillaume de Bertier de Sauvigny (Paris, 1976), p. 358.
30. Lyons to Russell, 23 December 1861, enclosed in a letter from Russell to Cowley, 8 January 1862. PRO: FO 519/199, Cowley Papers.
31. Émile Ollivier, *L'Empire libéral*, Vol. 5, p. 269.
32. Jurien to Chasseloup-Laubat, 28 December 1861. AN: BB[4] 799.
33. Russell to Cowley, 27 December 1861. PRO: FO 519/199, Cowley Papers.
34. Charles de Mazade, ' La Guerre du Mexique', *RDM*, Vol. 40, 1 August 1862, p. 745.
35. Russsell to Crampton, 19 January 1862. *State Papers*, Vol. 52, pp. 417–18.
36. Thouvenel to Flahault, 17 January 1862. AMAE: CP Angleterre Vol. 721.
37. Flahault to Thouvenel (private), 20 January 1862. AMAE: PA–AP 233 Thouvenel, Vol. 8.
38. Thouvenel to Flahault, 17 January 1862. L. Thouvenel, *op. cit.*, Vol. 2, pp. 225–6.
39. Cowley to Russell (private) Copy, 17 January 1862. PRO: FO 519/229, Cowley Papers. Emphasis given.
40. Russell to Cowley (private), 18 January 1862. PRO: FO 519/199, Cowley Papers.
41. Palmerston to Russell (private), 19 January 1862. PRO: Russell Papers. Quoted by C. H. Bock, *op. cit.*, pp. 343–4.
42. Flahault to Thouvenel (private), 20 January 1862. AMAE: PA–AP 233 Thouvenel.
43. Napoleon to Lorencez, quoted by M. Billault, Minister without portfolio, to *Corps législatif*, 26 June 1862. *AD*, Vol. 4, 1862, pp. 209–10.
44. Colonel Claremont to Lord Cowley, January 21 1862. PRO: FO 27/1431.
45. Russell to Crampton (telegram), 2 February 1862. PRO: FO 72/1028.

46. Palmerston to the House of Commons, 6 February 1862. *Parliamentary Debates, (Commons)*, Third Series, Vol. 165. Reported also in *Journal des Débats*, 9 February 1862.
47. Collantes to Prim, 22 January 1862. *AD*, Vol. 3, 1862, p. 347.
48. Collantes to Mon, 9 December 1861. *Ibid.*, pp. 314–15.
49. Charles de Mazade, 'L'Expédition du Mexique', p. 770.
50. Crampton to Russell (private), 4 February 1862. PRO: PRO 30/22/86, Russell Papers.
51. Collantes to Spanish Cortes, 8 January 1863. *AD*, Vol. 2, 1863, pp. 54–5.
52. *Ibid.*, p. 54.
53. Billault to Corps Législatif, 26 June 1862. *AD*, Vol. 4, 1862, pp. 176–7.
54. Hammond to Russell (private), 8 February 1862. PRO: PRO 30/22/41, Russell Papers.
55. Russell to Bloomfield, British Minister in Vienna, 13 February 1862. *State Papers*, Vol. 53, pp. 389–90.
56. *Ibid.*
57. *The Times* Correspondent in Mexico, 29 December 1861. *The Times*, 30 January 1862.
58. *The Times* Correspondent in Mexico, 20 January 1862. *The Times*, 4 March 1862.
59. *Le Temps*, 26 February 1862.
60. Charles de Mazade, 'L'Expédition du Mexique', pp. 768–9.

4   A Life of its Own

1. Wyke to Russell, 16 January 1862. *State Papers*, Vol. 53, pp. 395–6.
2. Proclamation to the Mexican Nation, 10 January 1862. *AD*, Vol. 3, 1862, pp. 359–60.
3. In report of Jurien to Thouvenel, 12 January 1862. Copy with report to Minister of Marine and Colonies, 15 January 1862. AN: BB^4 799, ff. 223–47
4. Jurien to Minister of Marine and Colonies, 1 January 1862. AN: BB^4 799, f. 175.
5. Mon to Collantes, 9 November 1861. *AD*, Vol. 3, 1862, pp. 315–16.
6. Thouvenel to Jurien (confidential), 11 November 1861. AMAE: CP Mexique, Vol. 57, quoted by Carl H. Bock, *Prelude to Tragedy: The Negotiation and Breakdown of the Tripartite Convention of London, October 31 1861* (Philadelphia, 1966), p. 522.
7. In report of Jurien to Thouvenel, 12 January 1862. Copy with report to Minister of Marine and Colonies, 15 January 1862. AN: BB^4 799, ff. 223–47.
8. Charles de Mazade, 'Le General Prim', *RDM*, Vol. 61, 15 January 1866, 540–44.
9. Captain of *Lavoisier* to Chasseloup-Laubat, 3 January 1862. AN: BB^4 799. f. 155.
10. Crampton to Russell (private), 7 January 1862. PRO PRO30/22–86 Russell Papers, Spain and Morocco 1859–1862.
11. Ralph Roeder, *Juarez and His Mexico* (New York, 1947), Vol. 1, p. 280.
12. See Nancy N. Barker, *Distaff Diplomacy: The Empress Eugénie and the Foreign Policy of the Second Empire* (Austin, Tx, 1967), 409–26. Although Barker

provides invaluable insight into the character and motives of Saligny as an envoy in Mexico, her argument that the Jecker bonds were Napoleon's pretext for imposing a monarchy are not well supported. See also Nancy N. Barker, 'France Disserved: The Dishonourable Career of Dubois de Saligny', in Nancy N. Barker and Marvin L. Brown (eds), *Diplomacy in an Age of Nationalism: Essays in Honor of Lynn Marshall Case* (The Hague, 1971), pp. 25–43, in which Saligny's correspondence with Thouvenel in March 1861 shows Thouvenel thought the petitions of bond holders should be pursued. In 1862, however, Thouvenel's opinion was greatly modified, but Barker does not show this.

13. Prim to Collantes, 14 January 1862. *AD*, Vol. 3, 1862, pp. 362–3.
14. Collective letter to the Juarez Government, 14 January 1862. *Ibid.*, pp. 364–5.
15. Émile Ollivier, *L'Empire libéral*, Vol. 5, pp. 369–70.
16. Jurien to Chasseloup-Laubat, 12 January 1862. AN: BB⁴ 799, f. 220.
17. Émile Ollivier, *L'Empire libéral*, Vol. 5, p. 249.
18. Jurien to Thouvenel (personal), 24 January 1862. AMAE: PA–AP 233 Thouvenel, Vol. 10.
19. Thomasset to Jurien, 31 January 1862, included with Jurien's reports of 28 January to Minister of Marine and Colonies. AN: BB⁴ 799.
20. Jurien to Thouvenel, 24 January 1862. AMAE: PA–AP 233 Thouvenel, Vol. 10.
21. Jurien to Minister of Marine and Colonies, 28 January 1862. AN: BB⁴ 799.
22. Wyke to Russell (private), 31 January 1862. PRO: PRO 30/22/74 Russell Papers.
23. *Ibid.*
24. Wyke to Russell, 31 January 1862. PRO: FO 50/364.
25. Prim to Collantes, 31 January 1862. *AD*, Vol. 3, 1862, p. 376.
26. Thouvenel to Jurien, 21 February 1862, coded telegraphic dispatch sent via Cadiz (r. 3 April). AN: BB⁴ 1817bis.
27. Thouvenel to Flahault, 22 February 1862. AMAE: CP Angleterre, Vol. 721.
28. Russell to Wyke, 25 February 1862. *State Papers*, Vol. 53, p. 393.
29. Hammond, Under Secretary of State for Foreign Affairs, to Secretary of the Admiralty, 10 March 1862. *State Papers*, Vol. 53, pp. 436–7.
30. Russell to Wyke, 11 March 1862. PRO: FO 50/363.
31. Flahault to Thouvenel, 11 March 1862. *AD*, Vol. 1, 1863, p. 312.
32. Barrot to Thouvenel, 26 February 1862. *AD*, Vol. 1, 1863, p. 317.
33. Collantes to Prim, 7 March 1862 (No. 86). *Ibid.*, pp. 374–5.
34. Collantes to Prim, 7 March 1862 (No. 83). *Ibid.*, pp. 378–9.
35. Thouvenel to Saligny, 28 February 1862. *Ibid.*, pp. 304–5.
36. Russell to Cowley, 3 March 1862. PRO: FO 519/199, Cowley Papers.
37. Cowley to Russell, 6 March 1862. PRO: FO 519/229, Cowley Papers.
38. Hammond to Russell (private), 8 February 1862. PRO: PRO 30/22/41, Russell Papers.
39. Cowley to Russell, 6 March 1862. PRO: FO 519/229, Cowley Papers.
40. Reported by Cowley to Russell, 14 March 1862. *State Papers*, Vol. 53, p. 440.
41. Thouvenel to Saligny 14 March 1862. *AD*, Vol. 1, 1863, pp. 314–15.
42. Émile Ollivier, *L'Empire libéral*, Vol. 5, p. 356. The 'Five' referred to by Ollivier were the first opposition deputies elected to the *Corps législatif* in 1857, or in by-elections shortly afterwards, who included most notably

Ollivier, who was later to head Napoleon's government, and Jules Favres, a Republican lawyer who in 1870 led the crowd to the *Hotel de Ville* to proclaim the Republic.

43. Achille Jubinal to *Corps législatif*, 13 March 1862. Quoted by Émile Ollivier, *L'Empire libéral*, Vol. 5, pp. 356–7.
44. Jules Favre to *Corps législatif*, 13 March 1862. Quoted by Frank Lally, *French Opposition to the Mexican Policy of the Second Empire* (Baltimore, 1931), p. 37.
45. Paul Gaulot, *L'Expédition du Mexique (1861–1867)*...(Paris, 1906), Vol. 1, p. vi.
46. Quoted by Frank E. Lally, *French Opposition to the Mexican Policy of the Second Empire* (Baltimore, 1931), p. 38.
47. Quoted by Émile Ollivier, *L'Empire libéral*, Vol. 5, pp. 357–8.
48. Jurien to Thouvenel (personal), 7 February 1862. AMAE PA–AP 233 Thouvenel, Vol. 10.
49. Frank Lally, *op. cit.*, p. 38.
50. P. G. Rabou, Caen, 7 July 1862. Quoted by Lynn M. Case (ed.), *French Opinion on the United States and Mexico 1860–1867*, (Archon Books, 1969 © 1936) p. 315.
51. Wyke to Russell, 12 February 1862. *State Papers*, Vol. 53, pp. 453–4.
52. Preliminary Convention of Soledad. *AD*, Vol. 3, 1862, pp. 386–7.
53. Prim to Collantes, 20 February 1862. *Ibid.*, pp. 382–6, and Procès-verbal of the twelfth conference of the Plenipotentiaries and Commanders of the allied Powers, 19 February 1862. *Ibid.*, pp. 396–7.
54. Prim to Collantes, 20 February 1862. *Ibid.*, p. 386.
55. Charles de Mazade, 'L'Expédition du Mexique', p. 500.
56. Jurien to Chasseloup Laubat, 22 February 1862. AN: BB⁴ 799.
57. Jurien to Chasseloup Laubat, 5 March 1862. AN: BB⁴ 799.
58. Jurien was promoted from Rear-Admiral to Vice-Admiral in January 1862, at the time of de Lorencez's departure, before advice reached Paris of the proclamation to the Mexicans and of the negotiations with Juarez.
59. Jurien to Thouvenel (personal), 2 March 1862. AMAE: PA–AP 233 Thouvenel, Vol. 10.
60. Jurien to Thouvenel (personal), 14 March 1862. AMAE: PA–AP 233 Thouvenel, Vol. 10.
61. Prim to Collantes, 17 March 1862. *AD*, Vol. 3, 1862, pp. 407–9.
62. Jurien to Prim, 13 March 1862. AN: BB⁴ 799.
63. Reported by Jurien to Chasseloup-Laubat, 17 March 1862. AN: BB⁴ 799.
64. Jurien to Prim, 20 March 1862. *AD*, Vol. 3, 1862, pp. 414–15.
65. *Ibid.*, pp. 415–16.
66. Prim to Jurien, 23 March 1862. *AD*, Vol. 3, 1862, pp. 419–20.
67. Wyke to Jurien, 27 March 1862. *State Papers*, Vol. 53, pp. 505–7.
68. Wyke to Russell, 27 March 1862. *Ibid.*, p. 502.
69. Jurien to Wyke, 29 March 1862. *State Papers*, Vol. 53, p. 511.
70. Wyke to Jurien, 29 March 1862. *State Papers*, Vol. 53, pp. 513–15.
71. Saligny to Jurien, 29 March 1862. AMAE: PA–AP 233 Thouvenel, Vol. 10.
72. Saligny to Jurien, 30 March 1862. AMAE: PA–AP 233 Thouvenel, Vol. 10
73. Thouvenel to Jurien, 21 February 1862 (r. 3 April). AMAE: CP Mexique, Vol. 58.
74. Proceedings of the Conference held at Orizaba 9 April 1862 between the representatives of the Allied Powers. *AD*, Vol. 3, 1862, pp. 421–33.

75. French Commandant Raze in Vera Cruz to Jurien, 26 February 1862. AN: BB⁴ 1813.
76. Unsigned letter to Thouvenel dated 4 March 1862. AMAE: PA–AP 233 Thouvenel, Vol. 10.
77. Proceedings of the Conference held at Orizaba 9 April 1862 between the representatives of the Allied Powers. *AD*, Vol. 3, 1862, pp. 421–33.
78. *Ibid.*
79. Saligny and Jurien to Doblado, 9 April 1862. *AD*, Vol. 3, 1862, p. 435.
80. Doblado to Saligny and Jurien, 11 April 1862. *Ibid.*, pp. 435–6.
81. Jurien to Chasseloup-Laubat, 11 April 1862. AN: BB⁴ 799.
82. *Ibid.*

5 'A Chaos of Difficulties'

1. Russell to Cowley, 2 April 1862. *State Papers*, Vol. 53, pp. 490–1.
2. Russell to Wyke, 1 April 1862. *Ibid.*, p. 488.
3. Russell to Wyke (private), 1 April 1862 (copy). PRO: PRO30/22/95 Rusell Papers, Central America 1859–65.
4. Member of *Corps législatif* (signature indecipherable) to Jurien, 17 March 1862. AN: BB⁴ 1812.
5. Saligny to General Rollin, 8 February 1862. AN: 400AP 62 Archives napoléon.
6. Thouvenel to Saligny, 20 March 1862. AMAE: CP Mexique, Vol. 58.
7. Muro to Collantes, 9 April 1862. *AD*, Vol. 3, 1862, pp. 403–4.
8. Russell to Crampton, 19 April 1862. *State Papers*, Vol. 53, pp. 497–8.
9. Russell to Wyke, 30 April 1862. *Ibid.*, pp. 519–20.
10. Thouvenel to Saligny, 30 April 1862. AMAE: CP Mexique, Vol. 58.
11. Cowley to Russell, 2 May 1862. *State Papers*, Vol. 53, p. 523.
12. Reported by Russell to Cowley, 5 May 1862. *Ibid.*, pp. 525–6.
13. Billault to *Corps législatif*, 26 June 1862. *AD*, Vol. 4, 1862, pp. 199–200
14. Wyke to Russell (private), 12 April 1862. PRO: PRO 30/22/74 Russell Papers.
15. Thouvenel to Flahault, 17 May 1862. L.Thouvenel, *Le Secret de l'Empereur* (Paris, 1889), pp. 301–2.
16. Palmerston to Russell, 19 June 1862. (PRO: PRO 30/22/22). Quoted by K. Bourne, *Britain and the Balance of Power in North America*, p. 255.
17. Marquis de la Havane, new Ambassador to France, to Collantes, 1 September 1862. *AD*, Vol. 2, 1863, pp. 29–30.
18. Jurien to Thouvenel (personal), 17 April 1862. AMAE: PA–AP 233 Thouvenel, Vol. 10.
19. Devarenne to Jurien, 31 May 1862. AN: BB⁴ 1814.
20. Lorencez to Randon, 26 April 1862. Service Historique de l'Armée de Terre (SHAT), Archives du Ministre de la Guerre, (AMG) G⁷ 1.
21. Thouvenel to Saligny, 31 May 1862. *AD*, Vol. 1, 1863, pp. 322–3.
22. Napoleon to Maximilian, 7 June 1862. Quoted by Egon Corti, *Maximilian and Charlotte of Mexico* (Archon Books, 1968 © 1928), pp. 372–3.
23. Napoleon to Lorencez, June 1862 (no exact date). *AD*, Vol. 2, 1863, pp. 72–3.
24. Napoleon to Maximilian, 14 January 1862. Quoted by Egon Corti, *op. cit.*, pp. 365–6. Maximilian to Napoleon, 22 January 1862. *Ibid.*, pp. 367–8.

25. Napoleon to Maximilian, 7 March 1862. Maximilian to Napoleon, 15 March 1862. *Ibid.*, pp. 371–2.
26. Napoleon III, 'Des Idées napoléoniennes', pp. 22–4.
27. Reported in *Le Temps*, 29 June 1862.
28. Billault to *Corps législatif*, 26 June 1862. *AD*, Vol. 4, 1862, pp. 209–10.
29. Émile Ollivier, *L'Empire libéral*, Vol. 5, p. 412.
30. Général Comte Fleury, *Souvenirs du Général Comte Fleury*, Vol. 2: *1859–1867*, (Paris, 1898), p. 265.
31. Napoleon to Lorencez, June 1862 (no exact date). *AD*, Vol. 2, 1863, pp. 72–3.
32. Saligny to Thouvenel (confidential), 8 May 1862. AMAE: CP Mexique, Vol. 58.
33. Lorencez to Randon, 22 May 1862. AMG: G[7] 1.
34. Lorencez to Randon, 24 May 1862. AMG: G[7] 1.
35. Saligny to Thouvenel, 26 May 1862. AMAE: CP Mexique, Vol. 58.
36. Randon to Napoleon, 2 July 1862. Quoted by Émile Ollivier, *L'Empire libéral*, Vol. 5, pp. 408–9.
37. Émile Ollivier, *L'Empire libéral*, Vol. 6, (Paris, 1902), pp. 451–2.
38. Lorencez to Randon, 25 August 1862. AMG: G[7]1.
39. Egon Corti, *op. cit.*, p. 221.
40. Lorencez to Napoleon, 23 June 1862. AN: 400AP 62, Archives napoléon.
41. Almonte to Napoleon, 24 June 1862. AN: 400AP 61, Archives napoléon.
42. Lorencez to Randon, 22 July 1862. AMG: G[7] 1.
43. Saligny to Rollin, 9 August 1862. AN: 400AP 62, Archives napoléon.
44. From a draft of a letter dated 14 July 1862, having exactly the same content as the letter written to General Forey 3 July 1862, but adding explicit instructions on what Forey was to do in Mexico on his arrival. This latter section of the draft talks of Forey in the third person, which makes it appear to be directions to be given to Forey by Randon. This is no doubt a letter to Marshal Randon, which is referred to in Randon's memoirs. See *Mémoires du Maréchal Randon*, Vol. 2 (Paris, 1877), p. 71. Another draft of a letter to Forey, dated 4 July explains Napoleon's reasons for accepting Saligny's views so far and stresses the importance of working with Saligny and that if he feels he cannot he is to tell the Emperor before he accepts the position of Commander. AN: 400AP 62, Archives napoléon.
45. A. J. and K. A. Hanna, *Napoleon III and Mexico: American Triumph over Monarchy* (Chapel Hill, 1971), pp. 77–9.
46. Dexter Perkins is the author of *The United States and Latin America; The History of the Monroe Doctrine; The Monroe Doctrine 1826–1867*, among other books on American Foreign Policy.
47. Michel Chevalier, *Mexico, Ancient and Modern* (London, 1864), Vol. 2, p. 216.
48. See, for example, Pierre de la Gorce, *Histoire du Second Empire*, Vol. IV (Paris, 1899), pp. 14–15.
49. Flahault to Thouvenel (personal), 25 January 1862. MDAE, PA–AP 233 Thouvenel, Vol. 8.
50. For discussions of economic motives see Shirley J. Black, *Napoleon III and the French Intervention in Mexico: A Quest for Silver* (PhD dissertation, University of Oklahoma, 1974).
51. Draft of letter Napoleon to Forey, dated in top left corner, 14 July 1862, in Napoleon's hand. See note 1 above. AN. 400AP 62, Archives napoléon.

52. Pierre de la Gorce, *Histoire du Second Empire* (Paris, 1899) Vol. IV, pp. 66–7.
53. *Ibid.*, pp. 81–2. Information on Generals Lorencez and Forey also obtained from their *états de Services* in the archives of the Ministère de la Guerre.
54. Note from Napoleon to Frossard, 5 July 1862. AN: AB XIX 172. The remark to General Lebœuf is mentioned by Émile Ollivier in *L'Empire libéral*, Vol. 5, p. 411.
55. Paul Gaulot, *L'Expédition du Mexique (1861–1867)* (Paris, 1906), Vol. 1, pp. 56-7.

6 The Will of the People?

1. Proclamation publiée par le général Forey à son arrivée à Vera-Cruz, le 24 septembre 1862. *AD*, Vol. 2, 1863, pp. 74–5.
2. Almonte to Napoleon, 8 October 1862. AN: 400AP 61, Archives napoléon.
3. Proclamation du général Forey au peuple mexicain, 3 November 1862. *AD*, Vol. 2, 1863, p. 76.
4. Forey to Randon, 9 November 1862 (r. 16 December 1862). AMG: G^7 1.
5. Forey to Napoleon, 27 November 1862. AN: 400AP 62, Archives napoléon.
6. Napoleon to Maximilian, 2 October 1863. Quoted by Egon Corti, *Maximilian and Charlotte of Mexico* (Archon Books, 1968 © 1928), p. 390.
7. Forey to Napoleon, 25 January 1863. AN: 400AP 62, Archives napoléon.
8. Forey to Fleury, 25 January 1863. AN: 400AP62, Archives napoléon.
9. Gallifet to Napoleon, 9 February 1863. AN: 400AP 62, Archives napoléon. Gaston Auguste, Marquis de Gallifet had been a military *aide-de-camp* to Napoleon in 1860, which would explain his familiarity with him. Later in the campaign he was Lieutenant-Colonel. He became a general in 1870, Governor of Paris in 1880, and in 1899 was briefly Minister of War.
10. Forey to Napoleon, 11 January 1863. AN: 400AP 62, Archives napoléon.
11. Henry Banford Parkes, *A History of Mexico* (London, 1962, © 1960), pp. 98–102.
12. See Chapter 1.
13. Napoleon to Forey, 14 February 1863. Quoted by Émile Ollivier, *L'Empire libéral*, Vol. 6, pp. 438–9.
14. Egon Corti, *op. cit.*, p. 221. Corti uses as the basis for these assumptions the letters from Napoleon to Forey referred to by Paul Gaulot, *L'Expédition du Mexique (1861–1867)* (Paris, 1906), in Vol. 1, p. 132. The letters quoted on this page were dated 1 November 1862, 17 December 1862 and 14 February 1863, but it is only the content of the last of these that Corti has made use of without actually mentioning the date.
15. Napoleon to Forey, 17 December 1862. Quoted by Paul Gaulot, *op. cit.*, Vol. 1, p. 132. Paul Gaulot authenticates his sources as original letters that were collected by Ernest Louet from people such as Marshal Bazaine who had confidential letters from Napoleon, Randon and Maximilian, among others. He also obtained material from Vienna, Brussels, Trieste and Miramar. These were placed in Gaulot's care when Louet died.
16. Gallifet to Napoleon, 9 February 1863. AN: 400AP 62, Archives napoléon.
17. Gallifet to Napoleon, 21 February 1863. AN: 400AP 62, Archives napoléon.
18. Napoleon to Forey, 14 April 1863. AN: 400AP 62, Archives napoléon.

19. Napoleon to Forey, 12 June 1863. AN: 400AP 42, Archives napoléon. This letter arrived in Mexico at the end of July 1863.
20. Almonte to Napoleon, 2 June 1863. AN: 400AP 61, Archives napoléon.
21. Saligny to Forey, 16 June 1863, reproduced in the manuscript, *Journal de la Campagne du Mexique*, de la Hayrie. AMG: MS 851.
22. *Ibid.*
23. Note signed by Almonte, undated and with no addressee. However, as it is among Almonte's letters to Napoleon in the Archives Napoléon in the Archives Nationales it is highly probable that it was included with one of his letters of advice to the Emperor. The heading states: 'Considérations sur les mesures qu'il y aurait à prendre, dès l'occupation de Mexico, par l'armée française, pour établir dans le pays une autorité gouvernementale préparatoire'. AN: 400AP 61, Archives napoléon.
24. Forey to Napoleon, 30 June 1863. AN: 400AP 62, Archives napoléon.
25. Almonte to Napoleon, 26 June 1863. AN: 400AP 61, Archives napoléon.
26. These letters were found in the Archives Nationales among the Archives napoléon, series 400AP 61–3. Included here were 36 letters from Forey, 29 from Almonte, 83 from Bazaine and a number from Lorencez. This series has not been used by previous historians of the campaign.
27. Général du Barail, *Mes Souvenirs, 1851–1864*, 2 vols (Paris 1898), Vol. 2, p. 478. General du Barail was a Colonel in the expeditionary forces in Mexico.
28. Paul Gaulot, *op. cit.*, Vol. 1, p. 30.
29. Saligny to Napoleon (n.d.). AN: ABXIX 172.
30. Salas was the most senior of Mexican generals, aged 72, who had been an interim president of the Republic for a month in 1846. According to Paul Gaulot he brought to the government no other strength than his worthiness, and could offer nothing but his signature. Paul Gaulot, *op. cit.*, Vol. 1, p. 138.
31. Forey to Drouyn de Lhuys, the new Minister of Foreign Affairs, 25 July 1863. AN: 400AP 62, Archives napoléon.
32. *Ibid.*
33. Forey to Randon, 10 August 1863. AMG: G^7 1.
34. Forey to Napoleon, 16 August 1863. AN: 400AP 62, Archives napoléon.
35. Napoleon to Maximilian, 21 June 1863, and telegram, Napoleon to Maximilian, 8 August 1863. Quoted by Egon Corti, *op. cit.*, pp. 376–7.
36. Maximilian to Napoleon, 10 August 1863. *Ibid.*, p. 378.
37. Napoleon to Maximilian, 15 August 1863. *Ibid.*, p. 379.
38. Maximilian to Napoleon, 26 August 1863. *Ibid.*, p. 380.
39. Maximilian to Napoleon, 12 September 1863. *Ibid.*, p. 382.
40. Drouyn de Lhuys to Bazaine, 17 August 1863. *AD*, Vol. 4, 1863, p. 289.
41. Général du Barail, *op. cit.*, Vol. 2, pp. 483–4.
42. Forey to Napoleon, probably 20 August 1863 according to Émile Ollivier, *L'Empire libéral*, Vol. 6, p. 448. A longer extract is quoted by Egon Corti, *op. cit.*, pp. 386–8, undated but appended to a letter from Napoleon to Maximilian, 25 September 1863.
43. Émile Ollivier, *L'Empire libéral*, Vol. 6, pp. 446–7.
44. Napoleon to Maximilian, 25 September 1863. Quoted by Egon Corti, *op. cit.*, p. 385.

45. See note 25 above.
46. Napoleon to Bazaine, 16 December 1863. Quoted by Paul Gaulot, *op. cit.*, Vol. 1, pp. 224–5.
47. Fleury to Bazaine, 12 December 1863. *Ibid.*, Vol. 1, pp. 232–3.
48. Charles de Mazade, 'L'Expédition du Mexique et la politique française', *RDM*, 48 (1 December 1863), pp. 675–706.

7 The Empire Does Mean Peace

1. Address at the opening of the Legislative Session, 5 November 1863. *AD*, Vol. 4, 1863, pp. 163–4.
2. *Exposé de la situation de l'empire présenté au Sénat et au Corps législatif,* November 1863 (Paris, 1863),Vol. 2, p. 111.
3. Maréchal Randon, *Mémoires du Maréchal Randon* (Paris, 1877), Vol. 2, p. 57.
4. Napoleon to European sovereigns, 4 November 1863. *AD*, Vol. 4, 1863, pp. 188–9.
5. Rechberg to Metternich, 17 November 1863. *AD*, Vol. 1, 1864, pp. 59–60.
6. Cowley to Russell, 5 November 1863. PRO: PRO30/22/59, Russell Papers.
7. Russell to Cowley, dispatch in cypher, 7 November 1863. PRO: FO27/1482.
8. Russell to Cowley, 12 November 1863. PRO: FO27/1482.
9. Bloomfield to Russell, 12 November 1863. PRO: PRO30/22/42, Russell Papers.
10. Drouyn de Lhuys to Marquis de Cadore, Chargé d'Affaires in London, 23 November 1863. *AD*, Vol. 1, 1864, p. 48.
11. Address by the Senate, presented to Napoleon 21 December 1863. *AD*, Vol. 1, 1864, pp. 81–2.
12. Comte Fleury (ed.), *Memoirs of the Empress Eugenie*, 2 vols (New York, 1920), Vol. 2, pp. 147–8.
13. Count de la Chapelle, *Posthumous Works and Unpublished Autographs of Napoleon III in Exile* (London, 1873), pp. 253–4. Hunt confided his discussions with Napoleon to the Count de la Chapelle, a close friend of Napoleon's when he was in exile in England.
14. *Ibid.*
15. *Ibid.*, pp. 254–6.
16. William E. Echard, *Napoleon III and the Concert of Europe* (Baton Rouge, 1983).
17. Charles Mackay, 'The French Conquest of Mexico', *Westminster and Foreign Quarterly Review*, Vol. 80, October 1863, pp. 335–6.
18. Larrabure, 'Rapport sur les crédits supplémentaires de 1863'. Quoted by Émile Ollivier, *L'Empire libéral*, Vol. 6, p. 460.
19. Bazaine to Napoleon, 24 October 1863. *Ibid.*, pp. 454–5.
20. Almonte to Napoleon, 27 October 1863. AN: 400AP 61, Archives napoléon.
21. Général du Barail, *Mes Souvenirs, 1851–1864* (Paris, 1898), Vol. 2, p. 496.
22. Report from the paper's correspondent in Mexico, 9 January 1864, published in *The Times*, 17 February 1864.
23. Michel Chevalier, *Mexico, Ancient and Modern* (London, 1864), Vol. 1, pp. xi–xii.
24. Egon Corti, *Maximilian and Charlotte of Mexico* (Archon Books, 1968 © 1928), pp. 272–3.

25. *Exposé de la Situation de l'Empire présenté au Sénat et au Corps législatif,* November 1863 (Paris, 1863), Vol. 2, p. 117.
26. Almonte to Napoleon, 27 October 1863. AN: 400AP 61, Archives napoléon.
27. Metternich to Rechberg, 14 December 1863. H. Salomon, *op. cit.,* pp. 532–3.
28. Report from Mexico, 16 December 1863, *The Times,* 20 January 1864.
29. Summary of the article in the *Moniteur* printed in *The Times,* 22 January 1864. The brochure referred to is possibly one entitled, *Solution de la question mexicaine,* by A. Malespine (Paris, 1864), a copy of which was found in AN: 223AP 16, Fonds Berryer.
30. Report of 9 January 1864, printed in *The Times,* 17 February 1864.
31. Charles de Mazade, 'L'Expédition du Mexique et la politique française', p. 705.
32. Charles Mackay, *op. cit.,* p. 316.
33. Napoleon to Prince Napoleon, 22 January 1863. Quoted by Ernest d'Hauterive, *The Second Empire and its Downfall. The Correspondence of the Emperor Napoleon III and his cousin Prince Napoleon.* Translated from the French by Herbert Wilson (London, n.d.), pp. 186–7.
34. *The Times,* 30 January 1864. This debate was reported in great detail in *The Times* during the last week of January 1864.
35. A. Malespine, *Solution de la question mexicaine* (brochure, Paris, 1864). AN: 223AP 16, Fonds Berryer.
36. Rouher was a lawyer and a Bonapartist and long-time friend of Napoleon, having been appointed Minister of Justice in the Second Republic. He had been an influential adviser to Napoleon since he first came to power, and the position he presently occupied as defender of government policy was one of considerable importance in the *Corps législatif.*
37. Quoted by Émile Ollivier, *L'Empire libéral,* Vol. 6, pp. 464–5.
38. *The Times,* 30 January 1864.

8   'A Noble and Chimerical Utopia'

1. Émile Ollivier, *L'Empire libéral,* Vol. 6, pp. 455–7.
2. Bazaine to Napoleon, 24 March 1864. Quoted by Émile Ollivier, *ibid.,* pp. 574–8.
3. Pierre de la Gorce, *Napoléon III et sa politique* (Paris, 1933), pp. 27–8.
4. Alain Minc, *Louis Napoléon revisité* (Paris, 1997), p. 189.
5. *Ibid.*
6. Montholon, the new French Minister in Mexico, to Drouyn de Lhuys, 28 April 1864. Quoted by Émile Ollivier, *op. cit.,* p. 578.
7. Egon Corti, *Maximilian and Charlotte of Mexico* (Archon Books, 1968 © 1928), pp. 305–6.
8. Napoleon to Maximilian, 28 March 1864. Quoted by Egon Corti, *op. cit.,* pp. 399–400.
9. Frossard to Napoleon, 1–5 April 1864. AN: 400AP 62, Archives napoléon.
10. Paul Gaulot, *L'Expédition du Mexique* (1861–1867) (Paris, 1906), Vol. 1, p. 297.
11. Napoleon to Frossard (telegraph), 5 April 1864. Quoted by Émile Ollivier, *op. cit.,* p. 585.

12. Leopold to Maximilian, 4 February 1864. Quoted by Egon Corti, *op. cit.*, p. 317.
13. Frossard to Napoleon, 7 April 1864. AN: 400AP 62, Archives napoléon.
14. Général Comte Fleury, *Souvenirs*, Vol. 2, pp. 265–7.
15. Convention conclue le 10 avril 1864 entre la France et le Mexique. *AD*, Vol. 3, 1864, pp. 312–14. See Appendix 2.
16. Metternich to Rechberg, 14 March 1864. H. Salomon, 'Le Prince Richard de Metternich et sa correspondance pendant son ambassade à Paris (1859–1871)', *La Revue de Paris*, 31(1), 1924, pp. 534–5.
17. Émile Ollivier, *op. cit.*, p. 586.
18. A. J. and K. A. Hanna, *Napoleon III and Mexico: American Triumph over Monarchy* (Chapel Hill, 1971), pp. 110–11.
19. *The Times*, 7 July 1864.
20. Napoleon to Maximilian, 16 November 1864. Quoted by Egon Corti, *op. cit.*, pp. 853–4.
21. A. J. and K. A. Hanna, *op. cit.*, pp. 126–7.
22. *The Times* correspondent in Mexico, 11 October 1864. Printed in *The Times*, 19 November 1864.
23. Randon to Bazaine, 28 June 1865. Quoted by Paul Gaulot, *op. cit.*, Vol. 2, pp. 137–8.
24. Bazaine to Randon, 27 July 1865. AMG: G⁷ 2.
25. Magne to Napoleon, 12 August 1865. AN: 400AP 62, Archives napoléon.
26. Comte Émile de Kératry, 'Le Mexique et les chances de salut du nouvel empire', *RDM*, Vol. 65, 15 September 1866, pp. 451.
27. Napoleon to Maximilian (no precise date given), quoted by Joan Haslip, *Imperial Adventures: Emperor Maximilian of Mexico and his Empress* (London, 1974 © 1971), p. 314.
28. Randon to Napoleon, 5 October 1865. Maréchal Randon, *Mémoires* (Paris, 1875 and 1877), Vol. 2, p. 101.
29. Napoleon to Bazaine, 29 November 1865. Quoted by Paul Gaulot, *op. cit.*, Vol. 2, pp. 210–11.
30. Napoleon to the chambers, January 1866. *Exposé de la situation de l'Empire présenté au Sénat et au Corps législatif*, January 1866, Vol. 4, p. 227.
31. Lord Clarendon reporting to Cowley a conversation with the French ambassador, 9 or 10 May 1866. Colonel the Hon. F. A. Wellesley (ed.), *The Paris Embassy during the Second Empire* (London, 1928), p. 303.
32. Napoleon to Drouyn de Lhuys, 11 June 1866. AN: 400AP 42, Archives napoléon.
33. Notes by Napoleon on foreign relations, no date. AN: 400AP 54, Archives napoléon. Reproduced as a letter of instruction from Lavalette to the Emperor's diplomatic agents and printed in *Moniteur*, 17 September 1866.
34. Albert Guérard, 'Cæsarian Democracy', *Napoleon III: Buffoon, Modern Dictator or Sphinx?* Edited by Samuel M. Osgood (Boston, 1963), pp. 57–8.
35. Albert Pingaud, 'La politique extérieure du Second Empire', *Revue Historique*, Vol. 156, November/December 1927, pp. 41–68.
36. William Echard, *Napoleon III and the Concert of Europe* (Baton Rouge, 1983), pp. 183–4.
37. Mazade to Eugenie, 17 July 1865. AN: ABXIX 174.
38. Pierre de la Gorce, *Napoléon III et sa politique*, pp. 37–9.

238 *Notes and References*

39. Bazaine to Randon, 28 January 1866. AMG: G^7 3.
40. Comte Fleury (ed.), *Memoirs*, Vol. 2, pp. 120–1.
41. The story of the illness of the Empress has been well recounted by Egon Corti in *Maximilian and Charlotte of Mexico*, and by Joan Haslip in *Imperial Adventurer: Emperor Maximilian of Mexico and his Empress*.
42. Napoleon to Castelnau, 15 September 1866. Quoted by Louis Sonolet, 'L'Agonie de l'Empire du Mexique: D'après des lettres et des notes inédites du Général Castelnau', *La Revue de Paris*, Vol. 34, 1927, p. 601.
43. Louis Sonolet, *ibid.*, p. 594.
44. Napoleon to Castelnau, 10 January 1867. Transatlantic cable. AN: 400AP 42.
45. Letters provided to Castelnau testifying to Bazaine's actions, dated 3 and 5 December 1866. Quoted by Louis Sonolet, *op. cit.*, pp. 869–70.
46. Bazaine to Randon, 10 January 1867. AN: 320AP 2, Bazaine.
47. Castelnau to Napoleon, 28 December 1866. Quoted by Louis Sonolet, *op. cit.*, pp. 879–82.
48. *Ibid.*
49. Egon Corti, *op. cit.*, pp. 765ff.

9   La Plus Grande Pensée du Règne?

1. Dano to Moustier, 1 September 1867. Quoted by A. J. and K. A. Hanna, *Napoleon III and Mexico: American Triumph over Monarchy* (Chapel Hill, 1971), p. 304.
2. Castelnau to Napoleon, 28 October 1866. Quoted by Louis Sonolet, 'L'Agonie de l'Empire du Mexique: D'après des lettres et des notes inédites du Général Castelnau', *La Revue de Paris*, 34 (1 August 1927), pp. 606–7.
3. Général du Barail, *Mes Souvenirs, 1851–1864* (Paris, 1898), Vol. 2, pp. 487–8.
4. Prince Jerome Napoleon to Napoleon, April 1855. Quoted by Ernest d'Hauterive, *The Second Empire and its Downfall* (London, n.d.), p. 78.
5. Randon to Napoleon, 3 June 1863. Maréchal Randon, *Mémoires*, Vol. 2 (Paris, 1877), pp. 81–2.
6. Mazade to Eugenie, 17 July 1865. AN: ABXIX 174.
7. Émile Ollivier, *L'Empire libéral*, Vol. 5, pp. 76–7.
8. William E. Echard, *Napoleon III and the Concert of Europe* (Baton Rouge, 1983), pp. 206–7.
9. Webb to Napoleon, 27 April 1866. AN: ABXIX 172.
10. Drouyn de Lhuys to Dano, 15 January 1866. *AD*, Vol. 3, 1866, pp. 340–3.
11. A. J. and K. A. Hanna, *op. cit.*, p. 153.
12. Napoleon to Drouyn de Lhuys, 19 October 1866. AN: 400AP 42, Archives napoléon.
13. See A. J. and K. A. Hanna, *op. cit.*, pp. xiii–xiv and 303.
14. C. Schefer, *La Grande Pensée de Napoléon III* (Paris, 1939), pp. 253–4.
15. *Ibid.*, pp. 260–1.
16. Ernest d'Hauterive, *op. cit.*, p. 10.
17. Comte Fleury, *Souvenirs*, pp. 52–3.
18. Émile Ollivier, *L'Empire libéral*, Vol. 3, pp. 77–8.
19. William H. C. Smith, *Napoleon III* (London, 1972), p. 169.

20. Richard Cobden in House of Commons debate, 5 July 1864. Quoted by Kenneth Bourne, *The Foreign Policy of Victorian England*, pp. 378–9.
21. William H. C. Smith, *Napoleon III: The Pursuit of Prestige* (London, 1991), p. 38.
22. See Chapter 6.
23. Jack Autrey Dabbs, 'The Indian Policy of the Second Empire', in Thomas E. Cotner and Carlos E. Castaneda (eds), *Essays in Mexican History* (Austin, TX, 1958), p. 115.
24. *Ibid.*, p. 117.
25. Eduardo Ruiz, *Historia de la guerra de Intervención en Michoacán* (Mexico, 1896), pp. 73–4. Quoted by Jack Dabbs, *op. cit.*, p. 118.
26. Jack Dabbs, *op. cit.*, p. 126.
27. Comte Fleury (ed.), *Memoirs*, Vol. 2, pp. 105–6.
28. Paul Gaulot, *L'Expédition du Mexique (1861–1867)* (Paris, 1906), Vol. 1, p. 19.
29. Albert Guérard, 'Caesarian Democracy', in *Napoleon III: Buffoon, Modern Dictator or Sphinx?* edited by Samuel M. Osgood (Boston, 1963), p. 65.
30. Napoleon III, 'Des Idées napoléoniennes', p. 171.
31. *Le Temps*, 10 January 1873.
32. Alain Corbin interviewed by Véronique Sales. 'Louis Napoléon, le mal-aimé', in *L'Histoire*, No. 211, June 1997, p. 24.
33. *La France*, reported in *La Presse*, 12 January 1873.
34. *Paris-Journal*, *ibid*.
35. *Moniteur Universel*, *ibid*.
36. Quoted by Count de la Chapelle, *Posthumous Works and unpublished Autographs of Napoleon III in Exile* (London, 1873), pp. 267–8.
37. *The Times*, 13 January 1873.
38. *The Times*, 10 January 1873.
39. Émile de Girardin. Extract from a comment in *Liberté*, reproduced in *La Presse*, 12 January 1873. Emphasis given.
40. Jean-Michel Gaillard, 'Sedan, 1870: L'Effondrement d'un Rêve Européen', *L'Histoire*, No. 211, June 1997, pp. 42–5.
41. Emile Lousse, 'The True Place of Napoleon III in the History of Europe', *Napoleon III and Europe*. Edited by Jacques de Launay (Brussels, 1965), p. 147.

Bibliography

Archival Sources

LONDON

Public Record Office

Foreign Office Records to 1878

General correspondence

France: FO 27/1377–FO 27/1382, FO 27/1397–FO 27/1400, FO 27/1412, FO 27/1419, FO 27/1431, FO 27/1482–FO 27/1483, FO 27/1497–FO 27/1498. Mexico: FO 50/327–FO 50/328, FO 50/334, FO 50/353–FO 50/354, FO 50/363–FO 50/365. Spain: FO 72/934, FO 72/940–FO 72/941, FO 72/1002, FO 72/1009–FO 72/1012, FO 72/1022, FO 72/1028–FO 72/1029.

Supplement to general correspondence

Mexico: FO 97/278–FO 97/279. Spain: FO 97/397.

Embassy Archives

France: FO 146/1009–FO 146/1010, FO 146/1014. Spain: FO 185/380–FO 185/381, FO 185/385–FO 185/387, FO 185/392. Mexico: FO 204/153–FO 204/154, FO 204/156, FO 204/159–FO 204/160, FO 204/163.

Private collections

Cowley Papers: FO 519/196–FO 519/200, FO 519/207, FO 519/229, FO 519/268, FO 519/272, FO 519/300–FO 519/301.
Russell Papers: PRO 30/22/29, PRO 30/22/41–PRO 30/22/42, PRO 30/22/56–PRO 30/22/57, PRO 30/22/59, PRO 30/22/62, PRO 30/22/70–PRO 30/22/71, PRO 30/22/74–PRO 30/22/76, PRO 30/22/86, PRO 30/22/95, PRO 30/22/105, PRO 30/22/115.
Bloomfield Papers: FO 356/32.

PARIS

Archives du Ministère des Affaires Étrangères

Correspondance politique

Angleterre: Vols 711, 719–21. Espagne: Vols 852, 859. Mexique: Vols 54–5, 58–9.

Papiers d'Agents – Archives Privées

PA–AP 009 Barrot, Vols 15–17. PA–AP 242 Gramont, Vol. 3. PA–AP 233 Thouvenel, Vols 3,8,10,17.

Mémoires et documents

Angleterre, Vol. 127. Mexique, Vol. 10.

Service Historique de l'Armée de Terre (Chateau de Vincennes)
Archives du Ministère de la Guerre

Expédition du Mexique (1862–1867)

G^7 1–3 Correspondence du général en chef avec le Ministre (1862–1867).
G^7 99 État-Major général: correspondence avec le Ministre, instructions de l'Empereur, correspondance générale (1862–1867).

Manuscripts

MR 851 de la Hayrie *Journal de la Campagne du Mexique*

Archives Nationales

Archives Privées

107AP 14 Archives Gallifet; 223AP 16 Fonds Berryer; 249AP 5 Archives Randon; 320AP 2 Papiers Bazaine; 400AP 41–4, 52, 54, 61–3, 68 Archives napoléon.

Dossiers du Cabinet de Napoléon III (papiers trouvés aux Tuileries en septembre 1870)

ABXIX 171–2 Documents relatifs à la guerre du Mexique. ABXIX 170, 173–5 Documents relatifs à tous les événements du règne de Napoléon III.

Fonds de la Marine

Campagnes
BB^4 799, 807, 810, 812, Expédition du Mexique 1861–1865. BB^4 1810, 1812, 1813, 1814, 1817bis, Papiers de l'Amiral Jurien de la Gravière.

Printed sources

Archives Diplomatiques: Recueil de Diplomatie et d'Histoire, 1862–67 (Kraus Reprint, Paris, 1969).

British Documents on Foreign Affairs: Reports and Papers from the Foreign Office Confidential Print. Part 1, Series F *Europe 1848–1914:* Vol. 9 *France 1847–1878,* Vol. 26 *Spain 1846–1896,* edited by Kenneth Bourne and D. Cameron Watts.

British and Foreign State Papers (Blue Books), Vols 51–4, 1860–64.

Exposé de la situation de l'Empire présenté au Senat et au Corps législatif January 1863 (Vol. 1); November 1863 (Vol. 2) (Paris, 1863); January 1866 (Vol. 4) (Paris, 1866).

The Papers of Queen Victoria on Foreign Affairs. Part 5: France and Belgium, 1848– 1900, edited by Kenneth Bourne (Bethesda, MD, 1990).

Parliamentary Debates, Third Series, Vols 161–2, 165–8.

Parliamentary Papers, Parts 1–3 Correspondence relating to Affairs in Mexico, presented to both Houses of Parliament by command of Her Majesty 1862 (London, 1862).

Parliamentary Papers, Correspondence respecting the Congress Proposed to be held at Paris, presented to both Houses of Parliament by Command of Her Majesty 1864 (London, 1864).

Secondary sources

Agulhon, Maurice, *The Republican Experiment 1848–1852,* translated by Janet Lloyd (Cambridge, 1989). Originally published in French as *1848 ou l'Apprentissage de la République 1848–1852* (Paris, 1973).

Ambes, Baron d', *Intimate Memoirs of Napoleon III: Personal Reminiscences of the Man and the Emperor,* 2 vols, edited and translated by A. R. Allinson (London, n.d.). These memoirs are considered suspect, not only because of the doubt surrounding the real identity of d'Ambes, but also because there is little evidence to support the role he claims to have played in various events during the Second Empire. See Christophe Bourachot, *Bibliographie critique des mémoires sur le Second Empire* (Paris, 1994).

Barail, Général du, *Mes Souvenirs, 1851–1864,* 2 vols (Paris, 1898).

Barker, Nancy Nichols, *Distaff Diplomacy: The Empress Eugénie and the Foreign Policy of the Second Empire* (Austin, TX, 1967).

—— 'France Disserved: The Dishonourable Career of Dubois de Saligny', in Nancy N. Barker and Marvin L. Brown, Jr (eds), *Diplomacy in an Age of Nationalism* (The Hague, 1971).

—— 'The French Legation in Mexico: Nexus of Interventionists', *French Historical Studies,* VIII (1974), pp. 409–26.

Bismarck, Otto Prince von, *Bismarck the Man and the Statesman being the Reflections and Reminiscences of Otto Prince von Bismarck,* translated from the German under the supervision of A. J. Butler (London,1898).

Black, Shirley, *Napoleon III and the French Intervention in Mexico: A Quest for Silver* (PhD dissertation, University of Oklahoma, 1974).

Blanchard, Marcel, 'Napoleon III: Aims, Achievements and Failures', in *Napoleon III: Buffoon, Modern Dictator or Sphinx?* edited by Samuel M. Osgood (Boston, 1963).

Blasio, José Luis, *Maximilian Emperor of Mexico: Memoirs of his Private Secretary José Luis Blasio*, translated from the original Spanish and edited by Robert Hammond Murray (Yale University Press, 1934).

Blayau, Noël, *Billault, ministre de Napoléon III d'après ses Papiers Personnels 1805–1863* (Paris, n.d.).

Blumberg, Arnold, 'French Government Justification for the Mexican Expedition, 1861–1867: A Study of Subtle Changes in the Management of Public Opinion Through Propaganda', *Proceedings of Western Society for French History*, Vol. 2, (1974), pp. 292–301.

Bock, Carl H., *Prelude to Tragedy: The Negotiation and Breakdown of the Tripartite Convention of London, October 31 1861* (Philadelphia, 1966).

Bourachot, Christophe, *Bibliographie critique des mémoires sur le Second Empire 2 décembre 1852–4 septembre 1870* (Paris, 1994).

Bourne Kenneth, 'The Clayton–Bulwer Treaty and the Decline of British Opposition to the Territorial Expansion of the United States, 1857–1860', *Journal of Modern History*, Vol. 33 (September 1961), pp. 287–91.

—— *The Foreign Policy of Victorian England 1830–1902* (London, 1970).

—— *Britain and the Balance of Power in North America 1815–1908* (London, 1967).

Bright, John, and Rogers, James E. Thorold (eds), *Speeches on Questions of Public Policy by Richard Cobden, MP* (London, 1878).

Bury, J. P. T., *Napoleon III and the Second French Empire* (London, 1975 © 1964).

Callcott, Wilfred Hardy, *Church and State in Mexico, 1822–1857* (New York, 1965 © 1926).

Campbell, Stuart L., *The Second Empire Revisited: A Study in French Historiography* (New Jersey, 1978).

Carr, Raymond, *Spain 1808–1939* (Oxford, 1975 © 1966).

Case, Lynn M. (ed.), *French Opinion on the United States and Mexico 1860–1867* (Archon Books, 1969 © 1936).

—— *Edouard Thouvenel et la Diplomatie du Second Empire*, translated into French by Guillaume de Bertier de Sauvaigny (Paris, 1976).

Cavendish, Francis W. H., *Society, Politics and Diplomacy 1820–1864: Passages from the Journal of Francis W. H. Cavendish* (London, 1913).

Chapelle, Count de la, *Posthumous Works and Unpublished Autographs of Napoleon III in Exile* (London, 1873).

Chevalier, Michel, 'L'Expédition du Mexique', *La Revue des Deux Mondes*, 38 (1 April 1862), pp. 513–61; (15 April 1862), pp. 879–918.

—— *Mexico, Ancient and Modern*, translated under the author's superintendence by Thomas Alpass, 2 vols (London, 1864).

Cobden, Richard, *The Political Writings of Richard Cobden* (London, 1878).

Conway, Moncure D., 'America, France and England', *Fortnightly Review*, 3 (January 1866), pp. 449–50.

Corbin, Alain, 'Louis Napoléon, le mal-aimé', Alain Corbin interviewed by Véronique Sales, *L'Histoire*, 211 (June 1997), pp. 24–5.

Corti, Egon Cæsar Count, *Maximilian and Charlotte of Mexico*, translated from the German by Catherine Alison Phillips (Archon Books, 1968 © 1928).

Dabbs, Jack Autrey, 'The Indian Policy of the Second Empire', in Thomas E. Cotner and Carlos E. Castañeda (eds), *Essays in Mexican History* (Austin, TX, 1958).

—— *The French Army in Mexico 1861–1867* (The Hague, 1963).

Dawson, Daniel, *The Mexican Adventure* (London, 1935).

Descola, Jean, 'L'Expédition du Mexique a commencé aux Tuileries', *La Revue des Deux Mondes*, 23 (1 December 1966), pp. 341–59.

Dunaway, C. A., 'Reasons for the Withdrawal of the French from Mexico', *Annual Report of the American Historical Association 1902*, Vol. 1, pp. 315–28 (Washington,1903).

Echard, William E., *Napoleon III and the Concert of Europe* (Baton Rouge, 1983).

Eudeville, Jean d', 'L'Avénement du Second Empire et les Traités de 1815', *La Revue de Paris*, 43(17), 1 September 1936, pp. 96–110.

Ferrell, Robert H., *Foundations of American Diplomacy 1775–1872* (Columbia, SC, 1969).

Filon, Augustin, *Recollections of the Empress Eugénie* (London, 1920).

Fleury, Général Comte, *Souvenirs du Général Cte Fleury*, Vol. 2: 1859–1867 (Paris, 1898).

—— (ed.), *Memoirs of the Empress Eugénie*, 2 vols (New York, 1920).

Gaillard, Jean-Michel, 'Sedan, 1870: L'effondrement d'un rêve européen', *L'Histoire*, 211 (June 1997), pp. 42–5.

Gaulot, Paul, *L'Expédition du Mexique (1861–1867): D'après les documents et souvenirs de Ernest Louet, Payeur en Chef du Corps Expéditionnaire*, 2 vols (Paris, 1906).

Gérard, Alice, *Le Second Empire: innovation et réaction* (Paris, 1973).

Giovanangeli, Bernard (ed.), *Pourquoi réhabiliter le Second Empire?* Actes du colloque organisé par le Souvenir Napoléonien, Palais des Congrès de Paris, 21 Octobre 1995.

Girard, Louis, *Napoléon III* (Paris, 1986).

Goetzmann, William H., *When the Eagle Screamed: The Romantic Horizon in American Diplomacy 1800–1860* (New York, 1966).

Gorce, Pierre de la, *Histoire du Second Empire*, Vol. 4, 12th edn (Paris 1899).

—— *Napoléon III et sa politique* (Paris, 1933).

Guedalla, Philip (ed.), *Palmerston* (London, 1950 © 1926).

—— *Gladstone and Palmerston, being the Correspondence of Lord Palmerston with Mr Gladstone 1851–1865* (London, 1928).

Guérard, Albert. 'Cæsarian Democracy', and 'A Forerunner of Woodrow Wilson' in *Napoleon III: Buffoon, Modern Dictator or Sphinx?* edited by Samuel M. Osgood (Boston, 1963).

Guiral, Pierre and Témime, Émile, 'L'Historiographie du Second Empire', *Revue d'Histoire Moderne et Contemporaine*, 21 (January–March 1974), pp. 1–17.

Hanna, A. J. and Hanna, K. A., *Napoleon III and Mexico: American Triumph over Monarchy* (Chapel Hill, 1971).

Haslip, Joan, *Imperial Adventurer: Emperor Maximilian of Mexico and his Empress* (London, 1974 © 1971).

Hauterive, Ernest d', *The Second Empire and its Downfall: The Correspondence of the Emperor Napoleon III and His Cousin Prince Napoleon*, translated from the French by Herbert Wilson (London, n.d.).

Hayes, Paul, *Modern British Foreign Policy: the Nineteenth Century 1814–1880* (London, 1975).

Hearnshaw, F. J. C., 'The European Revolution and After; 1848–1854', in *The Cambridge History of British Foreign Policy 1783–1919*, edited by Sir A. W. Ward and G. P. Gooch (Cambridge, 1923), Vol. 2: 1815–1866.

Henry, Paul, 'Napoléon III et les Balkans', in *Napoléon III et l'Europe*, edited by Jacques de Launay (Brussels, 1965).

Hobson, J. A., *Richard Cobden: The International Man* (London, 1919).

Hoskins, Halford L., 'French Views of the Monroe Doctrine and the Mexican Expedition', *Hispanic American Historical Review*, 4(1921), pp. 677–89.

Isser, Natalie, *The Second Empire and the Press: A Study of Government-inspired Brochures and French Foreign Policy in their Propaganda Milieu* (The Hague, 1974).

Journal des Débats (Paris) 1861–2, 1873.

Kératry, C^te^Émile de, 'Le Mexique et les chances de salut du Nouvel Empire', *La Revue des Deux Mondes*, 65 (15 September 1866), pp. 442–61.

Lally, Frank Edward, *French Opposition to the Mexican Policy of the Second Empire* (Baltimore, 1931).

Launay, Jacques de (ed.), *Napoléon III et l'Europe* (Brussels, 1965).

Lecaillon, Jean-François. *Napoléon III et le Mexique: Les illusions d'un grand dessein* (Paris, 1994).

Lollié, Frédéric, *Rêve d'Empereur: le destin et l'âme de Napoléon III* (Paris, 1913).

Lousse, Emile, 'The True Place of Napoleon III in the History of Europe', in *Napoléon III et l'Europe*, edited by Jacques de Launay (Brussels, 1965).

Mackay, Charles, 'The French Conquest of Mexico', *Westminster and Foreign Quarterly Review*, 80 (October 1863), pp. 313–44.

—— 'Maximilian', *Blackwood's Edinburgh Magazine*, 102 (August 1867), pp. 232–44.

McMillan, James F., *Napoleon III* (New York, 1991).

McPhee, Peter, *A Social History of France 1780–1880* (London, 1992).

Malespine, A., *Solution de la question mexicaine* (Brochure, Paris, 1864).

Malmesbury, Earl of, *Memoirs of an Ex-Minister: An Autobiography* (London, 1885).

Martin, Sir Theodore, *The Life of His Royal Highness the Prince Consort*, Vol. 5, 3rd edn (London, 1880).

Mazade, Charles de, 'L'Expédition du Mexique', *La Revue des Deux Mondes*, 37 (1 February 1862), pp. 761–70.

—— 'L'Expédition du Mexique', *La Revue des Deux Mondes*, 39 (15 May 1862), pp. 497–500.

—— 'La Guerre du Mexique et les puissances européennes', *La Revue des Deux Mondes*, 40 (1 August 1862), pp. 733–61.

—— 'La Question du Mexique dans le parlement espagnol', *La Revue des Deux Mondes*, 43 (15 January 1863), pp. 505–12.

—— 'Crise ministérielle en Espagne', *La Revue des Deux Mondes*, 43 (15 February 1863), pp. 1004–8.

—— 'L'Expédition du Mexique et la Politique Française', *La Revue des Deux Mondes*, 48 (1 December 1863), pp. 675–706.

—— 'La Paix durable et les publications politiques', *La Revue des Deux Mondes*, 48 (15 December 1863), pp. 996–1005.

—— 'Le Général Prim', *La Revue des Deux Mondes*, 61 (15 January 1866), pp. 540–44.

—— *Lettres à une inconnue*, Vol. 2 (Paris, 1893).

Mérimée, Prosper, *Lettres à M. Pannizzi 1850–1870*, 2 vols (Paris, 1881).

Metternich, Princesse Pauline de, *Souvenirs de la Princesse Pauline de Metternich (1859–1871)* (Paris, 1922).

Minc, Alain, *Louis Napoléon revisité* (Paris, 1997).

Motley, John Lothrop, *The Correspondence of John Lothrop Motley*, edited by George William Curtis, 2 vols (London, 1889).

Napolean III, *The Political and Historical Works of Louis Napoleon Bonaparte, President of the French Republic* (London, 1852; reprinted NY, 1972).

—— *History of Julius Cæsar*, 2 vols (Paris, 1865).

—— *Œuvres de Napoléon III*, 5 vols (Paris, 1869).

—— *Napoleonic Ideas: Des Idées Napoléoniennes, par le Prince Napoléon-Louis Bonaparte*, edited by Brison D. Gooch (London, 1967).

Nicolson, Harold T., *The Congress of Vienna: A Study in Allied Unity: 1812–1822* (London, 1946).

O'Connor, Richard, *The Cactus Throne: The Tragedy of Maximilian and Carlotta* (London, 1971).

Ollivier, Émile, *L'Empire Libéral*, Vol. 3 (Paris, 1898), Vol. 5 (Paris, 1900), Vol. 6 (Paris, 1902), Vol. 7 (Paris, 1903), Vol. 9 (Paris, 1904).

—— *Journal 1846–1869*, Vol. 2: *1861–1869*. Text choisie et annoté par Theodore Zeldin et Anne Troisier de Diaz (Paris, 1961).

—— 'Napoléon III: Son dessein international', *La Revue des Deux Mondes*, 146 (1 March 1898), pp. 49–84.

Osgood, Samuel M. (ed.), *Napoleon III: Buffoon, Modern Dictator or Sphinx?* (Boston, 1963).

Palm, Franklin Charles, *England and Napoleon III: A Study of the Rise of a Utopian Dictator* (Durham, NC, 1948).

Palmerston, Viscount, *Opinions and Policy of the Right Honourable Viscount Palmerston as Minister, Diplomatist and Statesman, during more than forty years of public life* (London, 1852; reprinted NY, 1972).

Parkes, Henry Bamford, *A History of Mexico* (London, 1962 © 1960).

Patterson, R.H., 'The Napoleonic Idea in Mexico', *Blackwood's Edinburgh Magazine*, 96 (July 1864), pp. 72–83.

Persigny, Duc de, *Mémoires du Duc de Persigny* (Paris, 1896).

Phelan, John Leddy, 'Pan-Latinism, French Intervention in Mexico (1861–1867) and the Genesis of the Idea of Latin America', in *Conciencia y Autenticidad Históricas* (edited by Juan A. Ortega y Medina) (Mexico, 1968).

Pingaud, Albert, 'La Politique Extérieure du Second Empire', *Revue Historique*, 156 (Nov/Dec 1927), pp. 41–68.

Plessis, Alain, *The Rise and Fall of the Second Empire 1852–1871*, translated by Jonathon Mandelbaum (Cambridge, 1987).

Poulet-Malassis, A., *Papiers Secrets et Correspondance du Second Empire*, 2 vols (Paris, 1871).

Poulton, Gary M., *Great Britain and the Intervention in Mexico, 1861–1865*. (PhD dissertation, Miami University, 1976).

Randon, Maréchal, *Mémoires du Maréchal Randon*, 2 vols (Paris, 1875 and 1877).

Reid, Rachel R., 'The Franco-Italian War, Syria and Poland 1859–1863', in *The Cambridge History of British Foreign Policy, 1783–1919, Vol. 2* (Cambridge, 1923).

Reinach, Joseph, 'Napoléon III et la Paix', *Revue Historique*, 36 (January to April 1921), pp. 161–219.

Renouvin, Pierre, *Histoire Diplomatique 1815–1914: Cours de 1928–1929* (Paris, 1929).

—— 'Napoleon III, Bismarck, and Cavour', in *Napoleon III: Buffoon, Modern Dictator or Sphinx?* edited by Samuel M. Osgood (Boston, 1963).

Reuter, Paul H. Jr, 'United States–French Relations Regarding French Intervention in Mexico : From the Tripartite Treaty to Querétaro', *Southern Quarterly*, 6(4), July 1968, pp. 469–89.

Richards, Edward W., 'Louis Napoleon and Central America', *Journal of Modern History*, 34(2), June 1962, pp. 178–84.

Ridley, Jasper, *Maximilian and Juárez* (London, 1993).

Robertson, William Spence, 'The Tripartite Treaty of London', *Hispanic American Historical Review*, 20(2), May 1940, pp. 167–89.

Roeder, Ralph, *Juarez and His Mexico*, 2 vols (New York, 1947).

Russell, John Earl, *Recollections and Suggestions 1813–1873* (London, 1875).

—— *L'Ambassade de Richard de Metternich à Paris* (Paris, 1931).

Salomon, Henry, 'Le Prince Richard de Metternich et sa correspondance pendant son ambassade à Paris (1859–1871)', *La Revue de Paris*, 31(1), 1924, pp. 507–41 and 762–804.

Schefer, Christian, *La Grande Pensée de Napoléon III: Les Origines de l'Expédition du Mexique (1858–1862)* (Paris, 1939).

Schnerb, Robert, *Rouher et le Second Empire* (Paris, 1949).

Senior, Nassau William, *Conversations with Distinguished Persons during the Second Empire*, 2 vols, edited by M. C. M. Simpson (London, 1880).

Silberschmidt, Max, *The United States and Europe: Rivals and Partners* (London, 1972).

Smith, William H. C., *Napoleon III* (London, 1972).

—— *Napoleon III: The Pursuit of Prestige* (London, 1991).

Sonolet, Louis, 'L'Agonie de l'Empire du Mexique: D'après des lettres et des notes inédites du Général Castelnau', *La Revue de Paris*, 34 (1 August 1927), pp. 590–625 and 862–98.

Temps, Le (Paris), 1861–1867.

Thompson, J. M., *Louis Napoleon and the Second Empire* (Oxford, 1965 © 1954).

Thouvenel, L., *Le Secret de l'Empereur: correspondance confidentielle et inédite échangée entre M. Thouvenel, le Duc de Gramont, et le Général Comte de Flahault, 1860–1863*, 2 vols (Paris, 1889).

Times, The (London), 1858–1864, 1873.

Tremenheere, J. H., 'The Empire of Mexico', *Quarterly Review*, 115 (April 1864), pp. 348–81.

Viel Castel, Count Horace de, *Memoirs of Count Horace de Viel Castel*, 2 vols, translated and edited by Charles Bousfield (London, 1888).

Wellesley, Colonel the Hon. F. A. (ed.), *The Paris Embassy during the Second Empire* (London, 1928).

Whately, Archbishop, *Historic Doubts relative to Napoleon Buonaparte*, 11th edn (London, 1852).

Williams, Roger L., 'A Tragedy of Good Intentions', *History Today*, 4(4) (1954), pp. 219–26.

Zeldin, Theodore, 'The Myth of Napoleon III', *History Today*, 8(2) (1958), pp. 103–9.

Index